D0636870

THE STARS ARE OUR ONLY WARMTH

Doing my rounds.

Tipperary-born Alice Leahy began her working life as a nurse and midwife and went to help the outsiders in our society through her Simon community work. She was Co-Founder and Director of TRUST from 1975–2015, and remains a director of The Alice Leahy Trust – a non-judgmental, befriending, social and health service for people who are homeless.

Alice is also a former Human Rights Commissioner and former Chairperson of the Sentence Review Group and is a contributor to public policy, a writer, commentator, broadcaster and lecturer, giving a voice and a helping hand to the marginalised.

Alice co-authored, with Anne Dempsey, *Not Just a Bed for the Night* (1995), and edited *With Trust in Place – Writing from the Outside* and *Wasting Time with People?* Alice has featured in social documentaries, including the film *A Fragile City* (1999) and documentary *Wasting Time with People?* (2010).

Alice was awarded an honorary fellowship from the Royal College of Surgeons in Ireland (1999), an honorary fellowship from The Royal College of Physicians of Ireland (2017), an honorary doctorate from University College Dublin (2003) and has been named Tipperary Person of the Year (2004). She has received many other awards, including Person of the Year (1988) and the Crystal Clear MSD Health Literacy Award (2009) for her life's work combating social exclusion. Alice always emphasizes that her work is a 'team effort'.

Catherine Cleary is a journalist, author and broadcaster. She began her career as a reporter with *The Irish Times* in 1994 and became security correspondent of *The Sunday Tribune*. She met Alice Leahy in the 1990s while reporting on social issues around crime and poverty. Catherine's publications include: *Life Sentence, Murder Victims and their Families* (2004) and *A Month of Somedays, How One Woman made the most of Now* (2012). She co-wrote *Counter Culture, The Sheridans' Guide to Cheese* in 2015. She also co-wrote and presented the RTÉ radio series *History on a Plate* with historian Juliana Adelman. She has been writing a weekly restaurant review in *The Irish Times* for the past seven years.

THE STARS ARE OUR ONLY WARMTH

Alice Leahy

A MEMOIR

with Catherine Cleary

THE O'BRIEN PRESS
DUBLIN

First published 2018 by The O'Brien Press Ltd.,
12 Terenure Road East, Rathgar, D06 HD27, Dublin 6, Ireland.
Tel: +353 1 4923333; Fax: +353 1 4922777
E-mail: books@obrien.ie
Website: www.obrien.ie
The O'Brien Press is a member of Publishing Ireland.

ISBN: 978-1-78849-025-2

Copyright for text © Alice Leahy with Catherine Cleary 2018
Copyright for typesetting, layout, design © The O'Brien Press Ltd. 2018

All rights reserved. No part of this publication may be reproduced or utilised in any form or by any means, electronic or mechanical, including photocopying, recording or in any information storage and retrieval system, without permission in writing from the publisher.

10 9 8 7 6 5 4 3 2 1
23 22 21 20 19 18

All author royalties to go to The Alice Leahy Trust
For further information on The Alice Leahy Trust www.aliceleahytrust.ie

Layout and design: The O'Brien Press Ltd.
Cover image: Alamy. Front flap: Author photograph courtesy of the *RTÉ Guide.*

Printed and bound by Scandbook AB, Sweden.
The paper in this book is produced using pulp from managed forests.

Last Night

Last night,
Two boys in the doorway,
I watched him cry,
Genuine tears of lost undesertion
You slept silently, mouth open
I wrapped the blanket around you.
They pass by in the hundreds,
Not knowing that the pavement is our pillow
And the stars are our only warmth

Tony Gill, July 2000

Me and Tony Gill.

Dedication

To my parents, Jack and Hannie Leahy

Thanks

'At times our own light goes out and is rekindled by a spark from another person. Each of us has cause to think with deep gratitude of those who have lighted the flame within us.'

Theologian, writer and philosopher Albert Schweitzer

There have been too many sparks to mention by name. They all know who they are. Some of them have died but their lives and memories still inspire me. Thank you to those who encouraged, supported, challenged and believed in me. My wonderful colleagues who work with me on a daily basis, our board of directors, our volunteers, donors and especially the people who use our service. Thanks to Michael O'Brien and his team, especially editor Susan Houlden in The O'Brien Press. And finally my husband, Charlie, who has supported me and put up with me over the years, especially in recent times with my endless talk of an eventful life lived.

Contents

My Impressions of Alice Leahy

Leabharlanna Fhine Gall

'A tireless advocate and agitator for those who literally have no homes to go to'

Pat Kenny

Something Alice said years ago, has remained indelibly etched on my memory. It was in the context of a radio programme, and we had been discussing the homeless people on the streets and their insistent begging. Listeners phoned in to complain that the homeless would only 'spend it on drink'. Alice quietly said, in reply, that the importance is in the giving, without being judgemental. Once we have given the money freely, the recipient is also free to spend it as they wish. And what might each of us do with a few Euro in a similar situation? I realised then that everything that Alice does is informed by kindness and compassion. But it does not mean that Alice is a soft touch: her work is tempered by the experience of a lifetime, and woe betide those in authority who might consider this gentle and genteel woman a pushover, because she is not, as many in positions of authority have found. She is a woman of passions – for her sainted husband Charlie, for her work, for travel, for Tipperary hurling, and for the exposure of bureaucratic humbug. She is fearless and outspoken. She identifies with absolute clarity the moment, in the bitterly cold winter of 1992, when the 'homelessness industry' began, and which made careers for many but did little to ease the problem.

I have known Alice for many years, but only as a citizen of Dublin. I knew that she was a qualified nurse who was moved to help the homeless, who for so many Dubliners had been an invisible presence on our streets. She had an outsider's eye to see what many of us were blind to. With Voluntary Services International (VSI), she discovered the redbrick tenements of Benburb Street, which we, as local Dublin children, were warned to avoid. We saw and smelt the poverty through the open hallways: Alice discovered the humanity. That's what makes Alice different.

So, it was wonderful to be invited – in the text that follows – into the world of the child that was Alice Leahy, in a tiny place called Annesgift in County Tipperary. She has always been eloquent in speech, but she is even more so on the page. She grew up in a world of reading by oil lamp or candlelight, of rainwater harvesting, of Sunlight soap, of milk, still warm from the cow, a world of fairy forts, of nettle soup and river swimming. But she was also born into the world of 'the big house', because her father worked for the owner of Annesgift, a Major Hughes. He and his young Dublin-born bride, Olivia Cruickshank, opened their home to the young Alice, and in so doing exposed her to a wider world and a different sensibility. Oh, to have known that young fearless Alice, in hand-me-down jodhpurs encouraging her mount, a Connemara pony up the soft silage mound and to gallop down again, oblivious to danger! A love of horses, an occasional flutter is a legacy that still endures. And she was also surrounded by several strong women, including her mother, ambitious and driven for local causes, who had a hand in preparing her for the challenges to come.

If she captures the world of rural Tipperary in the middle of the last century with a gimlet eye, Alice also does the same for her adopted home of sixties' Dublin. From these pages, I can smell the ether and the antiseptic corridors of The Royal City of Dublin Hospital in Baggot Street, with its smartly blazered porter, starched nursing aprons, godlike consultants, and the invisible red uniformed cleaners, some of whom had come from county homes, institutions or Magdalene laundries. Young Nurse Alice vividly describes the shy and reclusive Paddy Kavanagh of Raglan Road being physically terrified of encountering the boisterous Brendan Behan, and we can imagine Kavanagh discovering the kindness of Nurse Alice, who also, by the way, babysat the Behan children! I can once again find myself back in Margaret Gaj's restaurant, where all manner of revolutionary talk was on the menu. And that evocation of Dublin by Alice is still as precise for our contemporary city, which she walks every single day.

In reading this book, I was constantly reminded of the poem 'The Road Not Taken' by Robert Frost:

'I took the one less travelled by,
And that has made all the difference.'

There is no doubt that Alice, at every crossroads, has always chosen the less obvious, the more difficult path, as you will discover in this book. Alice might have been lost to us, to remain in England or Germany or even New Zealand. Or perhaps to become Matron of Baggot Street Hospital and to slowly climb the ladder of promotion in a patriarchal health service. Or become a HSE housing executive with a leather and chrome office suite. But of course, it was to be none of the above. She continues her vital work every weekday morning in the Iveagh buildings on Bride Road. A cup of tea, a shower, a foot massage, a change of clothes, a conversation, simple human contact, all these things make a real difference. The ghosts of many of those who climbed down those basement steps populate this book, as do the ghosts of those who inspired the foundations of Trust in 1975.

Alice has become a tireless advocate and agitator for those who literally have no homes to go to. To quote one politician: 'You don't say no to Alice Leahy!' She says unpalatable and sometimes un-PC things that rattle the cages of the policy makers and the powerful. But then as GK Chesterton so eloquently put it, 'I believe in getting into hot water; it keeps you clean.'

Pat Kenny

A Word from Alice about her Memoir

We get people ready for the day. It sounds so simple: a hot shower, clean clothes, a shave and a spray of aftershave or perfume. But imagine how your day would feel without them. I watched a man sitting in our front room recently. He had a mug of tea in his hands and a biscuit. He was dressed in warm dry clothes. And he sat listening to beautiful music playing on Lyric FM, lost in his thoughts. There was something special about it, being sat there in the calm, a respite from the noise, traffic, weather and people on the streets, a few steps up from our basement home.

Beauty and tranquility can be in short supply when you're living on the streets. It will be assumed you have slipped beyond the need for them. Lots of things will be assumed if you live in a doorway, a tent or a hostel. You will be labelled a client, a customer, a service user, a number. If I've learned anything, it is not to make assumptions about anyone. Boxes are not for people. At least, not while they're alive.

Almost every day I learn again how challenging it is to cope with the needs of people lost to drink or drugs, living rough or feeling like an outsider.

We met a young woman who pulled out her medical tubes and left her hospital ward, chased by a doctor trying to keep her there. She told us that rehab was a place to go and eat and build herself up, a pause rather than a full stop, before heading back into serious drinking. There was a man addicted to heroin who told us he didn't want any clean clothes. He could only get enough money for drugs if he stayed in his filthy clothes. We don't know if we'll see him alive again. There was the man who had been 'successfully' moved into independent living but came to us for a shave. In months of independent living his beard had grown down to his chest.

I'm called a veteran these days, as if I had returned from a war zone. In some ways I did. At the height of a promising nursing career I fell into step with people who didn't march to the beat of a typical life. This is the story of my untypical life, what I learned and saw and did in the company of those people over more than four decades.

To tell that story I worked with journalist Catherine Cleary. Collaboration has been a cornerstone of my work. And this book would not have seen the light of day without her. We talked about the past and visited people and places where I once worked or lived. We worked with an archive of material that I have been gathering since the start. Many of our conversations about ideas and experiences from the past circled back to today. I learned a lot about memory and how precise or foggy it can be when one life event is picked out of the flow and held up to the light for examination. As sticklers for facts, we worked hard to chase down any misremembered details but it is an occupational hazard of writing a memoir.

This has ended up becoming a book not just about the complexity of being homeless but also about the complexity of being human. We are struggling in a world where things have become so far removed from people. We run the risk of being isolated into lonely individuals whose worth is valued only by what we consume. I want to grasp the threads and pull the fabric back together again.

This is also a book about hope and the human spirit. It's something that needs to be nurtured in these challenging times especially for those who come after us. To find hope we need to step back a bit to see how far we have come. I hope this book will help that to happen.

Alice Leahy

Me, aged three and a half, with Gill at the main door of Annesgift, the Big House.

CHAPTER ONE

Annesgift

Fethard, County Tipperary

'There is always one moment in childhood when the door opens and lets the future in.'

Graham Greene, *The Power and the Glory* (1940)

I am sitting in my pram. Sawdust is piling in small drifts around the wheels. The smell is damp wood and stone. There are the sounds of horses and men in a busy farmyard. One of them is my father and he is chopping and stacking timber.

Memories flare like matches in the dark – bright and brief. Sometimes I wonder whether I truly remember this time in the wool room. Maybe it was something described to me so vividly that I threaded it into my own set of memories. In my seventies now I peer back through the window of my childhood, making new sense of things. Large chunks of time are lost and I'm left with shards.

These bursts and sparks from childhood are some of my strongest memories: blue sky summer days, glittering frosts, gossamer spider webs, tugging sheep's wool from the grip of a briar, the jolt of joy at finding a newly laid hen's egg, the tug of a newborn lamb sucking on the teat of a bottle.

I remember the knitted squares for Belgian refugees from World War II. Each one was bright, very much itself, like a memory. We sat on the floor knitting them in a room on a beautiful estate in the centre of south Tipperary. In winter a fire crackled in the grate. In summer the window was open and we could hear the crows squabbling in the tall trees. This was Annesgift, home, the place where I owned nothing and everything. A world where I belonged.

They were satisfying, those squares. You could knit one or two at a time, start something and finish it in the length of time it took to have a conversation. We cast on our stitches and turned the lengths of warm scratchy wool into something solid, all different colours, all the same size.

We sewed our squares together to make blankets. They were parcelled up and posted to Dominique Pire, a cleric helping refugees to rebuild their lives in Belgium after World War II. It was work that would earn him a Nobel Peace Prize. We pictured our knitted square blankets on the new beds and cots of people making new lives. The squares were small gestures that gave us the sense of being part of something bigger, a world outside life in Annesgift in fifties' Ireland.

My mother Johannah Crean (everyone called her Hannie) was born in the townland of Ardsallagh just outside Fethard in September 1919. 'It was all home births in those days,' she told me. Her earliest memory was her first day at school when she was four years old. Her sister and brother held her hands as they walked away from home. Her best friend, Patty Ahearne, lived down the road. Patty had 'dazzling red hair and a beautiful smile'.

My mother loved school and was gifted at maths but was required to finish her education after primary level. Secondary education had to be paid for and her family couldn't afford it.

Instead, she took a domestic science training course in Fethard and went to work, at the age of sixteen, in the office of O'Sullivan's chemist in the town. Later she worked in the market garden of the Church of Ireland rector Canon Patten, labelling flower and vegetable plants to be sent by rail to customers all over Ireland. When she was in her early twenties, she came to work at Annesgift and never left.

Annesgift is a handsome medium-sized Georgian country house hidden away from the road on nearly five hundred acres, just under three miles outside the Tipperary town of Fethard. The Clashawley river runs through the estate, splitting into two branches as it crosses the fields, one branch bigger than the other, before joining again into one river which flows into the Anner. The stone bridge that sits over the river at the entrance to the estate is, to my eye, the most beautiful place in Ireland. Wild garlic grows under the trees and trout swim in the river, luring the occasional otter to fish and hungry herons to stand watch on the banks.

The three-storey house with its long sash windows looks out across fertile fields, past tall cypress and oak trees to Slievenamon, or *Sliabh na mBan*, the mountain of the women.

The story I was told was that the house and lands were given as a wedding gift to the daughter of a wealthy landowner. In 1918 Major Jack Hughes brought his new bride, twenty-year-old Olivia Cruickshank, down from Dublin. He had been badly wounded in Flanders. Olivia had studied history at Trinity. The young newly-weds had experienced a lot by the time they came to live in Tipperary. Jack Hughes was recovering from the horror of World War I. A brother of Olivia's had been killed in the Dardanelles in northwestern Turkey in 1915.

The Annesgift Olivia Hughes arrived to in 1918 was a quiet place with a tangled history. The 1901 census shows how full of voices the house had been. Back then, Major Hughes was an eight-year-old boy. He had a five-year-old sister and a baby brother. His mother Kate was thirty-five. His father, John, was sixty. Kate Hughes, who was a Kerry woman, must have been a second wife. The major's father had two daughters in their twenties, not much younger than Kate. The live-in staff included a governess, a nurse and four servants, bringing the household to thirteen people. There is a Leahy listed amongst them, Ellen Leahy, my father's aunt who worked as the nurse in the house in 1901.

A decade on, the 1911 census shows a much diminished household. Kate Hughes was a forty-three-year-old widow, apparently alone in Annesgift with a gardener and two women listed as servants, nineteen-year-old Mary Cormick and my great aunt Ellen. Kate describes herself as a farmer. Sometime in the aftermath of the 1916 Rising she was driven out of the house and it was seized for a time, but not destroyed as many big houses were. It's difficult to know what exactly happened. The closest we get is something Olivia Hughes wrote much later for a foreword to a history of the churches of Fethard.

'My mother-in-law had been evicted from Annesgift, Jack's farm in a fertile and well-watered part of Tipperary. She never came back but lived in England. We settled down in Annesgift when the Sinn Féiners cleared out. The eviction didn't last long. Jack's workers were glad to see us again. The old steward who had worked all his life at Annesgift had wept bitterly when my mother-in-law was turned out.'

'Annesgift was a fine Georgian house with great windows,' Olivia Hughes wrote proudly. 'When one looked down the lawn there was a ring fort. There were many of these strange rings in the neighbourhood but none finer than ours which had a double ring and was crowned with fine ash trees. The first sign of spring was the return of the herons to the nest in the top of the trees.'

By the 1920s, when my mother was visiting Annesgift as a child, the house was humming with activity and work again; the farm was in full production. My father's father, Daniel Leahy, was the steward. He was born in a little house facing Annesgift House. Although the house is gone gooseberry bushes still grew there up until very recently remnants of his small fruit and vegetable garden. These were turbulent days of skirmishes and attacks during the War of Independence. Dan had to shelter under a small bridge on the estate when trees were being knocked around Annesgift to keep the black and tans from travelling between Fethard and Cashel. A group of black and tans had once swooped down on my mother's father, Martin Crean, who was a gardener in nearby Tullamaine Castle, as he walked the road. The British mercenaries mistook the large bough he was carrying on his shoulder for a gun. He was lucky not to be shot.

An annual highlight was the threshing dance, marking the end of the wheat harvest, where, in the time before combine harvesters, many hands were needed to separate the grains of wheat from their stalks, using a steam engine and a mill. The threshing took three days. Helpers came from neighbouring farms. It was hot dusty work, and my mother remembered Mrs Hughes working all day in the kitchen to prepare a hearty midday meal and afternoon tea.

On the last evening the workers and helpers went home and changed out of their work clothes to return for the threshing dance that went on all night into the early hours. Mrs Hughes sang with gusto at the threshing dance. Her party pieces included 'Way Down Upon the

The Leahy family. Me behind my father, my sister Eileen behind my mother. My brother Donal standing between us, with my brother Martin on my father's knee and my sister Mary on my mother's knee.

Swanee River', 'Annie Laurie' and 'Phil the Fluter's Ball'.

In the early forties my mother came to work at Annesgift, to help care for Mrs Hughes's mother, Elizabeth Cruickshank. Mrs Hughes's mother enjoyed jaunts in her pony and trap, with her nurse and my mother. The pony was flighty and would regularly rear up or set off at a gallop. This terrified the nurse and my mother but was a great source of glee to Mrs Cruickshank.

As a nurse's aid in Annesgift my mother started seeing my father John, or Jack as he was called. They had known each other in school. He worked on Annesgift farm and was a carer for the major's disabled cousin.

My parents' wedding was typical of its day, quiet and modest. Hannie wore a wedding suit – a skirt, blouse and jacket. Their 'honeymoon' consisted of a day trip to Melleray, the Abbey in Waterford. She moved into the small house where I was born, a four-roomed cottage on the edge of the estate beside the road.

The house came with the job of estate steward. Over my parents' long and happy lifetimes, the world of big houses, servants and masters, or 'high-ups' as my mother called them, faded and died. We are the last of a generation that remembers the big house and its army of workers.

I was the eldest, born in that sturdy little house on 1 December 1942. It never felt small because of the bigness of everything around us. I grew up feeling (maybe precociously) that Annesgift belonged to me, its fairy forts, the abundant kitchen garden, the boot and harness rooms with their tang of leather and linseed oil, the cool pantry where butter and cream were kept, the farm animals and all the wild animals: the squirrels, foxes, badgers and otters.

Four years later, my sister Eileen was born, then our brother Donal and finally the twins Martin and Mary. Our little house filled up. I spent what felt like hours staring out the tiny gable window of my bedroom, elbows leaning on the fragile wooden frame watching Slievenamon change. Its colours and shadows would lighten and darken, weather rippling and brewing across it.

We were not a family of huggers, but there was warmth and genuine caring for each other. My parents were hard-working and we learned by watching them. We grew up with a huge work ethic. Even though I was the eldest, my parents didn't lean on me for help with my younger siblings. My childhood felt carefree and independent.

Our house had a rose garden in the front with fat pink and yellow roses that filled the summer air with perfume along with the lilac and the honeysuckle. There were two rooms upstairs and two downstairs and the windows were very small. We had no running water or electricity. The only phone in the vicinity was in the big house. There were so few phones then that the number for Annesgift House was Fethard 10. Later when Godfreys up the road got the first television I would head up there with my siblings to sit and watch the screen, delicious chunks of Mrs Godfrey's currant bread in our hands.

We carried washing water from the river and kept it in a bucket. We collected rainwater in a barrel at the side of the house. Water for drinking and cooking came from a well. There was a scullery at the back of the house where my mother did all the washing with a washboard and a block of Sunlight Soap. It was back-straining work. She boiled the whites over the fire and made starch for them in the scullery. At the other side of the house there was a hen house. We had lots of hens, Rhode Island Reds, who would cluck and fuss around you when you went to find the eggs. There was a hen run, where chickens were hatched and raised.

Oil lamps and candles were the only source of light, along with the

Happy women with their lovely horse and dogs setting off for the day. Mrs Hughes and her mother Mrs Cruickshank in front, my mother Hannie behind Mrs Hughes with Nurse Connorton.

glow of the fire in winter. But there were always books in the sitting room. At night we sat around the fire and played cards, Snakes and Ladders or had a question time session. I still love sitting on the floor, although my knees no longer appreciate it. We always had an atlas in the house. We acted out parts from stories we had read in the paper. I loved elephants and had a beautiful book about them given to me by someone who visited the Hughes family.

We painted and drew and wrote and took turns to read the Curly

Wee cartoon strip in the *Irish Independent*. My mother wrote to people around the world until she died. One of her longest correspondences was with her childhood friend Patty Ahearne, she of the blazing red hair, who became a nun in South Africa.

Mammy cooked our meals over the fire. A large pot and kettle hung from the crane, an iron right-angled contraption that could be swung over the fire. She made rabbit stew and turned the boiling pot into an oven by closing the lid and putting burning embers on the top, to bake bread. She was famous for her brown bread. She would also roast a chicken in the pot oven, bake apples in the cinders and top the chicken with mushrooms if they were in season. We picked mushrooms in the fields, threading them onto a thick blade of grass, as we found them like jewels on a chain.

Daddy was tall and thin and kept himself very well. He was dogged with a nagging pain in his hip, either from a fall from a horse or a tumble down the stone basement steps at the back of Annesgift House. There is a black and white photograph of him taken in Annesgift kitchen garden in the forties wheeling a large wheelbarrow stuffed with cauliflowers and cabbages. He's wearing a tweed cap, a waistcoat and tweed jacket. Olivia Hughes is also in the picture, slightly out of focus, walking behind him in a sturdy tweed skirt and jacket over a woollen jumper, her lovely white hair in a halo like dandelion fluff around her head.

Whoever took the photograph was concentrating on the wheelbarrow full of produce. Those cabbages and cauliflowers and Daddy's young handsome face are in clear crisp focus.

He was a man who loved the famous Irish tenor John McCormack and later McCormack's successor on the world stage Clonmel tenor Frank Patterson. For years Daddy had an old gramophone on the sitting-room table. When the twins were born the sitting room became a bedroom so the gramophone was moved to my parents' room to make space. He was a secure, happy man with a quiet solid wisdom that doesn't come from books. I remember once getting into a sulk because I was going to a film, *The Seven Little Foys*, and could only afford the pit. 'You'll see exactly the same film from the pit as from the balcony,' Daddy told me. It's an idea that stuck with me: Your vantage point is less important than your vision.

He would scan the fields every day for anything out of place, a blown-down branch or debris. I can still see him walking among the trees of Annesgift and stopping to gaze into space, as if the cathedral of trees helped him to think like a church could help someone to pray.

If he found something out of place, he'd make sure that it was removed immediately. He was meticulous about time keeping, arriving for work on time, doing your work and finishing on time. He was always keeping notes, details about the farm animals of Annesgift. His leisure time consisted of a weekly trip to McCarthy's bar in Fethard, where he would talk to other men about the harvest, the animals and the state of the country. He took a great interest in his own area but also the wider issues of Ireland and beyond. In McCarthy's he always had two glasses of Guinness and a 'medium' which was the name given to a small bottle of stout.

He dug the vegetables from our garden for the dinner and he polished his own shoes. He read the *Farmers Weekly*, a thick yellow English magazine that came to Annesgift and was then passed on to us. My parents shared the labour of running our home and were adamant about respecting others. When my brother Donal arrived I was old enough to be struck by the gentleness with which he was handled. They showed me how to hold him in the bath and rinse his small head with a container of lukewarm water warmed specially.

There were nights in spring when something woke me and I would come down to find an orange box lined with newspaper drawn up to the fire. Inside there would be a newborn lamb. Its mother might have died or rejected it. The lamb was fed using a glass lemonade bottle with a black rubber teat on top. It was a job that I often did, the small creature sucking the milk down with a powerful tug, gazing calmly at you before it fell asleep in its box with a full belly of milk. We cleaned the glass bottle by putting sand into it and shaking it to scour off the milky clots before rinsing it out with water. I fell in love with every lamb and cried when they were taken back to the flock.

Our milk came straight from a cow, frothy and warm and strained through a cheesecloth, which was rinsed and hung on the line to flap in the wind. After I left home, my parents got their own cow, and called her Bluebell. Like us, she treated Annesgift as her own kingdom, regularly grazing in the lusher fields of the estate rather than sticking to our own smallholding of an acre. Our ducks too often wandered down through the fields to the river.

Animals were a big part of our lives. There's a picture of me with Gill, the Hughes's big shaggy dog, sitting on the steps of Annesgift when I was about three years old. I remember the old dog, not least because Gill bit me; he turned and caught me on the side of the nose with one of his fangs. I think I must have pinched him. Even though I still have the scar it never turned me off dogs.

Horses were and still are my first love. When I was a child the horses of Annesgift were working animals, strong calm beasts that pulled farm equipment. I would stand and stroke their hot necks, breathing in their warm smell. Four stone drinking troughs stood, one in each corner of the large farmyard at Annesgift. The working horses drank long cool draughts of water, the sweat steaming off them after their work in the fields. The stables around the yard were filled with clean straw for them to rest at night.

I learned to ride and was allowed to borrow a Connemara pony from the Annesgift stables. Someone gave me a pair of secondhand jodhpurs that I was thrilled to wear, not least because they were the nearest I got to wearing trousers. Both the pony and I were fearless. One of the many things we did was ride up and down the silage mound, the pony's hooves compressing the hill of freshly cut grass, surefooted and confident. The silage pit was the first of its kind in the area. It was more typical for summer grass to be turned into hay for winter feed. It's a small miracle that the pony never lost his footing on the shifting mound. The danger never occurred to me. I kept urging him up and down the slopes as often as his obedient legs would go.

I rode the larger dray horses up to the farrier at the crossroads to have them shod with no fear about taking these huge animals out onto the road. I loved to sit and watch the blacksmith, Davy O'Meara, work and talk to him about horses, smelling the flinty tang of the hot shoe iron. He shod the horses on a corner beside his house, under two large trees. I was fascinated by how flimsy the old shoes were, worn thin by use. The new set of shoes seemed so solid and permanent, ringing off the road as I clipped back home on the freshly shod horse.

My siblings and I spent our time in the farmyard, the big house and fields where our parents worked. All of Annesgift House was open to us apart from Ciss's rooms. Ciss Grady was the housekeeper and cook, and her living quarters in a side wing of the house were off limits for us children.

'There's poor Alice,' she used to always say when I came into view.

'Poor Alice' was her term of endearment for me.

In our own small garden we had an apple tree and potato drills. When the potatoes were harvested they were buried in a pit to give us a store to last through the winter. Behind Annesgift they had a large kitchen garden that produced food almost all year around. A small workshop nearby held the garden tools, the string and boxes, scissors and secateurs, forks and spades that were used to keep everything growing well.

The kitchen garden was an amazingly abundant place. There were large patches of parsley and rhubarb. Along one wall there were plums and apples. In the greenhouse they grew tomatoes and there were cold frames for cucumbers and marrows. At one end there was a cider apple orchard. We picked the apples for cider makers Bulmers. In late summer there were rows and rows of raspberries, gooseberries, redcurrants and blackcurrants. Much of these ended up as jam in Olivia Hughes's store room.

Another field closer to the river held an apple and pear orchard and Mrs Hughes kept beehives here. We thought her beekeeper's suit looked like something from outer space. William Leech's 1913 painting 'A Convent Garden, Brittany', a scene of a woman dressed head to toe in white, in a garden drenched in sunlight and summer green, always reminds me of Mrs Hughes working with her bees, although Leech was painting nuns in white rather than beekeepers. Mrs Hughes loved the bees, but they terrified us. Although we steered very clear of the hives, we still loved the sticky crunch of the honeycombs.

The wool room, where I have that first strong memory of sitting in my pram as the men worked, was just inside the stone arch entrance to the farmyard. A trestle made from strong timber beams would hold the larger trunks of trees so that they could be cut into rounds more easily. Upstairs from the wool room there was a loft that was always called the rabbit room. Each field on the farm had its own name.

Down the stone steps at the back of Annesgift lay a set of cool cellar rooms. To the right was the coal cellar. My sister Eileen still has a scar on her leg from a fall down there. To the left was the kitchen wing. The kitchen had a tiny sink and a huge Aga. There was a dumb waiter that was rarely used and a small cold room for jams and chutneys. A small dining room beside the kitchen held a large round table. In the middle was a wooden lazy Susan, a flat board that spun to allow you to swing the salt to someone on the other side of the table.

The cellar dairy was always freezing cold, winter or summer. Its cool stone counter was where eggs were stored, butter was made, the buttermilk saved for drinking. I never liked buttermilk, but I loved the bricks of bright yellow butter sometimes still wet and oozing with white buttermilk. My sister Eileen hated the butter but liked the buttermilk.

There were always crows nesting in the big trees around the farm but we knew the sounds of other birds. Olivia Hughes loved to teach us to identify the birdsong. Everything was learning and doing.

My brothers, Donal and Martin, played in their imaginary farm in the fields near our house. Eileen, Mary and I played shop in our makeshift 'cabby house', often with our cousin Joan from up the road. We polished up bits of broken glass, crockery and pebbles and sold them in the shop to our imaginary friends and relations who came to visit. Mud pies were our apple tarts.

We never kept geese but our neighbours did and we made pillows from the feathers. There was little or no waste of anything, including time. We embroidered old potato sacks into cushions. We knitted slippers using thick cardboard for the soles. Clothes were mended, darned or fixed and when something reached the end of its life it became a duster or filling for a cushion. We didn't call this recycling. It was just how things were done.

There was a rhythm to the day, to the season and to the year. There was a regularity to the arrival of the travelling families. Usually it was the Delaneys and they would call to my grandfather selling clothes pegs or tin-smithing once a month. They always had something to sell, and if they hadn't arrived at a certain point in the summer you would worry about them.

On St Stephen's Day we dressed up for the Wren Boys and in summer we dressed up for the carnival. Whole families got dressed up in elaborate costumes and a wild sense of carnival would take hold in the town. It was a brief opportunity to pretend to be someone or something else for a night.

In summer I often lay still as could be in the grass for what felt like hours and watched the fairy forts hoping to see the fairies, half thrilled and half terrified at the prospect. Mrs Hughes tried to teach us to swim in the river. We splashed around in the silty brown water and hauled ourselves out onto the warm stones. It was one of her few failures. None of us ever mastered swimming.

In winter I would go out into a frosty morning and take off my shoes to feel the grass crunch like glass under my feet. The thrill was finding a spider's web on a frozen morning, the tiny beads of dew turned to diamonds in the frozen air.

Major Hughes took us to Helvick when he went fishing and we brought back gleaming silver mackerel for dinner. He also took us to the races and I would go down to the parade enclosure before a race as proudly as if I owned the horse in question.

At home we sat down as a family to every meal, with a grace before meals that focused on gratitude for the good food we would eat. The family rosary was a daily ritual. The evening meal always ended with a dessert: custard or milk puddings, semolina tapioca (which I hated) or rice with a dollop of jam in the middle. Whenever we went to the seaside my mother would harvest carrageen moss to use it as a setting agent in puddings.

Healthcare was rudimentary. We lined up on winter mornings for a spoonful from the big brown bottle of malted cod liver oil. We rubbed the cold juice of raw potatoes on chilblains. We ate nettle soup. The wisdom went that if you had three servings of nettle soup before May you would be healthy for the year. I was always glad when my three servings were over because it was awful stuff. If you got a burn someone would be sent out to find a fern, not the furled up crinkly fern but a flatter-leafed variety with a brown stripe down the centre. This leaf was applied to the burn to treat it.

Happiness and a sense of belonging are the feelings I have from childhood. But there were bad days. My teeth weren't straight and the school dentist just pulled them out. I woke from the anaesthetic in the chair as he was pulling one of them and ended up with a long-standing phobia of dentists.

There was the day I broke my nose in a fall off a bike.

'I've the same right to be on the road as anyone else,' I declared hotly when someone suggested I shouldn't have been cycling in the middle of the road.

My mother told me later she took that bloody-nosed defiance in as a sign of the person I was going to become. Instead of going to hospital with my broken nose I was taken to Mrs Walsh, a distant relation of my mother, who was a bonesetter. She had no training in anatomy or orthopaedics. Bonesetting was considered a gift like healing. My nose was set by Mrs Walsh and that was the end of the matter.

* * *

In the shadow of *Sliabh na mBán*, the mountain of the women, the women of Annesgift were big personalities. Mammy and Olivia Hughes loomed the largest in my life, two strong generous-hearted women who rarely took no for an answer. Mrs Hughes, as we all knew her, was filled with energy and ideas, a feminist before her time, with a strong belief in sharing her privilege and wealth. The Hugheses had no children of their own so we were welcomed into their lives and their home, like a summer breeze on a hot stuffy day. It was Mrs Hughes who established our Macra na Tuaithe branch, where we knitted those squares for Dominique Pire. Around twenty years later I would visit Pire's University of Peace in Huy in Belgium to talk about co-operation and peace.

My friend Goldie Newport, whose family ran a newsagent and grocers in Fethard, describes Olivia Hughes as 'a woman who could not be curtailed'.

'She was wonderful,' Goldie said when we sat recently in her kitchen at the back of the now-closed family shop and remembered those times. 'She introduced us to all the beautiful things of life.' Mrs Hughes's enthusiasm for music, art, books and theatre was infectious. She encouraged women to reach further and empower themselves through their own hard work and hard-earned income.

There were strong women going back generations in my family. My maternal grandmother, Ellen Crean, had talented, busy hands. Her house was a short walk from ours. It stands there still, a cut-stone cottage beside the road slightly further back from Slievenamon than we were.

In good weather I would sit with her in her garden, with bees buzzing around her perfumed pink roses. She sat on a stool we called a 'furm', her hands flashing over some piece of work – intricate lace crochet or complicated knitting. Often she would hum as she worked. Michael William Balfe's 'I Dreamt I Dwelt in Marble Halls' was her favourite

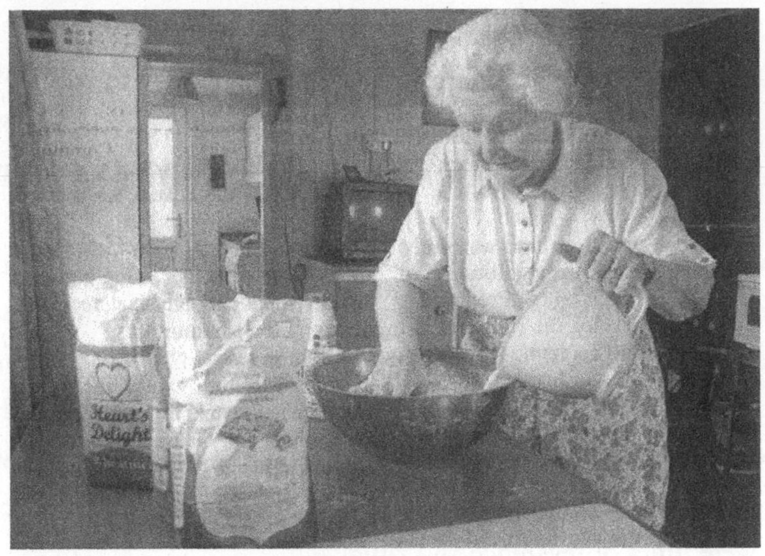

'Hannie still baking for Fethard Country Markets sixty years on' ran the headline in The Nationalist *in August 2008.*

song. It's another thread I have made my own as it is now mine.

Ellen Crean was always beautifully dressed and her shoes always shone. I have a thing about polished shoes. She had luminous skin and shiny hair, which she put down to washing it in rainwater.

Even though I was very young (she died when I was fifteen), she would talk to me about the women that she admired. All of them were women who had broken free of what was expected of them and made their way in the world. There was the opera singer Margaret Burke Sheridan, who was orphaned and used her talent to blaze a trail across Europe. There was the writer Annie Smithson whose novel *The Walk of a Queen* she loved. Annie Smithson was secretary and organiser of the Irish Nurses Organisation from 1929 until 1942, the year I was born.

My grandmother also spoke often about the many west of Ireland people she met during her years in America. Unlike them, my grandmother had returned from America and was back in her small house with her extended family dotted around her in the surrounding fields.

My grandmother and three of her sisters, who lived not too far away, were tall straight-backed women, slim and strong. They always wore long clothes with long aprons over them. Without washing machines a daily change of outfit was impossible. They never spoke about the war, any war. They lived in small-roomed houses that they kept spotless. There was always a little sitting room with a tablecloth on the table and good china in a cabinet. They sprinkled tea leaves on the stone floors to keep the dust down. They cooked over a fire in small fireplaces. A crucifix would often sit on a starched and ironed piece of linen. Holy water was sprinkled with a sprig from a tree picked specially for that purpose. They were times of reverence and ritual.

One of my great aunts was Aunt Jo, who struck me as a romantic figure. Great aunt Jo was always reading novels and she smoked. She worked as a nurse in Daisy Hill Hospital in Newry, and I still have a beautiful picture of her. Her hair is curled in an elaborate winged chignon under her nurse's hat, her uniform crisp and starched, everything cinched in at her tiny waist. Again, I wonder how much my admiration for glamorous Aunt Jo was another thread laid down, a direction that I followed into my own future when I went to train as a nurse.

My grandfather Dan, 'Daddy's father, loved throwing shadow animals with his hands on to walls to amuse us. His wife had died, when Daddy was a child, leaving him a widower with seven children: Daddy, five brothers and a sister. As the only girl, my aunt Alice took over her mother's role rearing her brothers, even though she was younger than some of them. When she grew up Aunt Lally, as we knew her, went to work in England for decades. She told me once about the love of her life who had been an English man. She came back home to live with her father and brother Mick and his family before getting a job as a housekeeper in a house outside Fethard owned by a Miss Selby-Bigge, a great huntswoman.

Aunt Lally retired in old age to a tiny house in Fethard, which she kept neat and sparkling as a doll's house. Her mother had been called Alice. My mother had an aunt Alice. It was very much a family name.

Uncle Mick lived the longest of the six boys in my father's family. He reared pigs and I was fascinated by the piglets. He grew parsley plants so full they were like heads of cabbage. Later when I lived in Dublin he would give me plants to bring back but I could keep them thriving like he could. Uncle Paddy, another brother, played music and wrote songs and poetry.

My mother's only brother, Willie, died aged ninety-three, two years before my mother. He had an immense knowledge of all sport up to his death, something we regret never recording.

My grandfather Dan died when I was in my mid-twenties and I was with him at the very end. Death and dying were given their place and time in the home. A death was not treated as something to be shunted out of sight. There was a pattern of visitors when someone lay dying: the priest, the doctor, neighbours and family. Endless pots of tea were made on the fire. Glasses of whiskey were given to the older men. There was space and time for the sharing of memories, murmured in the room next to where the dying person lay.

My grandfather was laid out at home in the brown shroud used at the time to dress and bury the dead. A widow wore black for a year after the death of her husband. Men wore black wool diamonds sewn onto their jacket sleeves as a mark of bereavement.

Years later when I was a nurse in intensive care I clashed with a priest over his handling of a dying woman. He had blundered in a self-important rush in to her bedside, slashing open the curtain, rudely shattering

Castlehiggins,
Fethard,
Co. Tipperary.
Telephone (052) 31172

If women ran the E.E.C.
No Butter Mountain you would see
Nor Nuclear Compounds there would be
To kill and poison you and me.
But if you would achieve this roll (role
And come out top in every poll
From I.C.A. you learn the skill
Your gifts and talents to fulfil
And friends to back you up, until
With courage you achieve your will
And rid us all from every ill.

Words by Mrs Hughes about the power of women, sent to me in letter form. Some things never change.

the peace and calm that had settled around her. I told him that was no way to behave.

Priests were not figures of fear for me. The closest I got to feeling overawed by them was when the Redemptorists came from Limerick to give a retreat. For the week of the retreat they would stand on the pulpit and thump it hard, sending spittle and dust flying as they ranted about sin and damnation. It was frightening and strange. But otherwise priests were just people to me. Everyone was just a person to me, masters and servants alike.

My parents were contented in their work but regretted that they didn't have a chance to get a better education. They had a social awareness, a knowledge of how important every voice was.

'Did you vote, Alice?' Daddy would always ask me after an election, even after I had left home. He wasn't interested in how I voted, just that I had voted. That was the essential thing.

My parents had lived through extraordinary days, with world war in the newspapers and civil war in violent skirmishes around them. They emerged from those days with the unspoken idea that lives were to be lived rather than pored over.

'Times were hard,' was as much as they would say about their lives before we arrived.

We walked to Coolmoyne National School, meeting up with friends as we went and gathering 'kippins', small scraps of wood for the schoolhouse fire. Like my mother, I liked school. Julia Ryan was one of my teachers. A Kerrywoman, she always wore nail varnish, which was unusual then. She encouraged us to sit still once a day, every day. It was not simply a way of keeping us quiet but as a way of encouraging us to just switch off and tune into the silence. It was mindfulness before its time and another habit I brought with me into adulthood.

Secondary school was different. The Presentation Convent in Fethard was the first place where I was made to feel different because of what others owned and we didn't. We had good tennis rackets, which came from Annesgift, but tennis lessons cost money, as did music, and my parents couldn't afford to pay for them.

I hated maths, but one nun insisted that I wouldn't be allowed to give it up.

'Your mother was brilliant at maths,' she told me. I was furious with her for forcing me to keep up the loathed subject.

Much of what I learned to do and be came from life in Annesgift and the projects and schemes that Mrs Hughes encouraged us to take on. If she saw a need she did something about it, often by press-ganging and encouraging (some might say bossing) other 'volunteers' to line up with her cause.

In the early twenties she had set up a public library and a coffee van for fair days in Fethard. A team of seven women were put on a voluntary rota to run the coffee van, a caravan that would be pulled into the square where the fair day was held. As Mammy noted, there was nothing voluntary about it. Mrs Hughes drew up a rota and you were on it, whether you wanted to be or not. They served tea, coffee or Bovril and hams were cooked in Annesgift for sandwiches.

Inspired by her great friend Muriel Gahan, Olivia Hughes's longest-lasting legacy to the town was the first branch of the Country Markets in Ireland in our home town in Fethard. Mrs Hughes and Muriel were friends from their school days in Alexandra College, Dublin, where they saw both sides of life in the divided city of early twentieth-century Dublin.

The former school friends were optimists and romantics. As a child, I saw Muriel come and go from Annesgift, bustling in with a fresh blast of energy and enthusiasm. Also in that circle of the Hughes's friends were the brothers Becher and Paddy Somerville-Large, clever, driven individuals who wanted to make the world a better place. I got to know Becher's wife, Beatrice, particularly well in later years. She became chairman of the Adelaide Hospital and I visited her up until her death.

In December 1930 Muriel Gahan had opened the doors of The Country Shop in Dublin at 23 St Stephen's Green. It had taken seven months of hard slog to take the building from a neglected former ink-works to the cafe, shop and gallery that I came to know and love when I moved to Dublin.

Eggs from Annesgift were sent by train to be sold in The Country Shop. Later, as a homesick nursing student in Dublin, the shop felt like a freshly baked slice of home. It traded, as a co-operative, for nearly half a century, closing in 1978. A miniature thatched cottage used to hang from the wall of the building on St Stephen's Green to mark its presence. The cottage was regularly nicked by students, who would bring it home as a trophy from a night out.

I learned a lot about self-belief and trusting your own instincts and abilities from these inspiring women. In my early teens I felt no qualms about taking to the stage to recite the Longford poet Pádraic Colum's poem 'An Old Woman of the Roads'.

In the early fifties we set up the Coolmoyne branch of Macra na Tuaithe, which later became Foróige. Mrs Hughes gave us the house annex for our meetings. We met regularly and had guest speakers and debates, as well as knitting those squares for Dominique Pire. There was nothing slapdash about it. We had a secretary, chair and treasurer.

There was more to the Macra na Tuaithe than speaking and meetings.

The first job when you joined was to take on a project. Major Hughes gave me six guinea pigs and a patch of grass down by the orchard, to rear them in a hutch. I fed them on thistles, carrot tops and grass. He helped me make contact with a laboratory in Trinity College Dublin, where they paid me for the guinea pigs, which were used for research.

The project was as much about accounting and management as it was about caring for the animals. At one stage I had sixty guinea pigs. When the animals had grown enough I strapped a special box to my bike, loaded in some guinea pigs and cycled to Fethard train station to put the box of guinea pigs on the train to Dublin. I sent a telegraph to Trinity to tell the lab staff to pick them up at the other end of the line. My sister Eileen had her own small business venture. She grew onions, lettuces and flowers which she sold at the Fethard Country Markets.

I entered my guinea pig project into the Young Farmer of the Year competition and went along to the final in the Cahir House Hotel, full of hope that I would win it.

'This competition is only open to farmers who own the land they farm,' boomed the voice of the senior official from the podium where the prizes were being given out.

I felt a flush of anger. The comment felt like a barb aimed solely at me. I was not a typical farmer, not part of the mainstream and had done something new. Later I realised this idea of working independently in the margins was something that would define my life.

In the fifties I wore a duffel coat, a practical, warm boiled wool coat with bone toggles. On cold nights my duffel coat added an extra layer to my bedclothes, another blanket to keep the chills out. I wore my hair mid-length with a big ribbon clipped on the top of my head. These were the days before girls wore jeans or trousers. It was all skirts, apart from my prized riding jodhpurs. My mother sent to Cassidy's for clothes from a catalogue and everything was handed down. The changes as I began to grow up were never discussed. There was no dramatic talk about periods or puberty. You just moved on with things and got used to each new thing.

In my mid-teens my proudest possession was a pair of white high heels that I wore everywhere. I cycled in them and would get off the bike to totter up the steep Railway Hill, wheeling the bike. I thought those white shoes were gorgeous.

Mammy loved clothes and was always nicely dressed. Mrs Hughes was no style icon to a teenager, always dressed in sensible brogues, tweed skirts and warm woolly jumpers.

I was planning my own future. In the run up to my Leaving Cert, the Newport family (my friend Goldie's parents) knew I had to travel three miles each way to school and invited me to have a hot lunch in their house every day. It was a kindness I never forgot. The kitchen table is still there, and the kitchen almost exactly as I remember it as a child, although the Newports' two shops, like many in small town Ireland, are closed and shuttered. Goldie's father made delicious ice cream.

As a child Goldie was given the treat of a soft scoop before the creamy ice cream was put into the freezer. A talented musician, Goldie still plays the organ in the local church, even though she has officially retired.

I longed to train as a vet but it was too expensive. Instead, I went to work as a chambermaid in the Ormond Hotel in Clonmel, to earn my fees for nursing school. Clonmel was a metropolis compared to Fethard. There was a Woolworths, with its special sugary smell of sweets, Lowry's shop and Boyd's hardware. Clonmel had a theatre, where we went to the opera in the Regal Theatre with Mrs Hughes and danced to Maurice Mulcahy's Orchestra in Collins Hall.

I had barely left Annesgift throughout my childhood. When I was seventeen, I spent six weeks at *An Grianán*, the Irish Countrywomen's Association College, in Termonfechin on a scholarship to learn domestic science. That was my only real experience of being away from home. I learned about budgeting, hygiene, butter making and horticulture. In many ways *An Grianán* formalised some of the skills I had been learning in Annesgift. I remember the cheesemaker, Mary Guilfoyle from Clare, dressed in white in her spotless chilly dairy. We could take a short walk to the seaside in the evening. It was a short time in a lovely place which had a connection to home because Mrs Hughes and Muriel Gahan had helped set it up.

That stay also helped me imagine how my grandmother felt when she went to America. You met other young people from the west of Ireland and worked together as a community. My only other big trip away from home had been with my mother to Manchester, when I was five, to visit her uncle who was a Christian Brother there. We travelled on the boat out of Dublin. It was a long tough journey in bad weather.

In June 1960 I cycled home from my last Leaving Cert exam, feeling light as air and beaming with happiness at the end of the exams. I spent the summer picking fruit and riding a large bay horse up and down the silage mound, last days of childhood spent doing childish things. In September I decided, as I wrote with all the earnestness of my eighteen years, 'to devote my life to the sick'. I wrote to hospitals all over Ireland and The Royal City of Dublin Hospital in Baggot Street said yes.

In the weeks before I left Tipperary, I worked in a hotel and tried to imagine myself as a nurse, taking temperatures, pulses and checking respiration. A list of required clothing was bought: Mary Hicks, the Cuban-heeled shoes, navy cardigans, and black stockings that I noted

Many hands make light work – everything ready for a Country Market morning in Fethard, in 1947. From left to right: Aunty Mary, Kitty Godfrey, Ciss, Olivia Hughes, Daddy, Catherine Trehy and Mammy. My sister Eileen is in the pram and Denis Godfrey is holding the basket.

would be 'so handy to cover any leg blemishes'. Then I took the train to Dublin for my interview.

It was a chilly autumn day when I pushed open the green door of Baggot Street Hospital, to be met with the strong smell of carbolic soap. The friendly hospital porter greeted me in his smart navy uniform, and I sat in the tiled hallway, waiting to be called to see matron. A stream of people: nurses, students, porters and patients, passed me as I quaked with nerves in the cold hall. At one stage, ambulance men wheeled in a patient, who looked blue from lack of oxygen.

A garda called to the desk to ask about someone. A patient left with bags packed. The postman made his deliveries, and I read the noticeboard in front of me advertising the nurses' dance in the Shelbourne Hotel. Another noticeboard showed the list of surgeons and physicians on duty that day. None of the names meant anything to me then.

I remember nothing of what I said in the interview in Matron's organised office. Afterwards, the Hughes's nephew Brendan Haythornthwaite took me to lunch in the zoo. Later, I got onto a crowded, stuffy train at Kingsbridge Station (now Heuston). By the end of the journey home to Fethard I had decided I was going to be a nurse. Shortly afterwards, I got word that my interview had been judged a success.

On a lovely light morning in early spring, with the sun just risen over Slievenamon, I waved goodbye to my family on the platform of Fethard Station, trying to keep the tears from spilling down my cheeks. All my belongings were in two small suitcases. It was a journey of just over a hundred miles, but it might as well have been several thousand.

Outside the train window I could see the familiar stations pass. Tractors with milk tankers were going to and from creameries, lorries filled with lime, horses and carts on the road, cattle grazing in fields, horses and riders exercising on the plains of the Curragh and then the Wellington monument in the Phoenix Park. We were in Dublin.

That world was already changing. Passenger trains to Fethard stopped in September 1963, leaving only goods trains using the line. Four years later, the line was closed down completely, one of many small country lines closed down in a series of short-sighted decisions.

I returned to Annesgift regularly, but my time in the shadow of Slievenamon was over. I was leaving that special world behind; I felt no trepidation or dread. I was young and full of excitement to get to what was next.

CHAPTER TWO

To Rule We Must First Obey

Training to be a Nurse

'No woman should take up the profession of nursing unless she is prepared for hard work, continual self-denial and constant subordination of her own will.'

My handwritten notes from nursing school

It was time to take a stand. We walked down the stairs to Matron's office. I lifted the brass monkey knocker on the handsome door. It dropped with a thump and I glanced around hoping for a smile of encouragement from my fellow protestors. But the corridor behind me was suddenly empty. My crowd had dissolved away. I was alone in front of that brass monkey knocker with Matron's voice behind the door.

'Come in,' she said.

Miss Farrell, the Matron, was an impeccably dressed woman. She was so tiny she was almost swamped by her handsome wooden desk. Although she was physically small in the world of the Royal Dublin City Hospital in 1961, she was the almighty ruler.

I swallowed hard and tried to keep my voice steady.

'We want to complain, Matron,' I said, 'about the rashers.'

The rashers we served to patients were so overcooked they would jump off the plate when you tried to cut them. Matron was a kind woman. She let the silence settle before saying quietly. 'Now, Nurse Leahy, would you go back up. Your mother wouldn't want you doing this type of thing.'

That was it. I was gently dismissed to my duties as an unquestioning, all-obeying nursing student.

Months earlier, I had arrived into the world of Baggot Street Hospital on the bus from the train station. I was just eighteen, fresh from the open space and peace of Annesgift. The hustle and bustle of the city that I saw from the bus window seemed exhausting.

'Baggot Street,' the conductor shouted announcing the stop. He handed me my cases and I stepped down off the bus into my new life. The nurses' home was a building behind the hospital, off Eastmoreland Place. It had been built in 1901 to house thirty nurses, each in their own small but separate room. Today it is part of the Dylan Hotel. I felt weary and homesick when I pressed the bell and waited. The door was opened by a slight middle-aged woman dressed in white. She brought me to a small cream-coloured cubicle on one of the upper floors, which would be my accommodation until we moved to a dormitory and finally a room towards the end of the four years of my training. Waiting for me in a neat pile on my bed was my uniform.

Those clothes felt very strange and new to me. There was a heavy cotton dress over which we wore a starched white apron with a belt and a separate white collar. I had my own black stockings, which were worn winter and summer, and those black shoes (or Mary Hicks, as we called them) with a small heel. In the years to come I would click along the corridors of the hospital with a distinctive brisk rhythm in these shoes and others like them. The finishing touch was a crisp white hat covering my hair, which had to be pinned up underneath. I was proud of my uniform and had to be. There would be regular uniform inspections, where a smudge or a crease would mean a reprimand. The hospital laundry was run with the same precision as the wards, so we were always smartly turned out.

Uniforms have fascinated me ever since. The state of someone's uniform will tell you a lot about how they feel about their job. People react differently to you when you're in uniform. And that can warp a uniform wearer's sense of who they are. It makes them feel separate, even alienated, from those around them. Uniforms can bring power with terrible consequences and are an easy way to hide vulnerability.

I had the day to myself that first day so I went for a walk around the neighbourhood, trying to get my bearings in the din of the city. That evening the girls who were to be my friends for years began to arrive. Mary and Margaret with their western accents, Ita with her softer Clare accent, Maureen and finally Kay, who was late arriving. Maureen was from Dublin and was tall and blonde. The rest of us shared a similar look, with darker hair and clear complexions, healthy young women up from the country. Here was our gang of six, a group of very different individuals. We would disagree about lots of things in the years ahead from county sporting prowess to medical opinions, but we became good friends.

That night we sat in the nurses' sitting room, with the blazing coal fire to ourselves, and chatted about everything from our futures as nurses to our home counties' chances in the All Ireland final. Later we learned the pecking order of the nurses' sitting room. The most senior nurses occupied the warmest armchairs by the fire. We new arrivals were relegated

Posing with my fellow nurses from the Royal City of Dublin Hospital, Baggot Street, in the garden of the Nurses' Home.

to the chillier end of the room and slowly, over the years, made our way to the good seats. That first night a loud knock on the door disturbed the chat and we were summoned to sister's office, which looked out on the lawn at the back of the nurses' home. Stiff and stately she told us our duties as student nurses.

We ate supper of toad-in-the-hole around a small table in the dining hall. The nurses around us gave us friendly smiles and reassured us, probably remembering their own first nights here. After supper we settled down in our beds and talked across the cubicles, pining for families and boyfriends. Slowly our lamenting ceased and we fell asleep between the cool white sheets of our new narrow beds.

A bell rang at 6am the next morning, and we could hear the footsteps of people already up and busy. It took me nearly an hour to wrestle my new uniform into some semblance of tidiness. Studs twisted and turned in the crooked collar, my apron proved tricky to overlap evenly. The cap seemed impossible to get at the right angle. Struggling into that new uniform gave me a strange sense of stepping out of one role and into another. I was no longer a schoolgirl but a young woman preparing to start a new life of responsibility. It felt glamorous and made me less afraid and unsure of myself. The uniform was armour. This wasn't like dressing up for a carnival, pretending to be someone. This was real, a new chapter.

Finally we went down to breakfast, a hearty meal of porridge, tea and eggs. Our final morning duty was to return to our rooms and make our beds. It never took me as long to try and make a bed. I spent a good fifteen minutes trying to perfect my 'hospital corners' until sister came to the rescue. With swift movements she had enveloped the bed sheet into crisp corners, making it look effortless.

By 10am we presented ourselves to matron at her office and were led to the lecture room to get a list of books. We walked to Fannin's of Grafton Street and carried the heavy medical text books and notebooks back to our rooms. They were full of baffling medical terms that made my head hurt and I felt uncertain that we would ever get used to them. Four years of study and apprenticeship stretched ahead of me, and I wondered if we would all complete the training. 'Will we leave to get married or will we go on to be truly dedicated nurses?' I wrote at the time. They seemed to be the only two options open to us as young women in sixties' Ireland, a life of service either in a hospital or in our own home.

Two months of study followed in the classroom on the ground floor of the nurses' home. Everything that seemed so new and fascinating at the start of term began to pale into boredom as we studied under the all-seeing eye of Home Sister.

In May I got my first pay cheque for £2 nine shillings and seven pence or roughly €3.12. It sounds absurdly low, but after taking in inflation it translated to around €75 in spending power today. I celebrated with a trip to Bewleys on Grafton Street. A cake stand filled with sticky cream buns and coffee slices marked my first flush of professional financial independence.

Then I faced my first day on the wards. It was terrifying and exhilarating. We were told to mark the fluid charts in ounces and cc's. We looked at each other hopelessly. A cc meant nothing to us. Doctors asked us for syringes fitted with appropriate needles – number one to number twenty. We had no notion of the difference. Visitors asked us which wards their friends were on and we looked at them blankly. By 3pm on that first day we sat down exhausted and shared our stories from the frontline, each one funnier than the next. Some friends were so tired and daunted by that first day that they planned to pack their bags that night and leave. But we got used to it. We learned the ropes and after six months we got our holidays.

* * *

Soon I felt at home in Baggot Street Hospital. It was its own world, with its characters and personalities, like Mr Jennings, the senior porter dressed in his smart navy blazer. His stern face was the first one I saw inside the door. He was of medium height and clean shaven with a high polish on his shoes and clean trimmed fingernails. He was very proud of his uniform and held himself well, with shoulders back and a tilt to his chin. In the hospital hierarchy he ranked alongside the matron in seniority. He instilled a confidence in us, knowing that somebody was watching the door. Beside his large wooden desk was the telephone exchange where telephonist Carmel Manning sat. Carmel had a pink complexion and wore glasses. She was visually impaired but never saw her poor sight as an obstacle to her work. She connected callers to the hospital to the doctors and nurses around the wards. Her husband Frank, who was a musician, was also visually impaired. Later I would come to realise how much knowledge Carmel had about what happened inside the walls of this building.

Nursing was an apprenticeship. We learned from our peers. Ward sisters passed on their strict culture of hygiene, pristine uniforms, courtesy and thrift. If we broke anything we paid for it from our wages. We spent hours standing at a big table in the middle of the ward rolling cotton wool into balls for use as swabs.

The hospital and the nurses' home felt like a community. We were all in it together: the porters, the domestic staff and the nurses. As student nurses, we scrubbed and cleaned alongside the cleaners. The tiles of the hospital shone and the whole building smelled of Jeyes fluid and carbolic acid. There was a huge brass steam steriliser, where instruments, cotton balls and other equipment were all sterilised for use. Equipment was not disposable. Even syringes were reused after sterilisation. In his history of the hospital, *Baggot St, A Short History of the Royal City of Dublin Hospital*, Professor Davis Coakley described how one doctor would plunge a syringe into wool wadding to test its straightness. If threads of wool got caught on the syringe it was rejected. A bent syringe made for a painful injection.

One of our jobs, as student nurses, was to take a tin bottle of Brasso and shine the brass steriliser to a bright gleam. The tangy polish dried in white chalky smears on the brass before you polished it off to reveal a burnished shine underneath.

There was hard physical labour, much of it difficult to do while trussed up in a stiff heavy uniform that had to be kept scrupulously clean. Beds were pulled out and the spaces under them dusted and cleaned. Practice made my hospital corners perfect. We cleaned the wheels of those beds and the lightbulbs that hung over them. Matron did rounds every morning and everything was checked from a housekeeping point of view, even under the beds.

In between our duties on the wards we sat in classes. I still have some neatly handwritten notes from my lectures. One lecture centred on the qualities of a good nurse. We were presented with an extraordinary set of rigorous and demanding ideas. We were expected to be somewhere on the spectrum between a saint and a superhuman. There was no room for mistakes. We were in a place where our actions could have serious consequences and that weight of responsibility was made clear.

'Every order should be carried out with the greatest exactness. Never guess out an order,' I wrote down carefully. 'If you do not understand ask someone who knows, or someone in authority. The essence of accuracy is truth. Be truthful in your work and in your dealings with everybody and in the performance of every duty. Avoid all exaggerations. Tell things just as they happen.'

Many of my notes read like instructions to a new army recruit. We weren't expected to click our heels and salute, but a junior-ranking nurse and a foot soldier had plenty in common. In another way, it was like being in a convent. Your duty, like a member of a religious order, was to obey and never to question. I wonder if the instructions would not have been so high-handed if we had been a group of men. Would there have been such an emphasis on knowing your place?

'In hospital there is a code of manners for every nurse to learn,' Home Sister told us, reading from a daunting list of requirements to the roomful of new recruits soaking up every word.

'This etiquette consists of showing respect to seniors and those in authority. It has nothing to do with social position and does not affect one's dignity,' she said.

'A nurse should never remain seated when spoken to by anybody of a higher rank, or when a visitor enters the ward. She should never push past the matron or a sister but should stand aside and let her pass. Should the matron enter the ward in the absence of the sister, the nurse, be she staff nurse or probationer, should come forward and see if she is wanted.

'This also holds good if any visitor enters the ward. It is usual for the nurse to open the door for the matron, seniors or staff nurse. She should never lean against a bed or table when addressed.'

This list of rules felt like a tall order for a long nursing shift. Straight-backed obedience meant you had to be ready to get to your feet and behave with exquisite manners at every moment in your shift, night or day. And you always had to know your place. 'The doctor and visiting staff are addressed as "sir" and not by their names,' Home Sister said. At that time the notion that a doctor might be 'madam' rather than 'sir' didn't feature in the instructions.

'A nurse must be punctual, good tempered, obedient and loyal to all rules in the foundation of the work,' Home Sister continued reading from that almost impossible list. 'She must also be active yet quiet, methodical, reliable, careful, clean, neat, observant, intelligent and economical, possessed with self control, gentleness, tact, sympathy and common sense, careful to respect professional etiquette and remembering what is due to those in authority, courteous in manner and attentive to patients' friends (a duty that nurses in pressure of their work are apt to overlook.)'

'To rule we must first obey,' I wrote that day. It seems a stirring line now to a young woman. They were ideas of their time when duty was a strong force in society and women were expected to be both obedient and authoritative. And yet underneath all this steel and crisply starched perfection there was a core idea about learning to care best for the people who needed it. To do that you had to be a decent human who liked and respected other humans, not a robot.

'A nurse must look upon her patients as individuals to be cared for personally, not merely as cases to be treated medically,' I wrote in my notes. They were people first, patients second.

As student nurses we got to know the domestic staff as we cleaned alongside them. Many of these women had come from institutions, county homes or Magdalene laundries, where they had been treated as slave labour from a young age. They left an institution to come and work in another institution and when they grew too old to work they died in an institution. They were ideal employees, obedient and unquestioning of authority. They knew who was boss. But they were a whole generation of women whose lives never got the chance to flourish, whose potential was daily flushed down the drain like the grimy water from a mop bucket.

Later in my career in Baggot Street, I worked with a cleaner called Kathleen, who was from Limerick, and she was wonderful at putting worried relations at ease. She was thin, had short, dark hair and seemed to fizz with a lively energy. She was not afraid to approach me or other nurses if she saw something she could do to help people.

'Is it alright if I make them a cup of tea sister?' she'd ask when she spotted someone or some family in distress. They might be standing in a huddle in the corridor outside a ward digesting some bad news or worried about a relative who was very ill.

I was always struck by Kathleen's empathy and ability to see things unfold that we might have missed. I imagine her other colleagues on other floors did the same.

Kathleen had her own issues. Perhaps the reason she could spot someone falling apart was that she worked hard to hold herself together. After a late night and a dash into work in the morning her lipstick could stray wildly off the mark in a way that would have been comical if it hadn't been sad.

Nellie Stewart, the hospital housekeeper, ruled the place for a long time. Plump with short hair, she had the air of someone in charge about her. She ruled with a firm hand but took a mother hen approach to her charges, making sure they were well looked after. She had her own kitchen on the ground floor, near the doctors' common room, where young doctors would come in at night after carousing or playing rugby in the local rugby clubs in Trinity or Old Wesley.

As student nurses we also cooked. Very badly. Mrs McNamara was the head cook in the big third floor kitchen that provided meals for staff

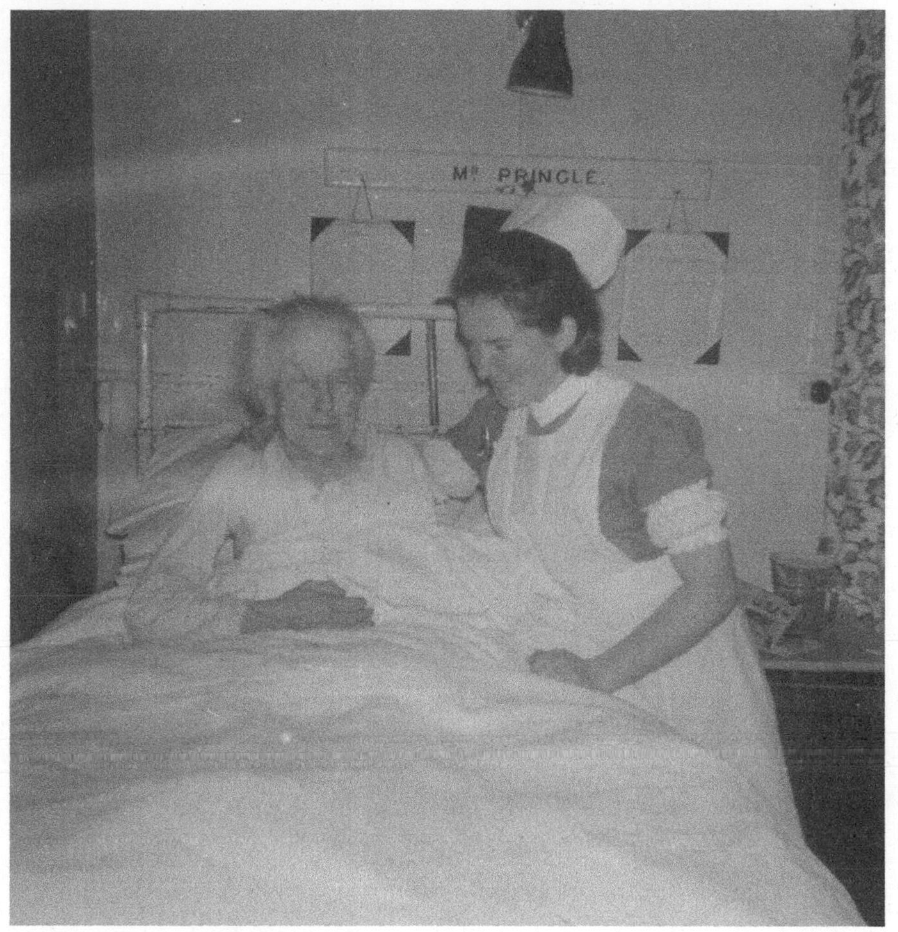

Connections from the past — a woman who knew my grandmother in the USA.

and patients. All you saw of her when you walked into the kitchen in the run up to lunch or tea was her broad back and strong arms stirring pots that filled the room with smells and hot steam. There was a large kitchen table in the middle of the room. As young nurses we ate at this table on night duty, bringing dinners of wildly varying quality, down to the night sister on a tray.

In the mornings we lit the fires, coaxing warmth into the wards and the staff offices. We cleaned the toilets on the ends of each floor.

There were several semi-private beds when I was a student, with curtains around them to give patients privacy. Those wards were sunny and bright, with flowers at most of the bedsides. Flowers aren't welcome in hospitals now. They are another loss to the tyranny of health and safety regulation.

I kept a diary as a student nurse and recorded the landmarks, the events and incidents that stood out. There are trivial things, like spilling Lysol disinfectant, thick and brown as coffee, all over my apron and stockings or remarking on how gorgeous a Bohemians' footballer patient was, after he'd been a patient in the hospital to have his appendix out. There were also profoundly serious things that I was encountering for the first time. I noted my first experience of death on a ward. It was a Miss Butler and she died in the Stoney Ward. That's all I noted, nothing about how she died, her age or circumstances. I'm certain we talked about death but we all came from a time when death was part of our childhoods. The fact that the people who died in the hospital weren't relatives probably made it easier to move on.

There was a ritual to a hospital death. We respected the dead and the manner of their dying. Patients were given the last rites. A crucifix and holy water would be brought to the bedside. No matter how busy the ward was someone always stayed with a dying patient. They were never left alone. In as much as we could in a busy hospital, death was afforded its own dignity and peace. Immediately after a death the body was left for an hour in stillness, to allow the spirit to be released. Then we washed the body to prepare it for the morgue or the undertaker.

But some deaths stopped me in my tracks. On a Good Friday afternoon around 3pm a man was brought in after a very bad car accident. He was young, darkly handsome and gravely injured. He lived for a short while but then died. I was struck by our similar ages. His death seemed wrong and sadder than any other I had encountered so far.

In my first summer of training a patient tried to commit suicide. It was a word that was rarely used and there was no concept that the mental health of patients should be the concern of a nurse. Our role was to fix them up physically, nothing more. In another diary entry I wrote about how horrible it had been to have a BID, or Brought in Dead, case, the term that used to be used in hospitals before the American DOA (dead on arrival) became more common.

The life of an apprentice nurse was a strange mixture of physical drudgery and challenging learning. In our precious time off we always got as far away from the hospital and nurses' home as our feet or bicycle wheels would carry us.

The cleaning, scrubbing, lifting and carrying was broken up with time in the classroom and learning at the elbow of a doctor or staff nurse. I was discussing things I had never talked about before: bodily functions, psychology, anatomy. We had studied some anatomy in school as part of domestic science but this was another level. There was a wonder about it.

In Baggot Street and other hospitals at the time there was a great emphasis on large spaces between the beds for hygiene. It seemed to work. We didn't have outbreaks of infection. If we were in the middle of a task and our shift finished we continued with the duty until it was done, regardless of the clock.

We had more contact with patients' families than would be the norm now. Patients would introduce us to their families when they visited the wards, so we were more exposed to the fears and anxieties of a family if a patient was very sick. Older colleagues encouraged us to be detached. We were not supposed to be emotional. We were being trained to suppress any natural distress in a difficult situation, and we were never encouraged to talk about our feelings. It was a huge help in doing the job, but I wonder now what that training does to you as a person, a life spent swallowing your emotions and briskly moving along to the next bed?

The uniform protected me, giving me some sense of detachment. But there was little thought about caring for the carers, the legions of women who put their hearts and backs into mending people physically and sometimes mentally. There was no place to go to talk about how you felt. Sometimes we would laugh about it all. Getting emotional about things was not felt to be helpful to your ability to be a nurse.

Later in my work I saw how people started to use language to distance themselves from distress and pain, to dis-entangle messy human emotion from a situation. Homeless people became 'clients' or 'service users'. A whole dictionary of corporate-speak was used to put a distance between the true realities of life and how it reads on paper in end-of-year figures and reports.

I learned how to sit with people and let them talk, sometimes from watching older doctors and nurses dealing with patients. One of those doctors was Professor Victor Synge, a nephew of playwright JM Synge. He had snow white hair and a walrus white moustache and wore heavy black-framed glasses. He was rarely seen out of his white coat, which he wore over a suit and tie. Medical students were terrified of Professor Synge. He kept them on their toes, likely to shoot a question at any one of them out of the blue, but he was extremely kind to patients. One day as he did his rounds of the ward he sat down to talk to a woman from Pembroke Road.

'How are you today,' he asked her.

'Not good, Doctor,' she said in a shaky voice that dissolved into tears.

'I'm worried about my cat at home while I'm here.'

Professor Synge pulled up a chair and sat beside her bed, held her hand, looked at her and listened to her, all the while being watched by a breathless group of medical students, and me, waiting attentively for him to move on to the next patient. It was a powerful lesson, about connecting with patients and being kind, even if you were the most important person in the room. 'Why are you late, sir?' Professor Synge once demanded as a hapless medical student arrived on rounds, flustered and rushing.

'Eh, there was a dead dog in the canal, Professor,' the young man spluttered.

'Right,' Professor Synge said, turning on his heel and marching out of the ward.

'Follow me.'

The story told is that he marched his group of bewildered students up to the canal to find the dead dog floating slowly along. He turned the canine corpse into a teaching exercise.

'First, I'd like you all to note the time and calculate, according to the movement of the body, and the distance it needs to travel at what time precisely this dead dog will arrive at the Grand Canal Basin,' he told them.

'Next, I'd like you to tell me what the cause of death of this unfortunate animal might have been,' he said.

'Finally,' he ordered. 'Do any of you know who should be contacted about this public health hazard? '

The poet Patrick Kavanagh was a patient during my first year of training. We were his local hospital in the heart of Dublin's literary district of Baggotonia. We were just down the road from Parson's Bookshop, a wonderful place in a corner building where Baggot Street meets the canal. It was run by a Miss O'Flaherty. It had a delightful smell of books, and you could lose yourself looking at the shelves. Kavanagh, who was in his late fifties at the time, seemed a very lonely character. I would see him sitting up in his bed sunk in his own thoughts.

Brendan Behan was also a regular patient, but a different character altogether. The two writers didn't get on. In his book *Dead as Doornails* Anthony Cronin claimed that Kavanagh was physically frightened of Behan, despite Kavanagh being the bigger man.

'Ah go on, nurse, take it,' Brendan Behan said to me one night in the outpatients' room beside accident and emergency, trying to press a couple of pound notes into my hand.

'No, Mr Behan. Thank you, but I can't,' I told him and walked away.

'Ah go on,' he said, following me, dead set on giving me the money to say thank you for looking after him on a previous visit. Someone came to my rescue and took him by the shoulder to explain that there was no way I could accept his gift.

Behan was often in and out of accident and emergency with a combination of ailments, chest trouble and health problems. I may not have even been the nurse who helped him but he wanted to make a gesture of thanks for his care.

Later during my time in Baggot Street I babysat his children, Blanaid and Paudge, for their mother Beatrice, who lived in Anglesea Road. A doctor in Baggot Street, Julia Grove-Raines, had digs in Beatrice's house and had introduced me to her.

Time off was rare, so I bought a bicycle and made my own little domain of Dublin galleries, museums and churches that I could reach easily to escape the smells and sounds of hospital life. I went to Robert Roberts for coffee, to Woolworths on Grafton Street and to dances in the Metropole Ballroom on O'Connell Street. Home from home was The Country Shop at 23 St Stephen's Green. Going down the stone steps to the basement I could smell the scones and bread baked there that morning. The tables had oil cloths and you drank tea out of hand-painted sturdy cups. Miss Keogh, one of two sisters, was always at the desk, and many of the women who had been writing to my mother when I was growing up were in and out of the building.

It was a real connection to Annesgift. Mammy would send up the accounts to The Country Shop. Life at home carried on without me. The animals grew and grazed. Fruits and vegetables had their seasons.

On warm days student nurses sat together in the gardens at the back of the hospital. The area is built up now. The mortuary and an anatomy lecture room with model skeletons were in the yard at the back of the main hospital. The laundry was in a separate yard near the tennis court which was set up on the lawn in the summer. I often sat there in the sun with a rubber cap on my head, strands of hair pulled through holes by my fellow student nurse Anne from Kildare. She would peroxide the strands and I would sit there letting them bleach in the sun for a set of home-made highlights.

Life was busier than I had ever known. I took on the challenge with my usual energy but it took its toll. I was too energetic. I threw myself into life and work without holding anything back. It took a whole chunk out of me. The life of a student nurse meant your time never felt like it was yours. When you weren't working you had to study or be prepared to be called on duty. I was tired and down at times. In my diary I noted I was 'on duty all day in my dreams'. I made mistakes, flooding the sluice room accidentally and nearly gassing the place by twisting the wrong dial on the gas steriliser.

Two years into my training I felt that life was getting on top of me. I stopped being able to fall asleep as soon as my head hit the pillow. Instead, I lay awake with my mind racing over events of the day. The next morning I would wake drained and exhausted. The pressure of work and training felt overwhelming and I felt I needed help. I made an appointment with one of the consultants, who prescribed a half gram three times a day of phenobarbitone, an epilepsy drug used to treat anxiety.

There was a strength and resilience needed to survive the nursing regime. Part of it came from who you were and the rest was instilled during your training. There was no place for weaker individuals. That might have been why some of the older nurses had a bad name as unfeeling women who followed orders until they were senior enough to give them. It's impossible to measure how damaged that generation of women were by the superhuman effort of constantly keeping their emotions under wraps. The demands of the training meant a complete subordination of your own will. The work of the women who went through this training and lived this life kept hospitals running on meagre resources. These women sacrificed their own lives and desires to the system, and their sacrifice went unnoticed by the wider world.

The ward sisters, in my student days, had huge responsibilities. I never saw them laugh or hold animated conversations. I could never imagine them in a warm embrace. Their strict and ordered lives seemed to turn them brittle. They were every bit as committed to their calling as women in the religious orders. Nursing was a vocation. I wonder how they felt on retirement, whether they felt that giving up family life, motherhood, or another more rewarding career was worth it in the end?

I think the independent streak that was instilled in me from childhood kept me from losing too much of who I was to the system.

My brief encounter with what passed for mental health support ended abruptly. The medication made me drowsy. I went to the cinema on Grafton Street and fell asleep during the film, so I stopped taking it. It was interesting to see how medication was being used to deal with the hurt of living, as it still is now. No matter how tough things got I never felt I had to give up nursing.

My childhood experience, moving between my own family and the Hugheses and their friends, gave me an example of how to be in the world, to be fully involved with things, and never intimidated by bullies, jargon or status. There was great energy, a shared energy in my childhood and I didn't realise at the time how powerful a foundation that could be.

A Tipperary home sister called Annie Grace stood out as the exception to the rule of the straitlaced sisters. She was more eccentric than her peers and had a real twinkle in her eye. She was happy to look the other way when someone was struggling to climb through a narrow window after missing curfew on a night out dancing. She was the sister with whom I got on best. I often felt the other sisters didn't like me. I was different, not willing to butter up the senior staff.

Seniority as a nurse was the only way a woman could climb the ladder in the hospital hierarchy in those early days. All of the consultants during my training years were men. The world was rigorously divided into female and male roles. Women were the nurses, cleaners and domestic staff. Men were in charge. Some of them took their status as consultants very seriously. A number of them had strong god complexes, which didn't take from their ability as a doctor but often made them difficult colleagues.

The domestic staff in their claret-coloured uniform were invisible to some people. Sometimes a doctor in a rush would literally trip over these women as if they were a mop and bucket. One day one of the cleaners was buffing a parquet floor, backbreaking work that's now done with mechanical polishers. At that time she was doing it with a heavy block of wood on a handle that pushed the polishing cloth over the floor. A consultant barrelled past her, with a flock of medical students in his slipstream, pushing her out of the way. She threw the floor buffer after him. I never saw her after that day. Her rage must have had serious consequences.

Dublin felt like a long way from Fethard. Without phone or barely imaginable technology like Skype I was as cut off as if I had crossed the Atlantic to America. My parents sent me the local paper in the post. It was folded in a special way and tied with string, with the address label and stamp on the newspaper itself. The ritual of unfolding this parcel of news from Tipperary and smoothing out the creases to pore over the headlines felt like a real connection with home. I wrote letters to grand aunts, cousins, my siblings. I wrote to my parents every week. Writing home was a habit I kept even after phones replaced the need to write letters. I wrote to Mammy regularly until she died in 2015.

They were lonely times. There was no time for romances. On night duty sometimes I would write scraps of poetry and imagine myself outside the hospital walls in a different life.

My visits home were short. It often took a day to get used to being back in that quiet place and then it would be nearly time to pack my bag to return to Dublin. Walking in the fields, reconnecting with nature, going to a dance, visiting relations were all part of the routine. These visits created another pressure. If you visited one you had to visit another. Uncle Mick and Auntie Mary always got a visit and Mrs Hughes.

I'd get the bus out to Newlands Cross and hitch home sometimes. Before those trips home I always had two jobs to do: a visit to Mackey's garden shop in Henry Street, to buy self-blanching celery plants or some other specific horticultural request for my father, and Lucky Coady's in Dame Street for a Sweepstakes ticket. There was a sense of excitement about a trip home. Mrs Hughes was always delighted to hear about my life in the city where she had grown up. I would always return to Dublin with home-made brown bread or a loaf of gingerbread in my bag.

Most people who came up from the country to work in Dublin would go home every weekend. Friday night marked an exodus out of the city. As a nurse my visits were much less frequent so I had to make Dublin more of a home than it might have been for other people my age.

Baggot Street Hospital was set up in 1832. It started as one large Georgian townhouse on Baggot Street bought by doctors from the College of Surgeons. At the end of the nineteenth century an adjoining house was demolished and the hospital was extended into its footprint. They took off the roof and added two storeys and the entire new building was put behind a single façade designed with a flourish in decorative yellow terracotta and red brick by architect Albert E Murray.

In its early days Baggot Street was funded by the wealthy citizens of Dublin 4 through subscriptions, donations and elaborate fundraising fairs held in the RDS. Its benefactors were rich, but most of its patients were poor. The hospital was a place where the servants of the rich could be cared for. The wealthy in the early nineteenth century were treated by private nurses and doctors in their own homes.

Today Baggot Street is a near-wreck. I couldn't have imagined a derelict future for the hospital back in the sixties when everything seemed so solid and permanent. The hospital felt like a world that could never fall into disrepair. We were in an institution with a hierarchy, where you could see your life mapped out in steps going from student nurse to qualified nurse, ward sister to matron.

It would have been easy to become institutionalised, to grow competent in some things and dependent in others. My childhood sense of a wider world helped me to avoid falling too comfortably into the confinement of this new narrower one.

My old room in the nurses' home is now a hotel room with thick carpet on the floor, a flat screen TV and heavy curtains on the narrow windows, underfloor heated bathrooms, and all the other five star accoutrements. The hospital trust sold the nurses' home to the developers of the Dylan Hotel in 1998.

In 2011, I was shortlisted for a Local Hero Award and part of the event was a stay in the hotel that was once my home as a student nurse. I felt weirdly sure the room I got was my old room from my student days. I lay awake that night, despite the luxury, feeling as if ghosts hovered around me, remembering my student days when we ran up from the fire in the sitting room to our icy cubicles, undressing as quickly as we could to dive under the chilly sheets and get warm again.

At the time of reliving my memories, the hospital is an almost empty building, in which a skeleton staff of health workers run various clinics. The building has been for sale since 2015. It will probably be turned into a hotel, luxury apartments or offices. The new owner has to provide a health care facility in the vicinity of the hospital as a condition of the purchase.

I visited to try to help spark memories of my time there as a student nurse. It was deeply depressing, a salutary lesson in the dangers of revisiting old haunts. I saw wards standing empty and ugly; beds gone; walls painted insipid yellow. Draughts whistled through the emptiness from cracked sash windows. Some of the old wards housed random piles of discarded equipment and debris, a children's bike seat beside some office equipment. Whole wings were cleared out, empty but for my memories of patients, nurses and doctors past. In one ward two buckets and a huge old zinc saucepan stood catching the drips from a seriously leaky ceiling.

Plaster had dropped in chunks on a stairwell and the pigeons clattered their wings in the dank wells and roof spaces outside. Sludge-coloured linoleum covered the old parquet floors, where I had walked miles over the years, clicking along in my Mary Hicks. Walking those empty corridors and climbing the stairs between the floors was spirit-sapping and sad. The building is a monument to everything that is wrong with the Irish healthcare system. It is a building about which nobody seems to care.

The heart and soul of the place has withered. All those years of labour that an army of women worked keeping the place gleamingly polished, are just a memory.

The old hospital is marooned in the heart of Dublin's business district. What was once Baggotonia, a place of poets and writers, has become the domain of bankers and accountants. The view of mountains we once had from the top floor ward is now obscured by new office buildings. Baggot Street Hospital is an obsolete time piece waiting for a consortium to spend the millions it will take to transform it into a luxurious place of work or leisure. The era of the small voluntary city hospitals is gone, swept away in the seventies when the government decided to abolish Dublin's network of smaller hospitals and focus everything on the large campus-style facilities of St James's, Beaumont, St Vincent's and Tallaght Hospitals.

It's only in recent years we see what was lost when those hospitals closed their doors. Clearly there are advantages to centralising resources and healthcare in one place, but I still feel it was a dreadful mistake to walk away from community-based services. Hospital care in Dublin is poorer for the loss of its small city hospitals like Mercer's Hospital, the Meath, Dr Steevens', Jervis St, the Richmond, Harcourt St Children's Hospital, the Adelaide Hospital, Hume St, Sir Patrick Dun's and the Royal City of Dublin Hospital on Baggot Street. Many of them were sold for private developments, putting public buildings into private hands. Hospitals were no longer small accessible places bedded in to the districts where people live and work. The danger with large hospitals is that they become self-contained bubbles where systematic dysfunction can thrive. And that hinders both decent care for patients and healthy work environments for doctors and nurses.

Baggot Street gave me a solid training as a nurse. But even in those early days in the sixties I started to see glimpses of people who would feature later in my life. There was Kitty, a woman around town. Everyone knew her. Kitty was small with a round face, strong features and rosy cheeks. She reminded me of the women Paul Henry painted so vividly, those strong raw faces of islanders in headscarves. She carried all her belongings in a set of bags and had beautiful skin. She wore old fashioned knickers with elastic, huge voluminous things, and she'd

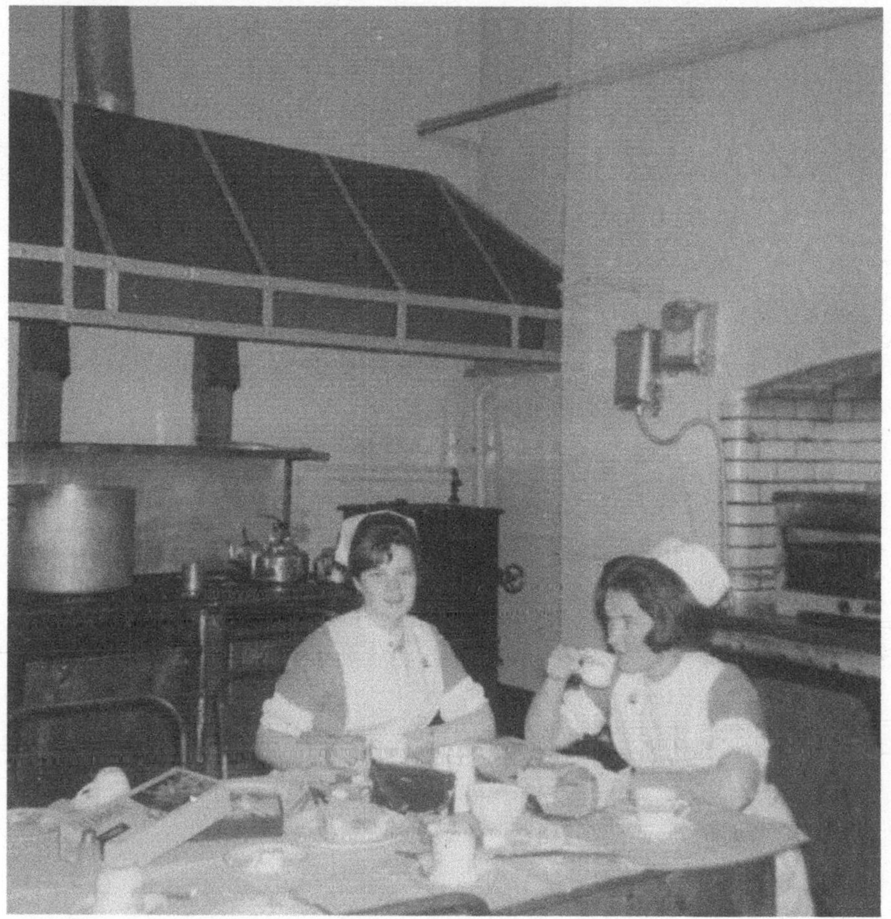

A tea break in the big old kitchen on night duty.

come to the toilets of different hospitals to wash them, hanging them up to drip dry in the toilets. We left her to it. She wasn't doing any harm. There were strict instructions from on high not to interfere with her routine and let her be.

When I was working in Simon a man who was known as Sligo on the streets came up to me. He was tall and rail thin, with dark hair, but he seemed strong. He was softly spoken and calm whenever I met him and always glad to get a bed. His skin was weathered and lined, a testament to his tough daily life. He was very well liked by everyone but was cut off from his roots in rural Ireland. He pressed a soft, folded five pound note into my hand and said quietly:

'You saved my life a lifetime ago,' he said.

He said he had had an operation for a hole in his heart when he was a boy, and I had nursed him in Baggot Street. I didn't remember him, but he remembered me. You meet people in life and you never see them again and you don't know the damage you might have done, or the good.

At the end of four years in Baggot Street I had learned a lot about life and nursing. I knew about sickness and death. I wanted to go to the other end of the process and learn about birth. Sitting in the nurses' sitting room up in the eaves of the hospital, I told my friends and colleagues that I was going to train as a midwife. I didn't think I could call myself a nurse without it. If someone asked me to come to their aid when they were having a baby, I wouldn't know what to do. It was time to leave Baggot Street and take the short trip over the River Liffey to the Rotunda.

CHAPTER THREE

Listening for a Heartbeat

New Life in the Rotunda

'A few more years and old you'll be
Friends, married, ill or dead perhaps ...
Please call again some day you pass,
It's nice to hear a voice at last.'
A poem I wrote about Mrs Hillers,
a Benburb Street resident, in 1968

A pinard horn looks like the earpiece of an early telephone. It's a hollow tube shaped like a trumpet, one end wider than the other. The pinard horn is a foetal stethoscope. Today it's been largely replaced by the electronic Doppler machine which broadcasts the pulsing whoosh of a baby's heartbeat in its mother's womb.

Learning to use my black Bakelite pinard horn was quite a skill. I had to push the wider end firmly against the tight skin of the woman's pregnant abdomen. Then I put my ear to the other end to listen. I was the only person who could hear the baby's heartbeat, unlike today when the Doppler shares the sound with everyone in the room. I had to concentrate and listen profoundly to detect weakness, an irregular rhythm or, in the worst, stomach-sinking scenario the absence of a heartbeat when a baby had died. We used touch, sight and those small sounds of the tiny heart to determine the condition of a baby. We had no scans to let us examine the foetus, measure its skull and determine its gender. The pinard horn was our hotline to the baby's life in utero.

From my first day in the Rotunda midwifery was hands on. And there was a sheer wonder to it. The taut warm skin of a pregnant woman, an ankle or an elbow rippling underneath as the baby moved, the tips of my fingers feeling tiny nubby toes behind a thin wall of muscle when I carried out one of my first internal examinations. The owner of those toes must be fifty now.

The Rotunda was an extraordinary place of history and community. I moved in to my room in the nurses' home on the grounds to begin life as a student midwife. My new uniform came from from Arnott's on Henry St. It had a coat and a storm cap. The Rotunda was an older hospital than the Royal Dublin City. The lying-in hospital was founded by the surgeon and impresario Bartholomew Mosse, in George's Lane (now South Great George's Street) in 1745, after he lost his first wife and eldest son during or shortly after childbirth. In 1748 Mosse bought the Rotunda site, and the Rotunda opened nine years later in 1757. Mosse was motivated by his personal loss and by concern about the abject poverty in the city and spent his short life fundraising for his hospital for the citizens of Dublin. It was an act of philanthropy which left him penniless when he died.

Shortly before I started midwifery training, I had spent a month in

St Patrick's Hospital in Cashel. I knew the old stone building from visits as a teenager when we used to bring books, papers, sweets and flowers to the residents who had no visitors. Then it was still remembered as the County Home, a former workhouse. The stigma and shame of the workhouse and the county home system, the place you went when you had run out of options, was something that flowed down through generations.

By February 1965, when I arrived in Cashel, St Patrick's was a hospital run by the Mercy nuns. Mother Aquinas, a distant relation of my mother, was matron there. I lived on John Street in Cashel with Nellie Dwyer and cycled home to Annesgift on days off. Some of the patients in St Patrick's were people that nobody wanted to know, longterm residents living out their lives forgotten by the outside world. Men of the road called for shelter. Later I would send a man who had been badly burnt in a fire down there to convalesce.

Attending a national conference on the Unmarried Mother (as they were known then) in the Irish Community, with Fr Donal O'Mahoney, 1970.

The horror of the workhouse was a fresh wound among the older generation. Mention the workhouse system and I always think of Johnny, a homeless man I would meet years after I left the Rotunda, who was from the Westland Row area of the city. He dropped into us in Trust regularly but would never ask for anything and kept his thoughts to himself. You always knew he liked a drink. His sister was a nun in England and she would ring Trust to talk to him and ask how he was managing with the drink. We had to reassure her with a little white lie and tell her he was fine because there was nothing she could do.

One day he ended up in Blanchardstown Hospital. Doctors discussing him at the end of his bed mentioned St James's Hospital, which reminded him of St Kevin's, the South Dublin Union county home. This upset him and he went out to the toilet and started to smoke. He was discovered and got into trouble, so he got out of his bed and walked in his bare feet the eight miles into the city centre, to get away from what he feared was the threat of being sent to the county home.

I caught up with him in an early house in Smithfield. I walked in out of the bright morning into the dim and dingy pub lit by the flickering cigarettes in the hands of the drinkers like stars in the sky.

'Jesus here she comes,' I heard Johnny say from the dark depths of the pub.

So we sat down with him and brought him back to Trust, fed him, cleaned him and got him into a hostel. He died not long afterwards, and we got permission from Glasnevin to bury him in an old grave so he didn't end up in a pauper's plot. Noel, one of our volunteers, made a wooden cross to mark his resting place.

The old county home in Cashel had left its past as a workhouse behind it during the short time I worked there. Today it's a wonderful health centre, proof that good things can happen in places with sombre pasts. Standards of cleanliness were as high there as in Baggot Street, but equipment was basic. They had one syringe. I used to wash the syringe and boil it up between uses to inject the two patients who were on Insulin and needed daily injections.

As a pupil midwife in the Rotunda I was able to put a face on that abstract idea of 'social issues.' They were in the haggard lines of malnourished women worn out by multiple pregnancies. The public wards of the Rotunda were a window into a part of Dublin that I had never encountered, despite living in the city for four years as a student nurse. Many of the women on the prenatal ward, where I spent most of my time, came from the kind of poverty I had never seen. In a time when contraception was illegal they had little control over their reproductive lives. The brown charts clipped to the ends of their beds often listed a baby born every year. Some of these babies were already condemned to a life of exclusion before they were born. I know I've met some of the children of those women in my work decades later, people whose heartbeats I listened for in their mother's womb with my black Bakelite pinard horn.

The patients in the Rotunda, unlike Baggot Street, were predominantly from Dublin, as were the cleaners and porters, which gave the hospital a great sense of community. We did one thing there, caring for mothers and their babies. In general medicine we dealt with a variety of issues and illnesses. Here in the Rotunda it was all about new life, with all its hope and promise.

The Rotunda had a sense of history and lives lived that seemed to come from the building itself. The chapel in the Rotunda, with its beautiful ceiling, was a special place, where I went for moments of reflection. If buildings have souls, then the Rotunda had an old and gentle one. I would often think about the babies who had been born here, had

Pride of place – Daddy (Jack) and his father Dan outside the door of our house.

grown up, aged and died, the generations of midwives who had walked the corridors in my shoes before me.

I hated the labour ward. It was a stressful place where the rhythm of birth was dictated by the clock, rather than its own natural progression. Bringing a baby into the world was a wonderful thing, but there was no time or space for the midwife to feel involved in the joy of the event on the busy labour ward. It felt more like a conveyor belt, where a birth had to be managed efficiently, rather than a special place where birthing was afforded its own space, dignity and time. The bleakest room was the cold tiled surgery with its dripping sinks and a pair of iron beds where women were induced, put on an oxytocin drip to speed up their labour.

One day, early on in my training, I watched the worst possible outcome unfold. With a loud wail a mother who had been put on a drip delivered her baby, and then an awful silence fell. The baby made no sound. The doctor in charge asked for help to resuscitate the baby, but it was too late. The newborn cry that we all hoped might pierce the horrible quiet never came. My heart was broken for the mother and I couldn't stop the tears rolling down my cheeks.

They were very different days with different rules. I often brought a cup of tea and a cigarette to a pregnant woman as she sat in bed on the prenatal ward. It seemed like almost everyone, doctors, nurses and patients, smoked like chimneys.

Part of my training involved home visits with the district nurse. In the Rotunda our district nurse was Biddy Butler. She was a Tipperary woman, which was a good bond between us, plumpish and healthy looking, with an air of quiet wisdom about her which inspired confidence both in me and in the women she would head out to see. Later, when I was on night duty, Biddy would always call up to have a chat.

She was a woman with a huge understanding of what the caring part of healthcare meant.

Biddy went out to visit mothers who had given birth in the hospital, or were about to give birth. We drove out in her car on those home visits, Biddy smoking at the wheel. When we arrived in the tough streets of the north inner city, like Corporation Street, Benburb Street and Sean McDermott Street, we always knew Biddy's car wouldn't be stolen. The men of the area knew and respected her.

We climbed up dark stairwells into small rooms hung with holy pictures. There would be a small table often covered with a blanket, no china or bookcases, no TV, maybe a watchful dog lying in a corner, thumping its tail or curling its lip, depending on its mood.

Biddy was always made to feel welcome. We didn't feel like we were intruding because we were there to celebrate the new baby or help an expectant mother. We were always offered tea. Biddy had a real bond with these mothers, despite the fact that she was from the heart of rural Ireland and they were Dubliners born and bred. She never talked down to people and was able to reassure the women that they and their babies were in good hands.

'Now, Mrs Brady, you need to look after yourself,' Biddy would say, sitting down with a woman hollowed out with tiredness. Often the woman would smile with relief, visibly relax in the knowledge that Biddy was here to take some of her load.

'Make sure you're eating and drinking, even cups of tea,' she would say kindly but firmly to the new mother.

'And get others to help you,' she'd add with a pointed look in the direction of a husband or older children. Although husbands often disappeared when Biddy arrived, leaving a cloud of Woodbine smoke in their wake.

At a conference decades later a policewoman in Scotland reminded me of the invaluable work of nurses like Biddy Butler and the power of the district nurse system to reach families alienated from authority. The Scottish policewoman had started life as a midwife, trained as a social worker and then joined the police. She talked about her work in the notorious Gorbals district of Glasgow. As a nurse she was accepted into the house of a family where the father was involved in crime because she was there to look after his child. But nurses weren't supposed to deal with the social issues they saw in these households. That was someone else's department.

There is a smell of poverty that I first came across in the crowded, damp and cold homes I visited with Biddy. I was going to become very familiar with that smell in years to come. It has changed little and you recognise it instantly because it never leaves you. It is the dankness of old unheated walls, mould and all that goes with that. The smell starts with the building, but has human smells layered on top that gave it a lingering quality.

Urban poverty was different to the poverty I had seen at home. No one had money in my circle of family at home, but they had space, wide green fields, big open skies and birdsong. Here poverty was four walls closing in on you and the noise and fumes and coal smoke fug of the city.

My other connection to the lives of the people of the north inner city was Margaret Bradley. She was the social worker attached to the Rotunda. In Baggot Street the social worker was known as the 'almoner', after the society set up in Britain in the forties, which later became the professional body of social workers. The word almoner came from the word alms, charity given to the poor. Margaret worked with hardship cases, usually the poorest of the Rotunda's patients and combined her job as a social worker with voluntary work in her spare time. She gave more than just her allotted hours to helping people. She was a big very friendly woman who, like Biddy, had great humanity. She had an office in the hospital, and I would often bring mothers to see her there.

I enjoyed the midwifery training and did well, getting the highest points in the house exam of that year's students. It wasn't all work. On Sunday nights we used to go down to the Four Courts Hotel to hear the Irish folk group, the Wolfe Tones. We went to the Metropole Ballroom for dances. In March 1966 I was out at a dance in Clery's Ballroom, a short walk from the nurses' home. That night we heard a huge explosion and went out to see that Nelson's Pillar had been blown up by the IRA. I picked up a piece of the rubble as a souvenir, but I must have thrown it away years later without realising what it was.

The sixties saw a lot of change at Annesgift. In the early part of the decade the Hugheses decided to sell the big house. They built a bungalow in Castlehiggins, at the other side of the town, a lovely house which came with a different view of Slievanamon. The housekeeper, Ciss Grady, went with them, moving into a little cottage across from them, where she grew her own vegetables and continued to do their housekeeping. They kept the piano and some of their paintings in the smaller house. They grew beautiful flowers in their garden. I continued to visit Mrs Hughes there often when I went home.

The For Sale sign went up at Annesgift, and my parents decided to wait and see what happened, even though their lives as tenants and employees of the estate were so tied up with the house. I felt they had an idea that you didn't need to own property to feel secure in your own home. In the end a Dutch tulip grower, called Tom Hulsebosch, bought the house and the land. And my parents remained in situ and in service,

Daddy caring for the farm animals and Mammy doing the wages for the tulip pickers and other farm workers.

Around the foot of Slievenamon the fields filled with acres of tulips – yellow, purple and red – rows and rows of gorgeous colour. Working at 'the bulbs' provided summer work for dozens of Fethard teenagers, who cycled out in their droves during the season to pick the bulbs churned up by the harvesters and pack them into crates. Daddy supervised the teenage workers, along with Mammy's brother Willie who had spent time in Holland learning the business. 'There was no messing when Jack [my father] was about,' one former bulb picker remembered in a piece on the local history site, the 'Fethard Notes'. 'Heads were down and the only break outside of the lunch was to go for a pee in the ditch. When supervision was less tight, you could expect a well-aimed bulb in the back of the head from some of the pot shots in the field. By evening, everybody was glad to get on their bikes and waste whatever energy was left in a race back to town.' Daddy handed out the wages on a Friday; for many teenagers it was their first pay packet. Mammy worked out the money and put it in the brown envelopes.

Tom Holseboch was married to a German woman and she helped me make contact with a German hospital to go there to work. I had always been fascinated by Germany, its language and culture.

In October 1967 I left the Rotunda for Kreiskrankenhaus Marienhöhe, a hospital near Aachen, travelling with Nora Collins, a nurse from Limerick.

Run by nuns of Our Lady of Schönstatt, the hospital was a small efficient operation. I lived in the nurses' home, and the nuns made me feel welcome and valued. I worked on a seventeen-bed ward doing a forty-seven-hour week for a salary of 400 deutschmarks a month (around £36), after taxes and board and lodging were deducted. I had a beautiful huge silver badge that I wore as part of my uniform. I remember a man, who was very ill, looking at the badge in wide-eyed terror. I guessed he was a veteran and reassured him, in my basic German, that I was Irish not English. The language barrier was a challenge. I would be struggling to find a German word and the Irish word would pop into my head. But I managed it. In November 1967 a letter arrived from Matron in the Rotunda.

'I would be glad if you would re-consider returning to pre-natal,' she wrote. 'Nurse McHale and Nurse Sheehan are both leaving in December, and Sister [Mary] Walsh, like myself is most anxious that you come back to us again.'

When I told the nuns in Germany I would be leaving to return to Ireland they asked me whether I needed any help finding my fare home, which was kind and seemed to go beyond the responsibilities of an employer.

In Christmas 1964, I had been living in digs on Iona Road, a house since bought by former Green MEP Patricia McKenna. In my time there Delia Cherry was the woman of the house. She was living with her aunt and was very much the caretaker of the place. She cooked for me, and if she made a cake there was always a slice to be had.

In Iona Road I first met Tim, whom I would meet many years later in the Iveagh Hostel. He used to call out to Delia's house on Saturdays to do the garden. He wore a wig, an awful-looking thing, and always arrived with a collection of bits and pieces he'd bought in the Bird Market in the Liberties. Delia trusted him, and if she was away she would make sure he had a key to let himself in. He used to sit by the fire and have a mug of tea on his break from the work in the garden. Then he'd show me his haul from the market. He was a simple man, and I only discovered more about him years later when I met him in the Iveagh Hostel.

Tim was a real miser. He used to hoard things. Once when there was a threatened strike at the Iveagh I asked him to give a radio interview. When he told his story, I understood some of the background to his miserly behaviour. He grew up in the tenements and lost his mother when he was a teenager. His father married again and effectively abandoned him. He survived by saving every penny he had. He would pocket hard-boiled eggs at breakfast just to give himself a store of food. When he came to the Iveagh, it was the first time in his life he had hot running water so he never moved out. They were great to him. Later we discovered he was a diabetic, and the Iveagh staff found the money he had been hoarding. 'He has money,' I told the matron, when he was admitted to Brú Caoimhín, then a geriatric hospital on Cork Street. 'Just make sure he gets what he needs.'

It was a real breakthrough one day in Trust when I said I didn't have money on me for a cup of coffee as I was heading out the door. 'I'll loan it to you,' Tim said. I think he must have worked collecting rents for a landlord. In the end, he lived out his life the way he wanted to live it, stubborn and dogged to the last.

When I had started as a staff nurse in April 1966 in the Rotunda prenatal ward, where women stayed for long periods with pregnancy complications, Mary Walsh was ward sister. She was a Connemara woman and, like many of that generation of nurses, she was strict. She had an ageless look about her, never losing the raw look of someone who had come up to Dublin from the country. She had reddish brown hair, wore glasses and never wore makeup. She had an almost nun-like lack of interest in her appearance. She loved the consultants. In her eyes they could do no wrong, and she was a gatekeeper guarding access to them with a sincerity and devotion. She had an uncanny ability to see when something was going wrong with a patient.

She was a tough boss, always insisting everything was done properly.

I think she saw in me the young nurse she had been once. She lived in the hospital, in a spartan room in the nurses' home, and even on her day off she could appear in the ward to see how everything was. Looking back on it now she seemed institutionalised, in a system that she was helping to maintain.

One of the aspects of hospital care that was never spoken about, but widely accepted, was the separation of single women (or unmarried mothers as we called them then) into a private room in the hospital. There were two single prenatal rooms set aside for single mothers, not luxurious but simple basic rooms. If they had a complicated pregnancy, they might spend several weeks in hospital. Mary Walsh was especially kind to them.

I think the separation had an element of kindness to it, rather than just an attempt to keep these women isolated. Unlike the other mothers, some of the single mothers would not be leaving hospital with their babies. The infants would be given up for adoption.

It might have been popular to see strict nurses like Mary Walsh as unfeeling authoritarians. But, deep down, she was one of many women who provided dedicated service without any thanks or talk of heroics. It didn't mitigate or excuse the system, but people like Mary Walsh represented something kind within its coldness.

During my time as a staff nurse on the prenatal ward, I worked long, demanding hours. Occasionally, I would carry out an unusual duty that I never questioned. I realise now it was part of a whole system set up to deal with Catholic adoptions. Father O'Neill was the priest in the Pro-Cathedral. He was a nice, quiet diocesan man. Every now and again, I was told to go, in uniform, with Fr O'Neill in his car to bring a baby that had been born in the Rotunda to a convent in Blackrock or to family homes elsewhere in the city and beyond.

We didn't ask questions. I never spoke to the mothers.

All of the unquestioning obedience drilled into us during our training came into play in this system. Knowing now that I was a cog in the machine that took babies from their mothers to give them to homes deemed to be more respectable is hard to understand looking back on it now. I know why people did not step forward to talk about things. Your silence was embedded in the culture of the times. I didn't talk to colleagues or friends about it. To do so went against everything you had been trained to do. Later on, when I met single mothers and the children who had grown up with gaping holes in their sense of who they were, I realised I should have been talking to the mothers, asking questions.

There is so much unearthing of details now about what happened in those days; it's appalling to realise that I was part, albeit a small part, of a system that did so much harm. Working closely with priests and nuns I also saw the good they did. In later decades, as the religious orders were demonised by revelations, those good deeds were swept away. The system allowed the State off the hook in caring for vulnerable women and children.

I noted in my diary in May 1968 that I went with Father O'Neill with two babies for adoption: one in Finglas and one near Clonliffe Road. In June I had a note concerning bringing babies to St Patrick's Infant Hospital, Temple Hill in Blackrock. Another note mentioned bringing a baby to Bray.

It's difficult to look at those brief notes now, considering our recent history, and realise that I was part of something I didn't understand. I'd like to think attitudes to single mothers have changed a lot, but the legacy of shame is something we deal with in Trust. At least two men we have contact with were adopted. Their search for meaning and identity is filled with hurt and the yearning of not being able to fill the gaps.

Temple Hill, the convent in Blackrock, was a beautiful building, grand and gleamingly clean inside. But does that mean it was a good place for a newborn recently separated from his or her mother? I once had a tour of a psychiatric unit and the medic was keen to point out how shiny and new it was. But sometimes those places can be less human than somewhere that is a little shabbier but contains more human warmth between the walls.

* * *

In the Rotunda private patients and public patients were never mixed. I dealt only with the public patients in the pre-natal wards. Most of them were from the north inner city, the north city suburbs and rural Ireland. The Rotunda might have had a reputation as a Church of Ireland maternity hospital, but I never felt there was a particularly Protestant ethos in the hospital. The one common trait among patients was that they were all pregnant and those women who were in long term on the pre-natal ward were experiencing problems. Private patients seemed to have easier lives, the same worries but not as many challenges.

The prenatal unit was where I spent most of my time in the Rotunda and I loved it. It was a large main ward and two other smaller eight-bed wards. The atmosphere was relaxed and friendly and there was more time to get to know the women, quite a few of whom knew each other as neighbours and friends. They often joked that their hospital stay was their only holiday. Many of them were sharp wits, able to put you in your place and not given to much reverence towards the consultants. Their humour was infectious and some of the doctors relaxed and enjoyed the banter. Dr Tony Richardson, a real heartthrob, had a small regiment of baby boys called Tony in his honour. The mothers were smart women, who could have gone far given the right opportunities. They had an energy and creativity that might have taken them anywhere.

My other contact with priests in the Rotunda was the opposite of that controlling Catholic culture which wrought so much damage in peoples' lives. There were many decent, caring people who worked as priests and nuns and felt a strong obligation to try to help alleviate poverty.

One of the clerics who impressed me was Father Donal O'Mahony. I met him in July 1968 after I saw an ad in the *Evening Press* for a Legion of Mary meeting, where they were looking for volunteers. A Capuchin, Father Donal was then known as Father Augustine. He had worked as a sports journalist with the *Irish Independent* before he joined the Capuchins, to begin living and working alongside the poor in inner-city Dublin. He became a peace campaigner and was the mediator who helped secure the release of the Dutch businessman Dr Tiede Herrema who was held captive by republicans Eddie Gallagher and Marion Coyle in 1975 for thirty-six days, in a kidnapping aimed at securing the release of three IRA prisoners. Father Donal later went on to found the homeless agency, Threshold.

In the late sixties and early seventies ideas from the wider civil rights movement had begun to filter into our consciousness. My social life began to revolve around visiting flats and working with the people who lived there. I started a voluntary social worker course in the Catholic Institute later that year.

Through Father Donal I got to know the families in Benburb Street. The five blocks of flats there had been built by Dublin City Council, in 1888, as an alternative to the Georgian tenements. At first the flats were solid and the 144 families who lived there were much better housed than their neighbours in tenements. But by the sixties the Benburb Street flats were badly in need of updating from their basic nineteenth-century level of comfort. The rooms were small. Each floor had one toilet and one cold water trough serving eight families. In the fifties the Corporation had begun sending tenants to Benburb Street after they'd been evicted for failing to pay their rent or a range of antisocial behaviour, including violence against other tenants. Older tenants found these new neighbours frightening and difficult. Squatters took over vacant flats. Children had nowhere to play.

I wasn't shocked by Benburb Street. I saw beyond the dirt and misery to the people, many of whom I had come to know in the Rotunda.

Mrs Hilliard was a widow in her eighties who lived alone in a flat on Benburb Street.

She came to the door wrapped in a blanket and leaning on her stick.

'Ah come in, chicken. Put on the kettle for the tea. Delighted to see you,' was her regular greeting. Her tiny room was divided in two. In one side she had a table with a rug over it and all her bits and pieces, her holy pictures hung around her on the walls. On the other side was her bedroom. She talked to me about life in the flats, how when it had been a happier community everyone could leave their doors open. She told me that I would be old myself someday. I was probably too young then to imagine ever being her age.

'Everybody gets to my stage,' she told me.

'If we're lucky,' I thought.

She kept a bottle of Guinness beside her bed. She appeared to me to be a very contented woman. She wasn't angry. She had her faith and she felt at home in Benburb Street. She was always delighted to get a visit.

Council officials and civil servants began to visit the flats to try and come up with solutions to the problems there. They took an interest

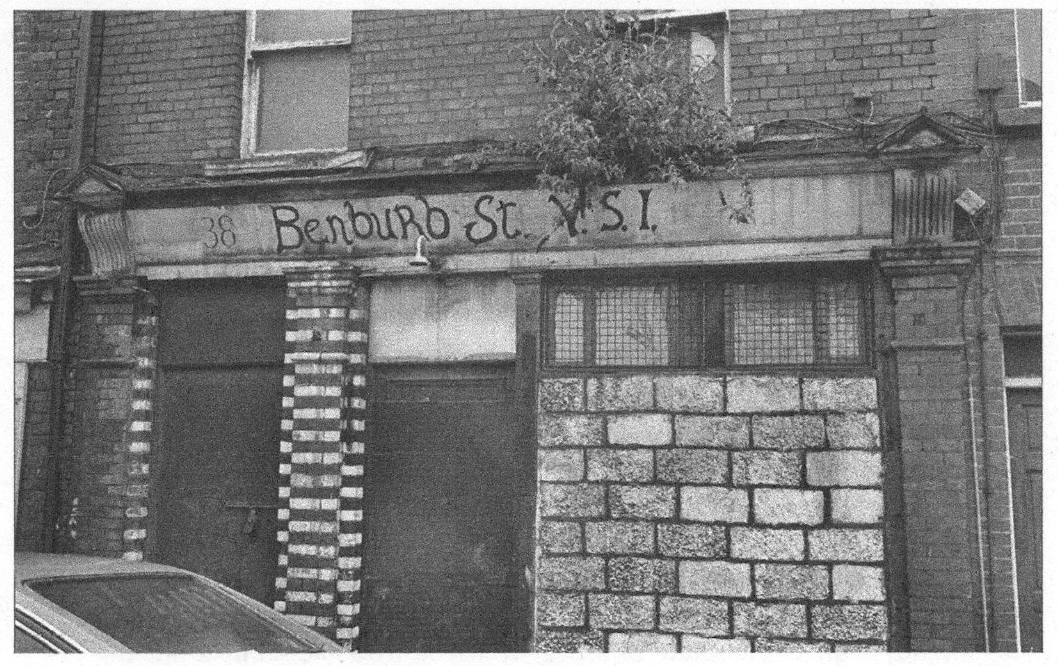

Benburb Street VSI, where we set up a Mothers' Group and installed a washing machine – what would today's women think?

in us volunteers and there was no huge feeling of difference between officials and volunteers. Those were the early days in the development of a social services system. People were able to forget about their labels and use their humanity to work with people and prevent them from becoming outsiders in a community.

If you wanted to do that kind of voluntary work now, you would have to go through an agency, which is probably being paid to find volunteers. You would be required to do a training course. I remember once a man at a conference talking about how his wife, who was an artist, was told she would have to do a training course if she wanted to teach art to older people.

It wasn't always easy to help people. One year we delivered hampers of food to families and a man came into the Rotunda and threw a raw chicken across the room towards us.

'Who do you think you are giving me a chicken? You can keep your fuckin' chicken,' he roared.

Benburb Street was a red-light area and one night I met a young Tipperary woman who had been dragged along the road by her hair by a pimp. She ended up in the Mater Hospital and had to have her beautiful black hair cut off because of her injuries. I brought her to buy a wig. A while after that I met her on O'Connell Street and asked her if she was using contraception.

'Don't worry, Alice,' she said. 'I'm on the pill and I take them all at once so I don't forget.'

The summer after starting to visit Benburb Street I worked in Rotherham in the north of England. I got a job in a nursing home through a friend, Anne O'Halloran from Baggot Street, who had set up a nursing agency. Anne had arrived into Baggot Street from Harcourt Street Children's Hospital six months after I started training. She was a glamorous woman from Kildare, my height, with fair hair and an enterprising zeal that would take her far. Someone once said Anne could dress in rags and still look like a model.

We lost touch when I went to the Rotunda and she left Ireland to set up a nursing agency in the north of England. By the time we got back in touch her business was thriving. I travelled over that summer for a spell of work. I was paid £19 7s and 6d a week (equivalent to around €350 today) which I noted was 'marvellous pay for so little work'.

Back in the Rotunda, in the autumn of 1969, my nursing life felt impossibly busy. I spoke to the matron about overcrowding on the wards and I broke down in front of the master, Dr Edwin Lillie. I was exhausted by the pace and demands of it all. Dr Lillie was a very kind and gentle man. My fascination with the work had waned and I wrote in my diary that it was time to leave 'for my own sake'.

The Rotunda had changed how I saw the city and its inhabitants, putting me at the start of the road that I would go down more fully. By the summer of 1970 I had decided to retrace my steps a little and go back to Baggot Street, first as staff nurse and then as night sister, swapping the daylight hours and bustle of the prenatal ward for the quieter dark hours of night duty in the Royal City of Dublin Hospital.

CHAPTER FOUR

My Calm Kingdom
Night Duty

'Our experience is not just our own property – it must be shared.'
Human rights activist Ela Bhatt

Things sound clearer in the dark. On the night shift, when the phone rang it was shriller. Voices boomed in the calm that settled over the wards, the offices and the long corridors, some of them lined with flowers. Each night at the start of my shift I asked the nurses to move patients' flowers out onto the corridors. Their perfume often lingered after they were moved back to bedsides the next day. Sometimes the night was too soothing. By 3am I often struggled to stay awake. In the fight to keep my eyes open, I would get up and walk down the corridor or climb the stairs to a ward.

As night sister in Baggot Street, the hospital was my kingdom. My shift, from 8pm to 8am, started in my office on the ground floor when staff nurses, one from each landing, came to give me their reports. These gave me a sense of how everyone had been during the day and how they were expected to be during the night. I had access to the sleeping tablets, which were kept with the other medicines in locked cabinets.

Call the midwife – me in my Rotunda District Uniform.

I loved night duty. All the frantic activity of the day was done and the city slept. I had medical duties but not as many as during the day. As night sister I was often as much a listener as a carer. Patients were more likely to call you to their bedsides to talk. The bustle of the daily routine on the ward was over; visitors were gone, and there was time to sit with a patient. Cups of tea could be made, and you could settle into a chair beside a bed for a few minutes. At night the hospital seemed to make more sense. It had a calmness and an order about it.

Secrets were told in those dark quiet hours. I had grown up with the idea that gossip was poisonous. As children we were discouraged from talking about other people, or spreading stories. Later, in my work, I think it helped me not to pry deeply into people's lives. If they wanted to talk, I would listen, but I wasn't there to dredge through their personal histories.

'Sister, I have to tell you something,' a young nurse whispered to me, stopping me as I passed her on a landing one night. The lights were dim, and the corridor was filled with the scent of flowers taken from bedsides overnight.

'I had an abortion in London and I want to tell my parents about it, but I don't know how,' she said in the same whisper.

She started to cry and I comforted her as best I could. We went back to my office, closed the door and sat down, as she told me about her secret journey to England.

I didn't judge her. I just listened. I was glad she felt comfortable enough to confide in me. There was something about the darkness that made it easier for her to talk to me. We talked late into the night. I think she must have felt some relief for having told me. The next morning the moment was gone. We never spoke about it again.

Baggot Street Hospital had changed in my time away from it. A night cook had been appointed so student nurses no longer had to cook for the staff. It was a relief for everyone, those who had to try and cook and those who had to try to eat the efforts.

I was beginning to understand some of the domestic staff and how their backgrounds in institutions influenced their behaviour. Institutions had taught them coping skills as children and young women that they carried into later life. They were watchful and finely tuned to the moods of others. Being one step ahead of a mood swing was a survival tactic in an institution. They mixed that acute sensitivity towards others with a toughness when it came to their own needs and feelings.

They worked extremely hard and were always anxious to please, acutely conscious of who was boss and who should be obeyed. The domestic staff who worked with private patients considered themselves to be higher up the pecking order. There was sadness in the eyes of many of them. They quietly looked out for the very young staff, nursing and medical. Many of these women were particularly helpful to visitors and reminded us all to ensure that visitors got proper attention.

They knew each corner of the hospital, having scrubbed and polished every inch of it. The hospital became their home. Some people looked through them as if they were invisible. But they took notice of everyone, watched, learned and knew a lot about how the institution that was Baggot Street ticked.

I met some of these women years later in the Regina Coeli hostel, which was run by the Legion of Mary, in the north inner city near what was St Brendan's Hospital. They were ending their days in an institution having been institutionalised from cradle to grave.

Night sister was my first senior nursing role and I was very conscious that I was on the next rung on the nursing ladder. I saw how the younger nurses, who had come up from the country like me, seemed just as awestruck by their role as I had been when I was in their stiff new Mary Hicks shoes a few years earlier.

I was younger than the other nursing sisters. Some people said at the time I was the youngest nursing sister in the country. Some of the fellow senior nurses were nice and helpful, but I never felt part of a sisterhood of colleagues. The age difference was one reason, but I was also beginning to look at things differently. I was (and still am) very direct. A direct woman can be seen as aggressive in a way that a direct man would never be. Directness could leave you misunderstood and isolated in a world that was increasingly becoming very polite and controlled.

After a night shift there was always something special about the crisp air of a newly minted city morning when I walked down the front steps of the hospital onto Baggot Street. The air had a sparkle even with the buses rumbling by belching exhaust fumes. I loved the city first thing in the morning. There was a sense of everyone beginning to be busy again, the lull of the night banished. Crossing the city, I could smell the brine of the tide in the Liffey, watch the gulls swooping on the night's debris on the way home to my bed in my digs on Iona Road.

On days off I often visited Paddy Somerville-Large in Vallombrosa, his house in Bray. Paddy and his brother Becher, a well-known eye specialist, were friends of the Hugheses. In 1934 Paddy had been involved in setting up the Mount Street Club in the city centre. The club, named jokingly to echo the name of the exclusive Kildare Street Club, was a co-operative set up for unemployed men in a renovated hotel in Mount Street. They had workshops, recreation rooms and a dining hall. Later they set up a city farm, sharing the food that was grown among the men who worked the land.

I got the bus down to Bray and Paddy would pick me up and drive me to their beautiful estate. It was a little like visiting Annesgift. They had an orchard and a large wooden kitchen table. They even had a wooden lazy Susan in the middle of the table. He drove me down to Fethard once, stopping off to show me the Quaker graveyard in Kildare. Becher Somerville-Large lived in Brooke Lawn, now King's Hospital School, and when my mother came up for Country Market meetings she would stay there. Their daughter Faith is now one of our special friends in Trust.

Hospitals in Dublin were still divided along religious lines in my time as a nurse. Patients were routinely asked about their religion when their medical history was taken. The Adelaide Hospital was run with a Protestant ethos. The Hughes family knew many of the senior Adelaide staff so as a child I had picked primroses from the ditches around Annesgift, wrapped them in newspaper and sent them up on the train to the Adelaide. It was a place that impressed me. It was an extremely well-run hospital, probably the best that I encountered in my years, but because I wasn't a Protestant I couldn't train there. Adelaide nurses had a very distinctive uniform, a navy dress with white polka dots, collar and cuffs finished with a crisp white apron over it and a sharply-cut cape. The Adelaide shared the Christian ethos of the voluntary hospitals, a belief that everyone was deserving of equal care.

Carmel McInerney was the new matron in Baggot Street when I arrived back from the Rotunda and I felt life wasn't easy for her. She had come from a religious background and seemed to have more in common with the younger nurses. She was slim, attractive and dressed with a young style not normally associated with how matrons dressed in their time off. She hadn't made her way up through the ranks in Baggot Street so she wasn't burdened with the responsibility of protecting the institution. People weren't always kind to her or about her. But I liked her. I think she struggled to fit in with the culture of the hospital but

Describe some of the favourite **memories** you have of me when I was a child . . .

Always bright and breezy full of self confidence

What was I **like** when I was a child?

Always bright and go ahead
Loved the outdoor life and animals
Wanted to be a vet but the money wasnt there to do the course

Describe what you **like** about me . . .

Very outspoken and know what you are talking about

My mother's thoughts on me growing up.

she was warm, chatty and very different to the typical matron. She was young at heart and had great ideas but she had no idea of what she was up against.

'Would you think of going for the job of matron yourself, Alice?' Becher Sommerville-Large asked me one day. He was on the board of the hospital. I said I wouldn't. The job never appealed to me. I think I was beginning to see how easy it would be to sacrifice yourself to an institutional life. It was a fork-in-the-road moment that I don't regret.

Up on the top floors of the hospital in the very late hours I felt like an observer of the world, watching over an orderly building of people sleeping. I've always loved looking out windows, a throwback to the hours spent as a child looking out at Slievenamon from my small bedroom window. In this cosy world it would have been easy to become cut off from the daylight life.

In the winter of 1970 I began to see fires starting around the city and rang Irishtown Garda Station to report them. The sergeant in charge got used to hearing me call.

'Where's the fire this time, Alice?' he'd say.

Later I found out an arsonist had been causing the fires. He was caught beside one of the blazes he had started.

Those years on night duty were the first time I saw a security man in a hospital. He often came around with his dog for a chat and both of them sat comfortably in my office. At one stage, I developed a terrible itch that I blamed on the dog, but a doctor discovered it was scabies. It's something I say to people when they're embarrassed to be diagnosed with scabies. The shame of those conditions associated with poverty is something you can alleviate when you can say, 'Don't worry. I've had it too.'

One night, a patient in the semi-private ward on the top floor called me to her bedside. She had jet black hair, so black it was almost blue like a crow's wing. She told me she wanted to tell my fortune.

'The nurses' dance is coming up and there's a medical student who's going to ask you to the dance,' she told me.

'He will say to you that you might be embarrassed to go with him because he's a student and you're a sister. You will go with him but there won't be any relationship between you both.

'And you're going to be asked by the hospital to do something completely different.'

I was going to 'meet a widower' who had four children and marry him, the woman said, and she gave me his initials: 'CB'. This part came true. The only small difference was that by the time I met a handsome taxi driver called Charles Best, he had three children. His eldest child had died at birth.

'And you're going to become well known.'

That night she called me back and asked me to ring her husband. The security man stopped me and we got talking on my way down to my office to make the phone call. The phone was ringing in the office when I walked in and it was the patient's husband. He said he wasn't surprised to hear she had been looking for him. She died very shortly afterwards.

The student she had predicted did come in a few nights later. And he stood shyly in the corner of my office and asked me to the dance, using almost exactly the words she had said. I said yes and wondered if any of the rest of her prediction would materialise in the way she said.

I continued to meet people who would drift in and out of my life for decades. Clive Snape, a doctor in Baggot Street, brought a young man to the office that he'd found in the basement with his wrists slashed in a half-hearted attempt at suicide. Clive took him to casualty and cleaned him up and dressed his wounds. He befriended the young man, encouraged him and kept in touch with him.

Years later, in Trust, I met the same man. He was getting his life together but was still without a home. He didn't remember meeting me in hospital all those years earlier. Then another few years on, I was walking by a café near Trust when a man in a fine suit and polished shoes, called me over.

'Alice, you don't remember me,' he said.

'No, but I recognise the smile,' I said.

It was the man I'd seen all those years ago with slashed wrists in Baggot Street, and again in Trust. He pulled his phone out of his pocket to show me a photograph of his son who had just made his First Communion. He was bursting with pride. Two things dawned on me after the encounter. Change doesn't happen overnight and that I'm not the only person who's been dealing with somebody. There is often a whole network of people who are trying to help someone. If I wonder what saved him, I think it was his youth and that great support network, including Clive Snape, in Baggot Street. People showed that they believed in him and they encouraged him to follow his passion, to be creative.

As the seventies progressed the culture of nursing was shifting. The idea that a nurse would continue to work long, arduous hours with unquestioning obedience was being challenged. On a chilly day in February 1970 more than 1,500 uniformed nurses in white dresses, stiff caps and capes marched from Parnell Square to Leinster House. The river of smartly turned out nurses of all ages made visible that largely invisible army of unsung women who had run the hospitals of Ireland diligently for decades. Organisers had predicted 450 nurses would attend, but more than three times that number turned up.

The protest was organised by the Irish Nurses' Organisation to seek a shorter working week, better pay and promotional opportunities. At the time nurses were expected to work eighty-five hours a fortnight, with student nurses enduring even longer hours. Nursing was quietly dismissed in official circles as a 'vocation' to which women (predominantly) dedicated their lives. This meant that proper pay and conditions didn't have to apply. The protesting nurses were met at Leinster House by a number of TDs, including Dr Noël Browne who had done so much to eradicate TB twenty years earlier.

I couldn't go on the march as I was on duty that day but the protest was an important part of the feminist movement in the seventies, a time when women were still regarded as second-class citizens, with their right to work severely curtailed by the law. Under the marriage ban nurses, and any other women working in the public service, had to give up their job as soon as they got married. That question that I wrote when I first started my nursing training – whether I would become a truly dedicated nurse or leave to get married – spelled out my limited options and those of other women of my generation. There were only two paths.

Early in 1971 I was called to a meeting with the board. I was, as the dying woman on the ward had predicted, going to be asked by the hospital to do something completely different and challenging. There were senior people who were quietly championing me since I returned to the hospital. One of them was the thoracic surgeon Keith Shaw.

Keith was a big man, very handsome and stately, in his forties at that time. He had a presence when he came into a ward. He was never flustered, and had a kind face behind big glasses. He was quiet, not the kind of man you'd throw your arms around, but he reminded me of Olivia Hughes and the way she used every opportunity to try and teach us something. Early on in my nursing life he had used a bronchoscopy as a teaching exercise. The procedure involved putting a tube down a patient's throat to look at the bronchus, the airway leading to the lungs. Keith Shaw was fishing for a portion of inhaled walnut. He showed us the shard of nut lodged in the patient's airway. We could see it clearly, thanks to his calm clear explanation of what we were looking at.

He taught naturally and fluently, rather than in any patronising way, talking to you as he was going along. This was the way of the hospital and nursing training. People shared their knowledge by doing. He had a way of making you feel you were capable by speaking about the procedure clearly and without medical jargon, and making it so interesting you felt you wanted to search for more knowledge.

Keith Shaw had worked in the forties to tackle TB, and in the sixties he began pioneering new heart surgery techniques, such as open heart surgery. He died in 2001 and the cardiac surgery unit in St James's Hospital is named after him.

I was called to that board meeting and was asked to go to London on a research trip. My job was to assess intensive care units with a view to the setting up of a new unit in Baggot Street. Within weeks I had packed my bags, walked out of Baggot Street and travelled to live and work at The London Hospital (now The Royal London Hospital) in Whitechapel, near the East End with its bustle of markets and traders.

Founded in 1740 in a single house the hospital was the first in Britain to establish formal hospital-based medical education. Like Baggot Street and the Rotunda, the London Hospital had a long, rich history as a teaching hospital. One of my childhood heroes, Edith Cavell had trained there. She was a British nurse who was executed in Belgium for helping French and British soldiers escape during the First World War.

I moved into the nurses' home at the hospital, bringing back memories of my days as a student. It was just like the nurses' home back in

Dublin. Nurses' homes felt like they were the same the world over. A young doctor friend I knew from Baggot Street was in London and he helped me to get to know the city, including a wonderful trip one night to the Royal Albert Hall. The visit had a huge sense of occasion and I wore my best skirt and blouse, which wouldn't have matched the ball-gowns and pearls of some of the women there.

My days were spent working on the wards and taking notes on complicated machinery. I had to figure out how the systems, both mechanical and human, worked in the intensive care ward. It was a challenge. I am not a machine person.

There were a number of consultants helping with the project from their base in Dublin, along with Keith Shaw. A registrar, Greg Shanik, was also involved. He went on to become a well-known vascular surgeon. He is as energetic now as he was then and keeps in regular contact with Trust.

Another Baggot Street doctor who later impressed me was the late Professor Aidan Halligan, who was invited by the then Minister for Health and Children, Mary Harney, in the nineties to run the health service. Wisely, he declined the offer and in 1999 went on to work in England as a director of clinical governance with the NHS and later deputy chief medical officer. It was our loss and England's gain. His lectures and writing inspired so many people thanks to his combination of intellect and compassion and continue to do so despite his early death at the age of just 57. Much of his work was based on demonstrating the importance of doctors, nurses and others working together in an environment where they learned from their mistakes. I considered him a real friend to me and to Trust and I am so glad our paths crossed. In 2010 Aidan helped set up an independent charity, Pathway, after a homeless man died outside a hospital where he was working. Pathway teams in hospitals across the UK work to try to ensure homeless people get better hospital treatment.

Oliver Connolly was a tall quiet junior doctor in Baggot Street towards the end of my time there. He later became a much-loved GP in the Liberties, which he cycled around on his bike. A quiet unassuming man who was widely read, he had an inner calm. He reminded me a little of Professor Synge, never judging people according to their status or treating them differently based on their rank in life. He also served as one of our Trustees.

Watching how the London Hospital ran its intensive care unit I noted that patients could be closely monitored by experienced staff and problems dealt with swiftly before they became more serious. 'These units save lives,' I wrote. But the unit could breed a culture where technique and equipment rather than the patient became the centre of attention. I saw how working on an intensive care unit could put enormous emotional strain on staff and that there was a 'tendency for the unit to develop into an elite organisation.'

The technical detail of all those machines has long since been forgotten. What stands out from my three months in London was a lecture I went to in March 1971. Organised by the London Medical Group, it was a talk on 'terminal pain', given by Dr Cicely Saunders, who was then medical director at St Christopher's Hospice, in south east London, which she had opened four years earlier. She became a key figure in the foundation of the hospice movement.

Saunders had trained as a nurse, went on to study social work and became a physician. The night I saw her speak she was in her fifties, charismatic and brilliant, when she stood up to speak. I can still remember the atmosphere in the room, crackling with interest and absolute attention to what she and others were saying. The lectures were mainly geared towards medical people but were attended by all kinds of people: theologians, philosophers, sociologists and lawyers. Eight years after I saw her speak, the Queen awarded her an OBE and later a DBE (Dame Commander of the British Empire, a higher award again), and she became Dame Cicely Saunders.

At the lecture that night she talked about so much more than straightforward medical treatment for dying patients. She warned about the dehumanising nature of intensive care thinking about a patient in terms of 'that monitor' or 'that ventilator' when attached to those machines 'is the father or husband of someone and that we should treat him as we would like those near and dear to us treated.'

She talked about pain, but not just the physical pain of sickness. She touched on the pain of loneliness and isolation, the pain of being a failure, a spiritual pain. Dr Saunders recommended the regular administration of pain relief like morphine or diamorphine. She said she didn't worry about addiction, but she didn't approve of legalised euthanasia. 'One might ask, "What has this to do with intensive care?" In my opinion a lot, because in this highly scientific age we mustn't forget that death should be dignified and peaceful,' she said.

I couldn't have agreed more. She gave a voice to those issues that had bothered me as a hands-on nurse. As I looked around the room, something clicked into place. Finally, here was a broad range of people from all kinds of disciplines talking about the things that really mattered. So many of the questions that I had about medicine, nurses and how we dealt with the humanity of the people we treated were being raised and dealt with here in London in the open, where people other than those involved in medicine could have a say. At home questions were left unasked or unanswered, buried in a layer of duty and obedience. The hospital culture I knew was all about knowing your place in a system that was designed to stifle rather than empower creative thinking.

Sally Trench was also at that lecture. At the age of sixteen she had left her comfortable home to live and work on the streets with homeless people. Five years later, she wrote *Bury Me in my Boots*, a book about her experiences which sold over a million copies. At one stage, MGM pitched the idea of turning her story into a musical. 'I had visions of Julie Andrews dancing around a bomb site singing: "Meths, glorious meths." I thought, no!' she once said.

Instead she fled to America and worked with drug addicts in Harlem. In the nineties she worked in war-ravaged Bosnia, organising aid convoys for children. She set up Project Spark, a youth support service in Yorkshire and later London. Spark was based on the idea of preventing young people falling into homelessness by providing a safety net for youngsters who were in danger of moving into lives of drug addiction or crime. Her thinking was that prevention was better than cure.

I had never come across a cross-disciplinary approach in the Irish healthcare system, before or since. The Saunders lecture felt like the opening of a door, allowing fresh thinking to be applied to the difficult things that doctors and nurses grappled with, but rarely discussed.

I returned home to Dublin and moved into a tiny bedsit in Leeson Park, which was nearer the hospital. I threw myself into setting up and running the Intensive Care Unit, which was opened in June 1971, by the then Tánaiste and Minister for Health Erskine Childers.

Overnight my calm kingdom of night duty had turned into the high-stress world of intensive care. By May 1972 the unit was described as 'one of the most advanced in the country,' by *Pulse* magazine, an Irish magazine aimed at doctors, which is no longer in print. There were four sections in the intensive care unit: a three-bed intensive care section, six-bed post-op recovery ward, a six-bed coronary care unit and a central nurses' station. The coronary unit was on call three days and had a houseman on duty twenty-four hours. The operating theatre was directly across from the entrance to the intensive care unit and another ten-bed thoracic unit was on the same floor.

I ran the unit with twenty-four staff nurses and two student doctors. Doctors from around the hospital tended to their own patients when they were in intensive care. I worked closely with the anaesthetist and the medical registrar to make any major decisions.

It was a mammoth task and an enormous responsibility. I got great support from the medical staff at all levels. We were often short-staffed and had to call on agency nurses. The facilities for staff to have rest breaks just to put their feet up were not available nor were opportunities for staff to discuss things in the way I had witnessed in The London Hospital. The pressure of the job had a fire-fighting feel to it. There was never time to step back and figure out the bigger picture.

I had welcomed the responsibility of running this new ground-breaking unit but it took its toll. The work was so specialised that most of the time it felt like we didn't have enough staff to run it as it should be run. The reliance on agency nurses, a huge part of today's hospital staffing system, meant a patchy service. There were days when I got skilled and experienced staff who could be trusted from the first moment. Other days the agency nurse could be someone you would have to keep a closer eye on because they had no relevant experience.

As someone with a senior position in the hospital I saw how quickly you could be wooed by the drug companies, invited to functions to promote their drugs. I went along to some but I began to feel uncomfortable with the scenario, the unsaid nature of what was going on:

hospitality given in return for lucrative contracts.

Clive Snape, the doctor who had brought in the young man in distress earlier in my career, was an English doctor working with us in Baggot Street. In the seventies being English in Ireland had its own challenges because of the political tensions in the north. Clive was a Bury soccer supporter, unusual when most medical students were rugby fans. He later went to work in Canada. One night a man was brought in from one of the border counties and his reaction to Clive reminded me of the expression on the German man's face during my time in the German hospital when he saw my badge and heard me speaking English. The man froze in the bed and his eyes bulged in his head when he heard Clive's accent. He was alarmed to be being treated, no matter how well, by the 'enemy'. Following years of conflict, English people were still viewed with suspicion by many Irish people then.

Everyday life was dramatic enough without anything else happening. But one morning I arrived for my shift and saw the matron and the local sergeant in her office. They were in a huddle and when they glanced up and saw me coming the huddle seemed to tighten. I got a sense that something was up so I didn't knock on the door to say good morning as I normally would.

Later I was summoned to the office and told that someone sitting in Neary's pub had overheard a conversation and reported it to gardaí.

'Alice from Baggot Street would be kidnapped on her way home from work' was what had been overheard.

I was one of only two Alices in the hospital. The other was a Chinese doctor called Alice Chang, who was a good friend.

The gardaí came up to interview me and asked if I could think of anyone who would threaten such a thing. I began to wonder if it had been someone I met through my work in Benburb Street. Was it somebody from those tough parts of the city where I had been doing voluntary work? How easy it was to jump to that conclusion, to label people, without thinking.

The seventies were paranoid times, so I agreed to move into the hospital for my safety, taking a tiny but comfortable room on one of the upper floors. My move didn't take long. I didn't have that many belongings to pack up. They offered me garda protection but I didn't want to scare the people I was working with in Benburb Street with the idea that I was trailing some kind of danger into their flats. I often wonder what kidnappers might have done. Would they had pulled up beside me in a van and bundled me inside? If they had been waiting for a ransom, it would have been a very long wait.

Sometime later I found out the person behind the threat was a nurse who had been working with me and who had wanted time off for personal reaons. I couldn't give her the time off. I wish I'd had a chance to talk to her and explain things. I think the conversation in Neary's might have been the drink talking.

I lived in Baggot Street for a few months until it was felt that the kidnap plot, if it ever existed, had gone. It seems preposterous now, but in the seventies, when political tensions around Northern Ireland were high, kidnapping was a feature of life – a threat had to be taken seriously. I left the hospital with my suitcases for another rented bedsit in the city. Baggot Street was no longer my home. It wouldn't be long before it was also no longer my workplace. I was about to take a leap into another world entirely.

That trip to London had unsettled me, in a good way. I got a glimpse of how nursing and medicine fitted into a wider sense of what it was to be human and vulnerable. Living away from Ireland for that short spell also made me hungry to see how other people lived. In September 1971

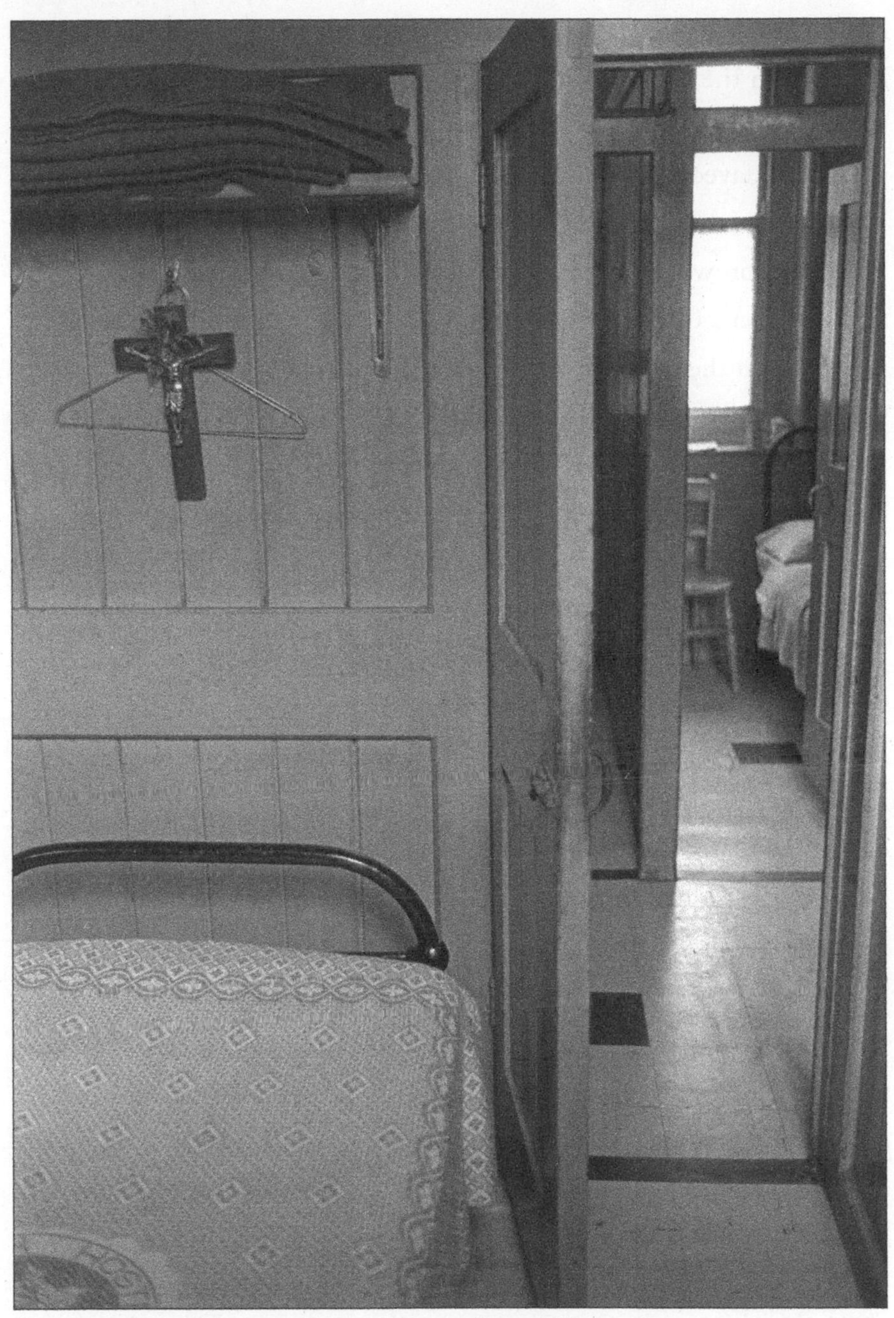

A cubicle in the Iveagh Hostel, in the early 1980s.

I had travelled across Europe on an organised camping holiday with a nurse from the Rotunda. On the flight to London we realised we had forgotten to pack mugs and cutlery so we pinched some from the hotel where we stayed that night. We felt a pang of guilt when we were leaving and gave the hotel porter £1 each on the way out to cover the costs.

In London we met up with the rest of our group: two other women and five men. Our driver Murray was a Scot who said he had hitch-hiked round the world twice so this was a short spin for him.

The hovercraft to Calais felt like being on a plane that skimmed the water. We camped in Cologne, on the banks of the Rhine. I had never seen anything like the poverty of northern and central Yugoslavia, which was then under Tito's rule. I noticed that the border guards never smiled. One day we threw away two overripe pears, and an old man picked them up and ate them. The market in Sarajevo was crammed with men and women in folk costumes, selling eggs, bread and cheese. I loved the beauty of the mountains. They seemed like a place where little had changed for centuries. The cows wore bells and women washed clothes by rivers and lakes. Ox-drawn carts were everywhere. Children stood by the side of the road selling berries from tins. When we didn't stop one boy threw a stone through the window, hitting one of the men but he wasn't badly hurt.

At the saltmines in Saltzburg we crossed a saltlake by ferry and had to slide down into the mine on a toboggan-type device which shot down the chute like whizzing down the bannisters. Half the mine was in Austria and the other half in Germany. We drove over two hundred miles to Dachau and found it closed for the visit of an Israeli minister. We camped nearby and visited the next day. I got a profound sense of being surrounded by the spirits of those who had died there. When I left, I found I couldn't speak for hours afterwards, and everyone else was the same. We carried the bleakness of the place away with us and were haunted by the question of how concentration camps could happen and whether they could ever happen again.

Our last night was in Belgium, just outside Bruges. The campsite was at the end of a lake. We were surrounded by apple trees on the camp, and the apples dropped thudding onto our tents throughout the night.

'There's lots more of course,' I wrote in a letter home, 'including the fellow who gave me a present of a real leather belt and ran down the street to tie a ribbon on my hair. But I had better finish off. Hoping you are all well.'

I had other suitors too. In March 1972 a young man from Carlow took me to see Leonard Cohen in the National Stadium. When we got back from the concert I told him bluntly.

'You're wasting your time. I really have no interest in you.'

My next trip, in July 1972, was to Russia with the same company that had organised the camping holiday. It was a nerve-wracking holiday. One of our group of ten women and five men was a deaf-mute man, who used sign language, and we all tried to learn some signing while we were on the trip. I had never come across sign language before. Russia was my first experience of heavy-handed security, booted men taking the seats out of our van to search it at the border. In one of the campsites we were robbed. I slept with my head at the door of my tent to keep my passport safe. Walking one night with a security man, he asked me about healthcare, and I figured out he knew I was a nurse. I suddenly realised that big brother was watching us.

In Leningrad our white van was stopped by police with sniffer dogs, and Brian, the driver, was taken in to custody. He was released shortly afterwards. When we crossed the border into Finland, it was an immense relief to get into a beautiful green countryside, where the air smelled so fresh we could relax. My friend Linda from New Zealand and I sat talking late into the night and shared that feeling of bliss at being in familiar green surroundings again. We travelled north to the North Cape, the most northerly tip of Norway, to see the midnight sun. We went home via Copenhagen and visited the Carlsberg brewery, where the rich smell of brewing filled the air, heady and yeasty, as we danced in the square.

In 1973 I got a tax rebate and used the money to fund a three-month leave of absence and a trip to Auckland in New Zealand, where one of my travelling friends, Linda, was getting married. The New Zealand trip was the first time since I had left Tipperary that there was time to soak in the peace and beauty of the countryside, rather than just passing through it on the way to somewhere else. At a rugby match I watched what might have been future All Blacks players as if it was a GAA match in a local village.

I travelled to Wellington to visit my mother's only sister who had gone to New Zealand a generation earlier. There was space to think and reflect about where I was heading in life. The lush green landscape was an escape but much of it reminded me of Ireland. I still have a dried silver fern that I picked there. I flew down to the South Island and visited other relations of my mother's.

When I returned from New Zealand, with lots of questions about what to do with my life, Billy Gibbons, the Church of Ireland chaplain who worked in Baggot Street, suggested I meet someone who was lecturing in social work in Trinity. The woman I spoke to was less than encouraging.

'You have worked so long in hospital, in a very structured discipline,' she said. 'Would you really be able to cope with and enjoy life as a student?'

I could see that she doubted my ability and I let her doubt shatter

Leabharlanna Fhine Gall

my dreams of going to Trinity, something I would never now allow to happen now. Much later I would give lectures in Trinity and meet students who wanted to come and learn from our work.

In the end, I didn't leave to go to college. Instead, a shockingly sad and senseless death was the spark for me to pack in my job in Baggot Street and leave hospital nursing forever.

CHAPTER FIVE

The Simon Shelter
In at the Deep End

'Tomorrow we will take up our struggle again.
Leave us to our sorrow today.'
From an appreciation of Sean Armstrong by Seamus Purseil

It was a bit like falling in love. I can still see Sean Armstrong sitting on the floor in a small bedsit in Dublin's Berkeley Road. He had a brown beard and his eyes shone with enthusiasm as he talked about his work with children and young people in Northern Ireland. He oozed charisma and a can-do spirit, talking about breaking down hatred and sectarianism. His words seemed to energise the room. We sat rapt, listening to Sean Armstrong speak about his work as a field officer with Voluntary Services International (VSI) in Belfast, where he organised children's parties and holidays for Catholic and Protestant children. He was someone who made us all feel like we could do great things, make a difference, change the world. It was 1972, a time when human rights movements were gaining ground and a generation was questioning how society was organised. Ideas were opening up and someone like Sean Armstrong was the embodiment of hope.

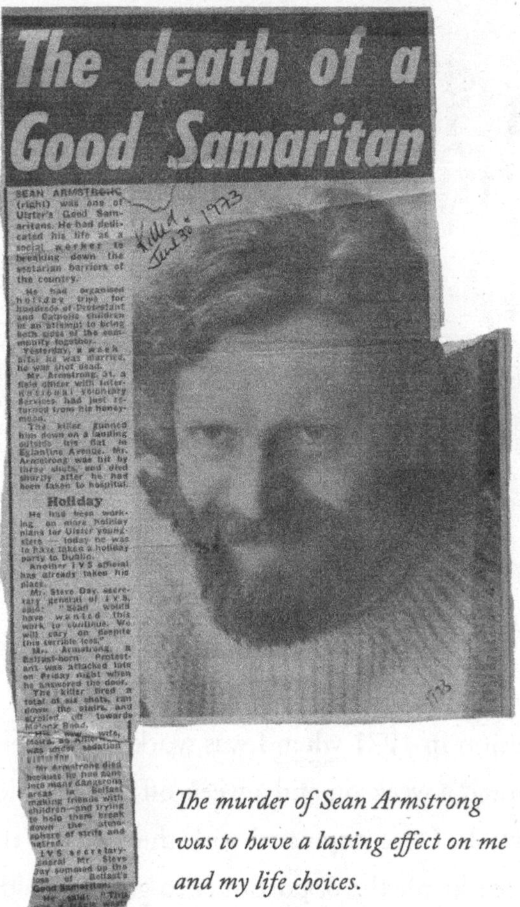

The death of a Good Samaritan

SEAN ARMSTRONG (right) was one of Ulster's Good Samaritans. He had dedicated his life as a social worker to breaking down the sectarian barriers of the country.

He had organised holiday trips for hundreds of Protestant and Catholic children in an attempt to bring both sides of the community together.

Yesterday, a week after he was married, he was shot dead.

Mr. Armstrong, 31, a field officer with International Voluntary Services, had just returned from his honeymoon.

The killer gunned him down on a landing outside his flat in Eglantine Avenue. Mr. Armstrong was hit by three shots, and died shortly after he had been taken to hospital.

Holiday

He had been working on more holiday plans for Ulster youngsters — today he was to have taken a holiday party to Dublin.

Another I V S official has already taken his place.

Mr. Steve Day, secretary general of I V S, said: "Sean would have wanted this work to continue. We will carry on despite this terrible loss."

Mr. Armstrong, a Belfast-born Protestant, was attacked late on Friday night when he answered the door.

The killer fired a total of six shots, ran down the stairs, and strolled off towards Malone Road.

His new wife, Moira, [illegible] was under sedation [illegible]

Mr Armstrong died because he had gone into many dangerous areas in Belfast making friends with children—and trying to help them break down the atmosphere of strife and hatred.

I V S secretary-general Mr Steve Day summed up the loss of Belfast's Good Samaritan.

He said: "This was a tragic waste [illegible]

The murder of Sean Armstrong was to have a lasting effect on me and my life choices.

Sometimes people make an impression on you that stays with you for the rest of your life, even if your paths only cross once, just briefly. Sean was that person for me. I only met him once, that night in the bedsit, where I was sitting with other members of VSI, listening to him talk about his work in Northern Ireland.

Founded in Switzerland in 1920 as a peace movement, VSI's Irish branch, based on the idea of social justice through practical assistance, had opened in 1965. Tenement living was still a feature of life in the city in the sixties. Dublin had a legacy of dire poverty.

I met VSI members working in the flats in Benburb Street and joined

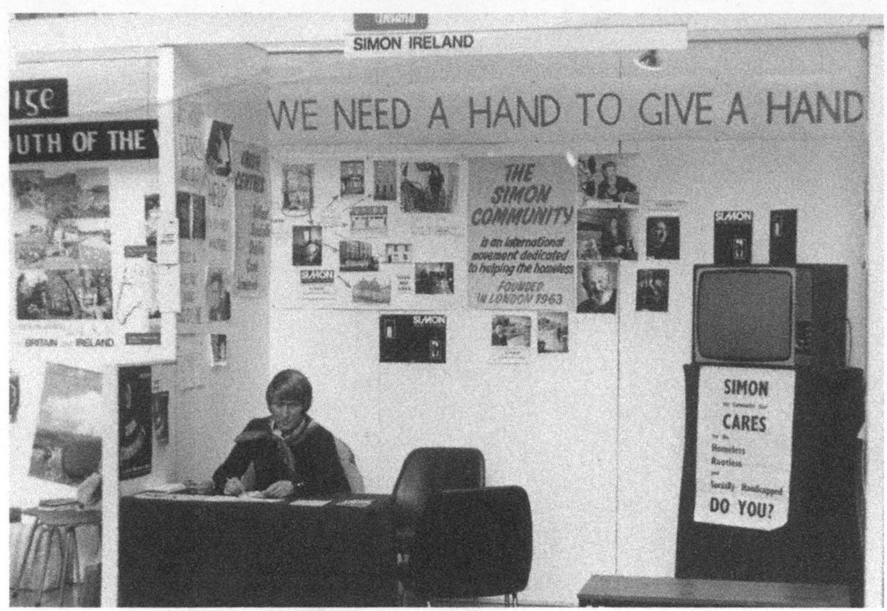

If I knew then what I know now. At the RDS where I asked Fred Donohoe to employ me.

the organisation in 1971 when I was working as night sister in Baggot Street. I worked a week-on and a week-off so was able to plan activities in my free week. I was impressed with the spirit of the VSI. They gave young people like me the opportunity to get involved in practical work to improve people's lives, and there was a fun social aspect to it, meeting like-minded people, both Irish and visitors from abroad, debating life and raising money. We wallpapered and painted the apartments of elderly residents. We fixed broken things, saw the gaps and tried to bridge them. We went on VSI work camps, where you would work so hard that you slept peacefully on the floor of a local hall after finishing with music and chatting late into the night.

In Benburb Street we sat in front of coal fires with older people in the flats who needed company and other things: fuel, bedding, repairs. Young mothers needed baby clothes, help with washing and a social space they could go to be a community together. We often left the flats with a long list of jobs to be done: windows to be repaired, doors painted, locks fixed. Our lists might be scribbled on the back of a cigarette box.

A report by VSI on Benburb Street in the seventies was a groundbreaking piece of research into the realities of life in this neglected public-housing scheme. It found that 519 people lived in the five Benburb Street blocks spread out between 139 flats. The flats had become a dumping ground for rent defaulters. Households ranged in size from one person to twelve. Most of the residents were unemployed and many of those who had jobs worked in unskilled, low paid and often seasonal work. Water and toilet facilities were poor, communal areas had been vandalised and there was nowhere for the children to play.

One of the human stories behind those grim statistics was outlined by journalist Eileen O'Brien in her 'social sort of column' in *The Irish Times*. In 1970 she visited a mother of nine living in Benburb Street and described the woman's living conditions. The family often shared a one-bedroomed flat with no water or toilet. They all slept in one room but for two of the bigger boys who slept on the floor in the kitchen. On the landing outside the woman's flat all the paint had peeled from the walls. The landing was littered with bedstead parts, broken toys and discarded food. The floor of the shared toilet on the landing was dotted with faeces. There was no glass in the windows of the landing, just thick wire netting with iron bars outside. There was nowhere to hang washing. The woman's husband had left two and half years earlier. She was nervous at night because there were always people sleeping on the landings. She hoped to go back to work when her children were older, she said. There were no playgrounds and the yards were filthy. Two of her sons went to a youth club. Her only break was an occasional trip to the Bingo.

In 1973 the *Catholic Standard* quoted widely from Eileen's article and described Benburb Street as 'a purgatorial street, where those who have defaulted in rent are sent as punishment.'

'Can we not avoid creating another Benburb Street?' the VSI report asked. 'The public experience of sub-standard housing and of eviction to such accommodation of rent-defaulters should show that the cost to the taxpayer in social welfare, medical services, law enforcement and prison maintenance is substantially greater than the lost income of rents.'

Sadly, many more Benburb Streets were created in the forty years since those words were written. St Michael's Estate, Fatima Mansions, and the Ballymun flats all fell into neglect and chaos, starting out hopefully and then used as dumping grounds for troubled people with the misery of heroin addiction added to the direness. The simple idea that massive social capital is created when the State provides good public housing has yet to take a real hold on public policy.

The VSI report made a real difference at the time. Benburb Street was raised as an issue in the Dáil, and the Corporation began to co-operate with volunteers, re-housing some families and enlarging some of the flats. Windsor Motors donated a house in the street to be used as a community centre. We installed a secondhand washing machine in the house and set up a women's club and a youth club.

The women loved to have a place where they could gather to celebrate a birthday or just share the tedium of wash day. The Corpo didn't put any obstacles in our way, and we never felt they were using us to do the things that they themselves should have been doing. It was a time when people wore fewer labels. You weren't defined by who you were: volunteer or Corpo official, which meant that we could work together effectively to really get things done.

We took the children up to the Dublin mountains, as part of the youth club activities. They were great days. For many of the children on those trips it was their first time outside the city. They had no connection with rural Ireland. It might have been the first time they'd ever seen cows or rabbits, long grass and wildflowers growing. There was the sheer excitement of jumping in a river, running wild in a field or forest. Child protection issues are important but there was an innocence and a joy of appreciating nature that happened on those trips, just looking at butterflies, the wonder of it all.

VSI was a fascinating organisation. It felt utterly democratic. I can't remember anyone being defined as the head person and that was part of what made it so energising. Everyone felt that they were part of something that worked and we all had a very clear purpose: we were there to make life better for people.

A lot of the people I met in those early VSI days went on to senior positions in Irish life. I don't remember anyone going into politics, but there were bankers, architects and civil servants. We often see civil servants as a separate vaguely bloodless breed. But these were people who saw voluntary work as something necessary to life in the public service. We were idealists with a will to get on with doing the jobs that blatantly needed doing. If someone made a mistake, and there were lots of mistakes, you just spoke about it and got on with it. We weren't stifled by procedures or political correctness.

The main office was in Merrion Square and we had meetings there and in the homes of volunteers like the meeting that night in Berkeley Street, the first and last time I saw Sean Armstrong.

It was easy to look at the situation in Northern Ireland in the seventies and see nothing but impossibilities. Sean wasn't confined by those barriers. He was simply a decent human being, trying to show the young people around him how much they had in common by giving them the shared joys of a holiday together.

Barriers and boxes are a big part of working with the poor. People today think I must be a nun or working with Father so and so or Brother so and so. If you're working with people who are poor, you're still expected to be a nun or to be aligned to some religion. Sean clearly didn't see it like that. He was from a Protestant background but wasn't confined by that. As Seamus Purseil wrote about Sean: 'Many of his friends knew nothing of what religious denomination he had been born into. Sean didn't care.' That sense of being more than your label really chimed with me. I had that sense of freedom from childhood, the belief that religion was neither a passport nor an obstacle to anything.

In June 1973, months after I'd met him, Sean's new wife opened the door of their flat in Eglantine Avenue to a stranger. The couple had been married a week earlier and had honeymooned in Scotland. The man walked up the hall of the flat, according to Sean's mother, Dr Hylda Armstrong who was interviewed by journalist Alf McCreary for his book *Profiles in Courage*. The man asked Sean 'Are you Robert Sean Armstrong?' Sean said yes, thinking the stranger was a parent of one of the children with whom he worked. The man pulled a gun and shot Sean once in the stomach and twice in the back as he tried to escape into the bathroom. No one has ever been convicted for the killing.

I woke up in Dublin to the awful news of his murder on the radio. I felt sick, with a stomach-churning sense of shock and loss. It made no sense, given that I had only met Sean once. But I walked around the city that day in a daze. As the rest of the world seemed to be getting on with life I had suddenly dropped outside the normality of daily routine and busyness. I was overwhelmed with sadness for someone I barely knew, and bewilderment that the city could carry on when something so savage and hopeless had happened. It seemed incredible that life could just continue as it had the day before when he was still alive and part of the world, a source of inspiration and hope to someone like me. I was numbed by the news.

The numbness lifted and I felt the reality of his death during the outpouring of sorrow at his funeral service in St Anne's Cathedral in Belfast. The cathedral was packed with people of all ages and denominations. Sean's wife told the funeral mass about a dream a friend of Sean's had had the night before Sean died. The man had dreamed of a huge oak tree being felled and little shoots coming up all around the fallen tree.

Sean's death made me question my own life. His murder was as hopeless and pitiless a death as anyone could imagine. It brought home the seriousness of life for me. Losing someone so young (Sean was 31), who seemed so full of life and potential, was the shock I needed to see that life was short. The vision of little shoots growing up around a fallen oak stayed with me. Sean had tapped into something in my psyche, the vague but strong feelings I had about overcoming obstacles and divisions, whether they're created by religion, or class or income or gender.

Sean's great gift, that had so impressed me that first and only night we met, was his ability to connect with people. He sat in a room and talked in a way that made us all feel more empowered, part of a shared humanity.

As a senior nurse in a high-powered, stressful role in a hospital, I was helping people, but I was doing it from the confines of a strict hospital system, closed in by barriers and labels and structures. Sean's death was the spark I needed to step out of those shoes and leave the only working world I had ever known.

* * *

'Well I'll make an appointment for you to see a psychiatrist,' the consultant in Baggot Street said in a flat voice. There was no glint of fun in his eyes. He was utterly serious. He thought I was mad.

His words left a sour feeling in my stomach. I didn't have to give my notice to him but I felt duty bound to tell him I was leaving. I was turning my back on my important job, as sister-in-charge of their brand new intensive care unit, a job for life with a pension at the end. I was going to live and work in Simon at 9 and 10 Sarsfield Quay, a night shelter which backed onto Benburb Street flats. In his eyes I wasn't taking a brave step into a more meaningful life but jumping off the career ladder and landing squarely in the filth of the gutter.

Realistically I didn't expect him to pat me on the back and tell me what a wonderful choice I was making, but I didn't expect to be offered psychiatric help either. The consultant wasn't the only one who thought I was mad. Some of my nursing colleagues cut me off. Doing something this different turned me from a friend into something of an embarrassment that they couldn't seem to understand. As word spread around the hospital, I noticed people's shocked reactions but I didn't let them get to me. I hadn't had a breakdown, as many people seemed to think. I had had a breakthrough.

Years later, one of them came over to me in Marks and Spencer's. She had seen me on television the night before. This seemed to have validated me in her eyes. I had gone from mad Alice to someone she was proud to have known.

I travelled home to my parents' house and, as we sat by the fire that night, I talked to them about my decision. I kept the grittier details of the Simon Community and its chaos, danger and grime, to myself, sketching in where I was going to live, rather than painting a more vivid picture.

They listened quietly.

'Are you sure, Alice?' Daddy asked me.

'Is there any danger you might fall off the edge yourself?'

They weren't worried about the decision to give up a permanent pensionable job or at my choice to work with homeless people. They were part of a rural way of life where 'men of the road' and residents of the County Home were part of the community, known and not feared. But they were worried that living with damaged people could be damaging. Exposure to all that human pain and chaos might blister and crack the shell of my own life. I wasn't frightened by that prospect. But it was a smart question and they were entirely right to ask it. I think they knew after my trip to New Zealand that I wanted a change. If they were going to lose me to something they would rather it was the Simon Shelter in Dublin than a New Zealand hospital on the other side of the world.

Dublin Simon Community was set up after a visit to Trinity College Dublin by its English founder Anton Wallich-Clifford. He was a former Capuchin who had joined the RAF and fought in the Second World War. He left religious life and became a probation officer in London after the war. In 1963 he set up Simon to help people like the homeless groups who gathered around fires drinking methylated spirits on bombed-out sites in the East End. The name came from Simon of Cyrene, the man who helped Christ carry the cross. Simon was set up to help the rejects or those people who were seen as too difficult to be reached by existing charities because of violent behaviour, chronic alcoholism and mental health issues. These people often ended up in the criminal justice system. The emphasis of Simon was on human warmth and contact and the creation of a real community.

Wallich-Clifford was an inspiring speaker. His words moved people to action. The Dublin Simon Community started after he visited

Dublin to give a lecture at UCD. One of the men listening that night was Larry Masterson, who would go on to shape *The Late Late Show* into the ratings hit that it is. The talk was so galvinising that Larry and several other people in the audience got together and set up a soup run the following week. Father Frank O'Leary, a Franciscan priest, found them a premises in Winetavern Street in 1969 and that was the beginning of the Dublin Simon Community.

At its heart, Simon was trying to restore hope to people living desolate lives by showing them that someone cared about them. Loneliness was the 'greatest social cancer of our age', founder Anton Wallich-Clifford once said. It was loneliness that forced people to drop out of society. The people he met were those who were pushed in on themselves by painful childhoods in broken homes, orphanages or institutions. One of the principles of the Irish branch of Simon stated: 'Simon comes in where others leave off, to meet the need where the need is greatest.'

The Simon philosophy drew from experiments in community living of the time, including those of American journalist and social activist Dorothy Day, The French priest Abbe Pierre, who set up communities across France in the forties, Mario Borelli, who lived with street children in Naples in the fifties, psychiatrist Maxwell Jones, who founded the Henderson Hospital as a therapeutic community for young people in Surrey, and the English Reverend Bram Peake, who turned his west-London church into a halfway house for homeless former prisoners.

I had come to know the work of Simon on Sarsfield Quay when I worked in Benburb Street. Two crumbling near-derelict buildings, numbers 9 and 10 Sarsfield Quay, had been given to the organisation by the St Vincent de Paul Society, who had been given the buildings by Dublin Corporation. They had boarded-up shopfronts at street level. On the upper floors the old windows were patched and crooked. The smell that greeted you at the door was that familiar smell of poverty, damp, mould and coal fire tang, with a layer of Jeyes Fluid on top, to try and mask the stench of sewage that seeped up occasionally from under the floorboards.

Sean's death and that sense of the enormous work he was doing helped me to make up my mind about leaving nursing. Once that clicked into place, I didn't lie awake debating it in my head. I was delighted to have made the decision. It wasn't something I felt I had to discuss with friends or colleagues. I felt most of them wouldn't understand what I was doing. I was certain that it was the right move for me so I applied to be a full-time Simon worker. My training as a nurse would be a real asset.

Despite knowing in my head this was the right move for me, I was aware that this was a serious career swerve. I was going to be taking a salary cut, working a 120-hour week for an allowance of £3.50 (the equivalent of around €44) a week. So I assumed they would welcome my skills and sacrifice with open arms. I was very unimpressed to be asked to do an assessment interview. The panel was made up of experienced Simon workers and a psychologist. They wanted to see if I was mature and self-aware enough to cope with the challenges. I was told that after a month's probation I would be re-assessed. I didn't like the interview. They seemed to doubt my ability to work in chaos coming as I was from an organised hospital background. They wanted to know how I would deal with violence and dirt. It was a rigorous grilling and a real interrogation of my motives. Part of me wanted to walk out in a huff and never go back. But I didn't.

The Shelter was open to anyone who called in off the street or was brought there by gardaí, referred by hospitals or members of the public. Most of the residents were people who had been sleeping in derelict

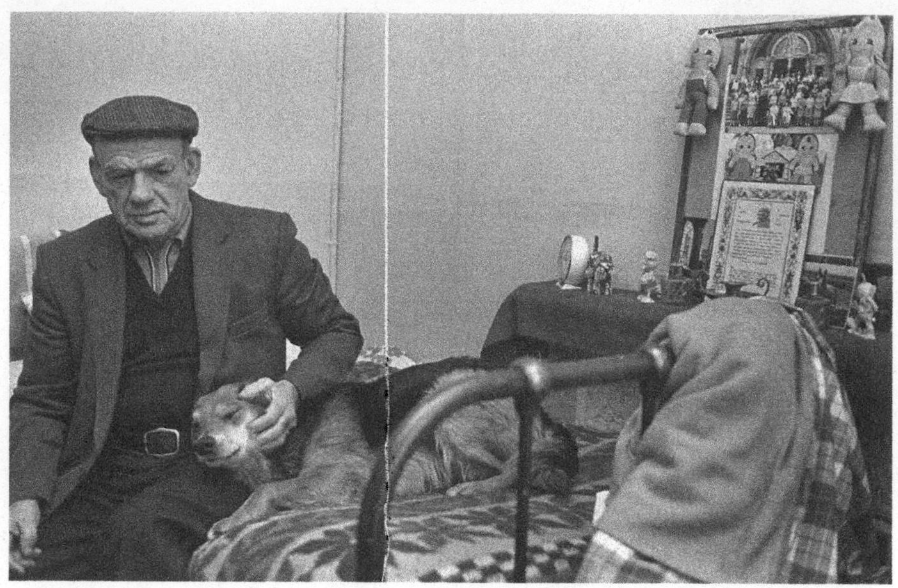

Man's best friend – with Christy, a Simon resident.

buildings, benches and doorways, begging for money and often committing petty crimes. Many of them had been barred from the main hostels for violence, stealing or bed wetting. Prison was the only place where they could get basic security and a roof over their heads.

This was the deep end. The Simon Shelter was an intense experiment in community living. *The Irish Times* journalist Eugene McEldowney put it: 'If you thought working for Simon meant getting a warm glow from handing out soup to grateful derelicts before skipping off to the next debutante's ball forget it. Simon is about caring. It's about living 24 hours a day with alcoholics and drug abusers and ex-mental patients under the same roof. It's about cadging vegetables from early morning traders so there'll be something to put in the stew you'll have to make when you get back to the wet house. It's about trying to put a roaring drunk to bed when he doesn't want to go. It's about getting jolted out of your sleep at four o'clock in the morning when some other drunk decides he does want to go, but hasn't seen the necessity of getting back to the house before closing time. Sometimes it's about giving out soup to derelicts, who are sometimes grateful.'

The Simon Shelter was set up to provide food, warmth, shelter, a bed and companionship. The basic rules of the shelter are ones we have in The Alice Leahy Trust today. No drinking, drug taking or violence was allowed on the premises. The Simon philosophy was to aim to put itself out of existence as soon as possible with the creation of a caring society outside the decrepit walls of the shelter. We had the same idea when we set up Trust.

Number 9 was set up as a therapeutic community, housing between nine and fourteen residents ranging in age from seventeen to seventy. Number 10 was the night shelter, or a wet hostel. Residents were not allowed to drink in the night shelter but they would be admitted even if they were very drunk.

Having a wet and dry house next door to each other was challenging. Before I arrived in November 1971 residents took over the wet house after a fight with a worker and began throwing things out the window. A bed was thrown down and landed on a car outside. The guards arrived and used the bed as a battering ram to get into the house and arrest the men.

We had breakfast meetings every morning and house meetings once a week. All the residents could talk about their pent-up feelings and make complaints or suggestions. The other full-time workers when I joined Simon were men, most of them younger than me. Simon was a real community, where workers and residents lived cheek by jowl in the same conditions, eating the same food, sleeping under the same leaky old roof. At weekends or on days off you could go home.

The wind snaked in through cracked doors and out again through rattling windows. We ate our meals with the residents around a big shared table. They cooked with us, went to the market with us, cleaned up the plates, pots and cutlery together. The senior worker always kept a diary of events that day, trying to keep some order on all the disorder.

I slept in a small shared room on the first floor, with four beds in it for the full-time workers. I always insisted we had clean sheets and kept a good supply of DDT to keep our beds free of fleas and lice. One night I woke up to feel the weight of someone fast asleep and snoring on my feet, a resident who had stumbled into the room and collapsed on my bed. I was so tired most evenings that I fell sound asleep as soon as my head hit the pillow, despite the din. There was always noise, someone clattering up the stairs, banging on the outside door to be let in, shouting or singing.

Luke, a young drug addict, used to sit by the fire in the shelter. He had the slight build of a young jockey, full of energy much of it self-destructive. He would usually arrive high as a kite roaring and running around, and it took a lot of ingenuity to calm him down and get him settled. My tactic was to offer him a cup of tea, a mug of soup or a cigarette. A Woodbine could work wonders if someone came in in a state, but you had to make sure you had enough for everyone.

Eventually, like a whirlwind that had run out its course, Luke would settle. I lost touch with him for nearly twenty years until he came into us in Trust one day. He hadn't changed but his behaviour was less frightening. He told us he had lived abroad. He became a regular in Trust and when he died the gardaí couldn't find any relatives. So he was buried in our plot in Glasnevin.

I kept my bedsit in Ranelagh as a refuge from the chaos. It was a nice cosy place, with a kitchenette and a large wardrobe, which was an unusual feature of bedsits at that time. I didn't have many things but I had books. One night when Simon founder Anton Wallich-Clifford was visiting Ireland he slept on the floor of my bedsit. I woke up and found him sitting down and saying the rosary. He was deeply religious but not interested in converting anyone else.

Sometimes the shelter was so busy people slept where they could find a quiet corner, under tables, on chairs in front of the dying embers of a fire. There was a constant feeling that anything might happen, good or bad. There was chaos, but there was also warmth, humour and acceptance of who we all were. We were living intensely real lives. We weren't protected or hindered by the 'them-and-us' barriers that existed for all the other professionals who routinely dealt with the people who came through the doors of Simon: the prison officers, guards, social workers, doctors. We didn't have a label, or if we did we wore it lightly. Everyone, residents and workers, was part of a community.

It was a step into the unknown for me, but experienced full-time workers showed me the ropes and also gave me a sketchy briefing about the more difficult regulars.

'Watch out for Crack when he first comes in. He likes to make a bit of a drama,' someone told me.

Crack was a small, fat, energetic man. He threw his bulk around and always made a scene when he blustered in off the street. Normally it didn't take much to calm him down.

But one night was different.

He started with the usual roaring and shouting and then picked up a kitchen knife that someone had been using to chop vegetables. He started to walk across the room swinging the knife from side to side, eyeing everyone to see what this new twist in his drama would bring.

'C'mon,' he said. 'Come near me and I'll kill ye.'

Everyone froze.

I knew I had to get between him and the other residents, who could easily pick up a knife and start a full-blown battle. I had the advice of the full-time worker who had warned me about Crack's love of drama in my mind as I walked calmly towards him. I kept my eyes on Crack but knew that there were workers in the room who would help me if he made a lunge. I took a deep calming breath.

'C'mon now. Give us the knife, Crack,' I said quietly.

We locked eyes and for a moment. Crack's eyes were wide, with the look of someone who might do anything. Then he dropped his gaze, bravado deflating like a balloon, and I reached out both hands took his wrist gently and loosened his grip on the knife handle.

He was quiet as a lamb afterwards. I'm not sure he ever meant to do anything other than cause a ruckus.

I felt the fear of what could have happened like a cold trickle down my neck after the adrenalin had drained away. But there was always someone around you could talk to about that. Afterwards, I wondered if being a woman had been a protection. I felt sure he was never going to stab me. Sometimes being a woman could spark animosity in men who had difficulty relating to women. But everyone was different.

I don't remember being frightened at the idea of living and working with homeless people. I never felt the people I would meet were dangerous. I think I had a confidence in myself as a person. I had always tried to talk to everyone as an equal, another human being, without the baggage of fear or prejudice.

Sport is a great way to connect with people. It allows us to tell our stories, to locate ourselves in a place, to dream big dreams for ourselves and our team. I always read the sports pages. My father's cousin Eileen lived in Manchester and made me a lifelong Manchester United fan. I even wrote a poem about the Munich Air Disaster. Rugby was part of my life because Major Hughes played it. Soccer became a part of my life later. Soccer players' names are often given by people who come into Trust when they don't want to give their real names. We've had more Roy Keanes in Trust than any other player.

The energy people get from watching their sports stars, their connection with the GAA, is such a powerful force for good. Sport can save people. Prowess on the playing field can make someone shine even when they're struggling in other areas of their life. Sport, even more than politics, is a common language. Women aren't expected to know or be interested in sport. It's a shared ground that I've always enjoyed talking about.

The *Irish Press* journalist Tom McPhail was a fellow worker in Simon. He was a wonderful man, a real mix of thinker and doer. He could work long, back-breaking hours, changing beds, shaking DDT on the mattresses, coping with the burst pipes, clearing blocked sinks or toilets; the regular seepage up through the floorboards. Then at night he would think and talk and write about our lives and what we were doing.

He captured a day in the life of the shelter so vividly in an article published in the *Evening Press* in January 1974, just a few months after I had joined:

'It is 7am on Sarsfield Quay with the mute fronts of the boarded-up shops and houses still gripped in frost. But already the winos are moving out from their refuge of night for the refuge of their days. Faces stubbled, eyes hard and seeking they shuffle up the Quays to that refuge – in Smithfield, in the market, in the nearest open pub. The early pubs are throbbing with the life of the dawn people.

'For the winos with a regular begging patch and the craft to avoid being barred in these pubs a pint or two of Guinness soaks and soothes their trembling bodies. The outcasts count out their coins of conscience, begged the night before by change and return to the streets clutching their flagons of cider. The wine shops are not yet open ...'

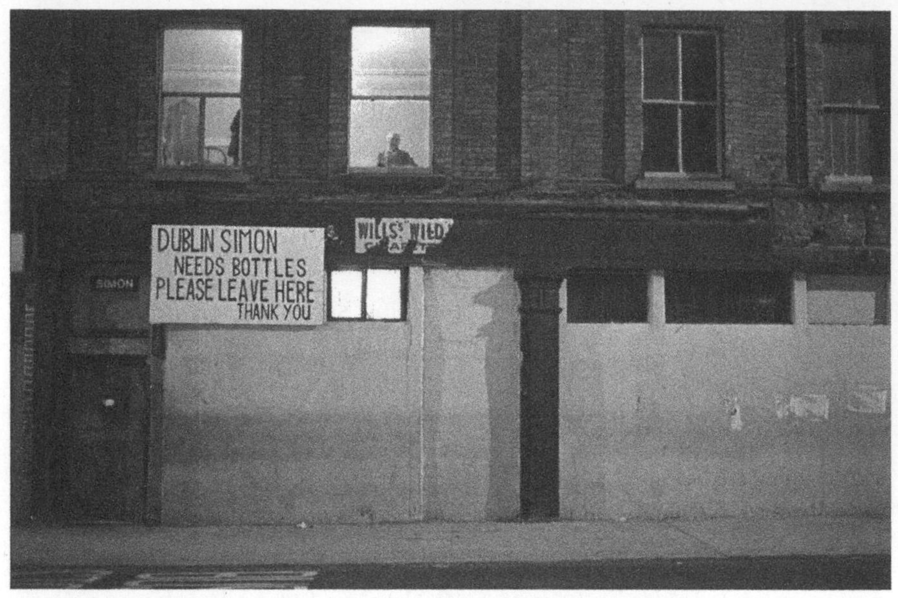

Behind closed doors – Dublin Simon, late 1970s.

At the end he described our night-time routine:

'It is after midnight now. The braces are put on the door for the night. The night worker will be up until dawn to let in the stragglers. Those more fortunate are in bed. Others stretch out under the table, on the landing in the hall. Chairs are pulled towards the fire for the telling of tales that will go on until sunrise. We drift into the residential house and sink tired and dazed into chairs around the upstairs fire for the nightly ritual of coffee and cigarettes. We exchange shattered hopes, moments of human kindness that have made this day whole.

'As a Simon worker you don't look for success rate or measure progress in terms of months. Many of these people are at the end of the road. You're working in the problem end with many terminal cases and it is soul destroying but vital.'

My background as a nurse in a highly organised hospital system meant the chaos often got to me. I had gone from a world that was controlled and run efficiently by women into one that was dominated by men, wonderful men who managed the service and the damaged men who used it. It was the first time I encountered regular violent outbursts, verbal and physical. The efficient ward sister in me could see how time, money and food was going to waste, how endless meetings soaked up time that could be used to get things done, to fix and clean and organise our surroundings.

Psychologist Ian Hart and Dermot McMahon, a former psychiatric nurse, worked in Simon when I was there. They were both extremely helpful and generous with their knowledge and time. Ian was a quiet and very caring man. He loved the people in Simon and his professional experience added so much to Simon's work. I was once elbow deep in a sink downstairs, trying to clear a blocked drain with a wire coat hanger, as Ian stood talking about the personality of one of the residents.

'Would he not talk and work?' I thought, a bit peeved.

But Ian was too likeable for me to be annoyed for long. Working as a research officer with the Economic and Social Research Institute (ESRI), Ian wrote a book about what he learned, called *Dublin Simon Community 1971–1976, An Exploration*. He talked about the idea that the difficult homeless people we were caring for were not easily fixed. What he called 'supportive help' was more appropriate than rehabilitation. 'The problems of Simon's people were social and educational rather than medical,' he said.

It's a difficult idea to take on board when people start working with homeless people, that the best you can do is give them a safe space where they can be clean and comfortable. In a study of residents he found that 39 per cent of the residents in the shelter and residential houses had been in prison. Twelve per cent had been in institutions for children or adolescents. Ian described three types of life histories that frequently arrived at the doors of Simon. They were people with disastrous pasts. 'Many had had miserable lives through little fault of their own,' he said.

The first common story was that of the returned alcoholic, who had left poverty in rural Ireland to work in England but found it desperately lonely and drank to combat that isolation before returning to Dublin to become down and out. The second was the alcoholic habitual offender, an illegitimate child reared in an institution, who had left without any social skills and fallen into petty crime and homelessness. The third was the person whose parents had died young and they had been put into an institution or lived with an older sibling, where they were not made welcome before they ended up on the streets and in Simon. They carried the social stigma of shame, which only lifted when they were drinking. These were people who had nothing and were going nowhere.

The therapeutic community at Simon was modelled on psychiatrist Maxwell Jones's Henderson Hospital in Surrey. Workers were sent to visit the hospital and I asked to be sent. I wasn't. They sent a young male worker instead. By coincidence, the worker they sent was Peter Gahan, a nephew of Muriel Gahan who I'd known from childhood as Olivia Hughes's great friend.

In Simon we workers talked a lot about the work of RD Laing, the Glasgow-born psychiatrist who challenged the orthodoxy of psychiatry, the labels that psychiatrists put on people when they behaved in certain ways and the medication that invariably followed such a diagnosis. Laing fascinated me because he questioned this easy labelling of people. He believed in the idea of therapeutic communities and the power they can have to change lives. These discussions in the broken-down office as we were finishing up for the night, after a day spent cleaning, cooking and coping with the chaos, were such a contrast to the physical labour of working in Simon. It was a hippie age. We could all wear our long clothes and Laing's ideas were part of that. In his book *The Divided Self*, he outlined how he believed we exist in the world according to the ways that other people define us.

The complexity of life under the roof in Sarsfield Quay and the fluid nature of our roles as humans sharing that space taught me how it was easier to deal with people where everybody's role is clearly defined. As a nurse I played a part when I talked to a patient. After performing that role for long enough you spoke from a script, taking on the persona of a nurse, a professional veneer that protected you from the raw emotions that swirled around illness and hospitals. I didn't have that veneer in Simon. It made my interactions with people more connected and much more complicated. It's much easier to look straight ahead, not to question things and to relegate everyone to a label, ourselves included, consciously or unconsciously. Life can get very uncomfortable if you're questioning things.

Christy was one of the regulars in the shelter. He was balding and wore a flat cap which rounded out his strong features. He wasn't a large man but he had an amazing charisma and could exert a strange power over people. When he wasn't drinking he was quiet, dull almost, and often sunken into himself. At the mildly drunk stage he was charming, thoughtful and interesting. When wildly drunk he became Hombre, a character from a film he'd seen. You stayed away from Hombre. After I'd been away on a break from the shelter he came in one night, saw me and threw his arms around me. I felt that for him I embodied three women in his life he wanted to love but couldn't: his mother, a lover, and a nun or teacher. Christy spent his childhood in a reformatory and blamed his mother for abandoning him. That rage and sadness engulfed him when he was drinking.

I got to know other Simon regulars well. Most of them, like Christy, are dead now, some of them having lived surprisingly long lives. John and Mary were well known around Dublin. When they weren't in Simon, they stayed in a garden shed in the garden of a rector on the South Circular Road. Duncan was the poster boy of those days, a real charmer who was loved by all. Paddy was proud as punch that he knew a woman in Guinness and used to make his way over to the brewery every day for free bottles of stout. Mary from Clare had been a nurse in London before she became homeless and I brought in my old textbooks for her to take a look at them. Her eyes lit up as she leafed through the pages, remembering her own training.

The city's homeless problem was worsening. In 1973 Simon counted 92 people sleeping rough, compared to 50 people in 1969. This looks like a smaller number compared to today's figures. In November 2017 the rough sleeper count reached its highest ever with 184 people sleep-

A happy couple – Simon residents, 1970s.

ing on the streets of Dublin. On the face of it, the figures have doubled, but the story and make-up of Irish society has a part to play in the statistics. Fifty-three of the rough sleepers in 2017 were not Irish and a further 51 did not have their nationality ascertained. In the seventies the rough sleeper population was almost entirely Irish.

We had an ancient shopping trolley that I trundled down to the markets, with the help of a resident, the wheels often falling off it as we man-handled it over the cobbles. The stallholders were generous and I loved the fresh clean smell of vegetables and flowers after a night in the shelter. We would call back by Martin & Joyce butchers on the corner of Benburb Street to pick up bones for the stews, Sweeney's Chemist on the quays for bandages and the bakery in Manor Street, where they gave us bread for free.

Dorothy Goodchild was a former nurse and part-time worker. She loved doing night duty in the shelter. She was English and her husband Vernon was a member of the choir in St Patrick's Cathedral. She ran the shelter in her own quiet way, never raising her voice. She always arrived in time with delicious homemade shortbread and packets of Woodbines. She left the place spotless before she left for home in Malahide the next morning.

Life was intense as a Simon worker and some of the workers were damaged by it. We had sensitivity group meetings to ensure workers didn't go off the rails.

These were held in a building on Harcourt Street beside The Four Provinces dancehall (or Four Ps as it was known), which later became The Television Club. It was relief enough to be out of the shelter to air our views. We sat in a circle on the floor, with psychologist Ian Hart, and opened up.

'Could he not get on with helping me instead of talking all the time?'

was a regular complaint of mine. I had little patience for hearing somebody talking when they could be rolling up their sleeves and doing something.

They were useful times to reflect and step off the treadmill of endless work. People could get very burned out and they brought with them their own problems and skills. I think my experience of working with the VSI and in the Rotunda gave me a good grounding. I suspect if I hadn't had that my time in Simon would have been much tougher.

I could see the difficulty of what Simon was trying to achieve in the model of a real community of residents and workers. 'Residents should be on the committee of the community if it is to be a community in the real sense of the word,' I wrote at the time in a frustrated letter where I expressed my frustration about the culture of 'talk day in, day out' rather than action and the shocking waste of food, money and man-power due to a lack of organisation.

We were allowed to be human in the middle of discussions, to get angry and say what we felt. I've been to case conferences since where walls of jargon and outcomes and performance indicators are built around the messy human situations being discussed around polished tables. Simon was far from perfect, but it was striving to be a real community, the only one I've seen apart from one in Amsterdam that I visited later on a Council of Europe fellowship.

Building a real community is difficult, but I think we have to dare to dream.

In hospitals where I had worked I had been slotted into a system, not a perfect system, but one that was solid and structured. In Simon we were making our world up as we went along.

Simon was also my first introduction to the world of prisons, a place that is hidden from most of us who are lucky enough never to be sent there. Being down and out was still a crime in the seventies. Under the Vagrancy Act people could be arrested for begging, 'wandering abroad without visible means of support' and drunkenness. Hundreds of people were charged and convicted under the act. In 1973, the year I went to work in Simon, 248 men and women were sent to prison for the offences of begging, wandering abroad or drunkenness.

A lot of people we dealt with in Simon ended up in prison, either under the Vagrancy Act or through petty crime. Prison today has become the place people go to get psychiatric care. They get another label, drop another notch down in society, when they walk through the gates: the label of criminal.

Most of the people I met in Simon loved going to prison. It gave their lives a structure that they didn't have on the streets. They knew the officers and their fellow prisoners. For many of them prison was just another link in the chain of institutions they had lived in all their lives.

On my first prison visit I walked up to Mountjoy, or the Joy, as it's called, from Sarsfield Quay. Turning off the North Circular Road, the office was the first port of entry. It was a prefab with seats around the side and two toilets. The prefab filled with smoke as people sat smoking waiting for their visit.

'Alice Leahy to see ...,' I said handing the cigarettes, or clothes or sweets that I was bringing to the prisoner to the prison officer behind the desk. I sat down to wait. Sometime later the telephone rang and the officer mumbled something to the caller, looked up, nodded in my direction and said, 'Alice Leahy.'

This was the stage when you walked towards the grey stone face of Mountjoy. Built in 1850, a copy of London's Pentonville Prison, four wings radiating out from a central circle. Walking up the pathway towards the small door within a larger door I could feel the weight and bleakness of the building. There was nothing green or growing once I stepped inside. The sky above was the only bit of nature left. It didn't smell of poverty like flats could. The air was stale and dead.

I could hear the clinking of keys on chains as the door was opened and I stepped into the tiny space where my name was checked. Beyond that another prison officer stood with a chain and keys to open a heavy iron gate, which clanged shut behind me, and brought me to the visiting area. People moved slowly, deliberately in these small hemmed in places, as if it was important to keep a lid on any energy, even your own, or else all hell could break loose.

The visiting area was a room with a long table, visitors on one side, prisoners on the other. There were no screens or glass, so the half dozen or so prisoners all chatted away with no privacy. Prison officers stood in the room but they kept in the background. The twenty minutes flew. I can't remember who I was visiting on that first trip, but we would have chatted about people we both knew outside. It all looked like a normal group of people chatting in what was a completely abnormal setting.

When the prison officers were around, there was a kind of rapport between prisoners and officers. I often wonder if the people who ended up in prison had had opportunities how differently their lives might have been. Prison is a home for poverty, financial poverty and the poverty of circumstances.

The women's prison felt like going into a dungeon. In the fifties the old women's prison had been given over to the young offenders St Patrick's Institution, and the women prisoners were moved to the basement of St Patrick's. They remained in that basement until 1990 when they were moved to a wing of St Patrick's, and in 1999 they were moved to the Dochas Centre, a purpose-built prison. *Dochas* is Irish for hope. Our two main prisons are called Hope and Joy. Until those improvements happened, I visited women in their cells in that dungeon like basement. Those rooms were dismal, windows high up in thick walls and cells decorated with pictures, photographs of family, sadness everywhere, almost thickening the stale air.

Despite the appalling conditions for women prisoners in the seventies some women liked going inside. Their lives had depths of sadness that could buckle the human spirit. Prison was a roof, a bed, company and some support.

I first met Pauline Leonard in Simon. She was one of the younger women we saw in the shelter, and the guards from the Bridewell often brought her to us when she was drunk. When she was sober she was great. She challenged us all. Her life was difficult, but she was getting on with it and she had the energy to give out, in a way that would make you look at your own vulnerability. She often came in to us having slashed her wrists. I would take her up to Dr Steevens' Hospital. As a former nurse, it was easier for me to take people to the voluntary hospitals. I didn't have to wait in line or go through the red tape of form-filling. Pauline's life and her eventual awful death was to play a huge part in our work in Trust and the making of a poverty industry around homelessness. But that was some way in the future.

Most of the Simon residents were men but there were some women. Some of them were older women who were great to have lived to the age they did, considering the hardship of their existence. One of them was Bernie. She came in one night to the shelter thin, filthy and miserable, quaking with sickness. The only hospital I could bring her to was Baggot Street, and my heart sank when I saw the doctor in charge that night walk over to us because he was so clean-cut and handsome and Bernie was in such a state.

The doctor's name was Philip Kennedy and I didn't know him from my time in Baggot Street. He had been in St Vincent's. He had matinee-idol looks, and Bernie took one look at him and threw her thin filthy arms around him. I couldn't believe it. The two of them stood in that embrace in the tiled hall of the hospital. I thought this polished young man would recoil in horror, but Philip smiled and returned Bernie's hug.

Judging him by his appearance, I would never have suspected he had met anyone like Bernie. But he wasn't thrown by the encounter because he had been out there meeting people who were homeless. I had this view of him as a well-got man, living on a different planet to people like Bernie.

Life in Simon had begun to take its toll on me and I was planning to take a break and go to work in Sheffield with my friend Anne's nursing agency. As well as an opportunity to step back into the clean and starched world of nursing, it was also a chance to earn some money.

We started chatting. I told him about my plans to go to England. He said he'd go down with me to Simon when I got back. I gave him Anne's address and said I'd keep in touch.

Yorkshire was a step back into a calm, organised life again. Anne had made a huge success of her nursing agency. It was the largest in the north of England and I had the pick of the jobs there. I worked in Batchelor's peas factory as an in-factory nurse in case of accidents and in a steel foundry in Sheffield. That foundry was where I really felt I was winging it. I didn't have the skills to deal with a major industrial accident. I prayed every night that the shift would pass without incident. The nicest place I worked was the Claremont Hospital, a private nursing home run by Mercy Nuns. It had all the hallmarks of the best places run by nuns. It was clean and bright and the patients were treated well. At night, we went around with mugs of hot Horlicks before bedtime. It was a world away from Sarsfield Quay.

I had two visits to Sheffield. On the second visit I moved into Anne's house in Rotherham to mind it while she was away. It was a beautiful, comfortable house with a well-stocked drinks cabinet and cut-glass crystal. My colleague from Simon, the journalist Tom McPhail paid for Mary, a Simon resident, to come and visit me in Sheffield as she had a sister there. I met her in Liverpool when she arrived off the boat. She stood out with her scarf on her head and her belongings in a string bag. She was thin and waif like and seemed to be carrying everything she owned in that little bag. She moved into the house for a short while, fitting in quite easily. She would get up every morning and have her shower. Then one day she got drunk and started shouting on a bus. The other passengers widened their eyes and tutted at her behaviour. She had a sister who was working in a pub near the markets area. In the end she decided to stay on in Sheffield with her sister. She returned to Dublin for a brief visit and went back again to Sheffield. I don't know how her life worked out but she seemed to be on a more even keel after the move.

Two things came through the letterbox of Anne's house in Rotherham that were gateways to the next stage of life. The first was a letter from Philip Kennedy.

'I have been down to Sarsfield Quay. Quite a lot and things are happening,' he wrote before launching into a ramble through some of those happenings which brought me vividly back to the world of Simon. 'Christy is on the dry since, excepting a few days' drinking, though as I write who knows? … Paddy S may at last be getting his glasses. He is very aggressive and his eye hurts because there is nobody to put in the ointment.' Like me, Philip Kennedy could see how Simon's medical response could be run better.

'Do you know there is a tremendous drugs cupboard … but all under lock and key and not being used! And the hangovers and vomiting in the morning are being borne with stupid stoicism.'

Anne's husband was a GP. And the second thing that came through the door was a medical magazine containing a report by CHAR, the Campaign for the Homeless and Rootless, about the medical needs of homeless people. I could do something like this, I thought as I read the report. No one had studied the medical needs of the homeless of Dublin. The CHAR pamphlet planted a seed in my head. There was a job going in the national office of Simon Ireland and I felt I could use it as a base to do some kind of a report on the medical problems of homeless people in Dublin and beyond.

I could have missed seeing that pamphlet and never had the idea. But another door had swung open by chance and it was one that would lead to the setting up of Trust.

CHAPTER SIX

The Elephant Catchers

'How wonderful it is that nobody need wait a single moment before starting to improve the world.'

Anne Frank's The Diary of a Young Girl

The Model Lodging House was at the end of Benburb Street Flats. It was a closed world, unknown to me despite all my visits to the flats. I had never walked through the door of The Model before I arrived there with my questionnaire in the seventies. I didn't know it was there.

The Model was a hostel for single homeless people run by Dublin Corporation for almost a century. It was opened by Dublin Lord Mayor Thomas Sexton in 1888 as a seventy-two-bed lodging house where a bed for the night cost 4d. The original complex included a house for the manager and a wash-house with two male and two female baths.

By the time I stepped through the door nearly ninety years later it was a hostel for homeless men with eighty-four beds. I would earn grudging respect in the shape of a steaming mug of tea eventually, but there was no welcome mat for me on those first visits. I was met with the smell of cooking. Through the door on the left lay a large kitchen with a huge gas cooker. Something always seemed to be bubbling on the stove, even first thing in the morning. It could be a pig's head, some kind of stew or coddle, a Dublin favourite.

Inside the entrance to the large 'dining room' there were small lockers, like cubbyholes you might see in the lobby of a modern apartment block. Each of the men who lived in The Model had his own cubbyhole where he kept his cooking equipment. This was typically a small saucepan, a mug and a spoon – the most basic equipment needed to make a meal for one. A picture of those cooking utensils said so much about those men, all similar, but different, like shoes lined up in a family home, except lonelier.

Many of the residents of the Model were dignified, independent men. They worked in the gardens of private homes or in the grounds of convents or churches around the city. Later, when I got to know the city's homeless services better, I discovered there were fifteen organisations giving out food, most of them run by religious orders. Lots of the men in The Model were too proud to use the food centres and cooked for themselves every day.

I had come home from England and succeeded in getting the job as the assistant national director of Simon Ireland. Almost immediately after I took up the role, I started my research with a view to finding out what were the medical needs of the homeless population. The Model was a man's world and they did not welcome me, a woman and a nurse when I first arrived with my two-page questionnaire in the spring of 1974.

I would make the rounds of eight other hostels in Dublin in the course of my research, to find out more about the people who lived there. I was assessing the needs of homeless people in Dublin, Limerick,

Dundalk, Killarney and Cork, and the attitudes of the medical staff they encountered. But more importantly, for what lay ahead, I was making connections with the network of people and places in Dublin involved in caring for homeless people. In those early days I was often met with suspicion and wariness. I didn't let that put me off. I met stony faces with my brightest smile. It helped that I was working for Simon, an organisation which didn't give me a label as a nurse or social worker. I had the freedom to interact with people one human to another.

Later I got to know the superintendent at The Model very well. John Hayes's claim to fame was that he knew the then ex-Minister for Finance Charlie Haughey. John was very helpful to me as my relationship with the place developed. I knew I was accepted when a mug of tea was offered on a visit. The tea was an invitation to sit down with the staff and chat. The Model became one of the places I really liked to visit early in the morning. They took a great interest in those men's lives and tried to help in any way they could.

It was an honour to be invited back to The Model as the renamed and upgraded hostel, Oak House many years later. Oak House was run by Dublin City Council and many men lived comfortable and safe lives in the new facility, with their own rooms and a communal sitting room. Mick, a Wicklow man, who came to us in the early days of Trust, spent years there as a resident. He arrived drenched one morning after falling into the duck pond in St Stephen's Green. We got him clean and dry and tried to help him find a place to stay. Thanks to the work of a community welfare officer he accepted a room in Oak House.

He kept returning to us in Trust up until very recently, forming a bond with our nurse Mary Kelly. When he grew very ill she linked in with his medical team, visited him regularly until he died in the hospice in 2017.

After my round of hostel visits, I would walk or cycle back to the Simon Ireland head office. It was in a cramped cubby hole in the basement of the old *Irish Times* building on Fleet Street. Journalist Tom McPhail helped me write the report and Nancy Giles, a former VSI colleague, typed it up in her office in Ballsbridge.

In Simon Ireland Dick Shannon was my boss. Our small office was dominated by a huge table covered with green felt. Dick typed with one finger on an old manual typewriter. He was very quiet and thorough, a serious-minded man of great integrity and a spiritual calmness. He worked extremely hard but never looked for any plaudits. He went on to train as a barrister in later life and then became a priest. He was not one for gossip or small talk.

We cooked up daily batches of soup on a gas cooker set into a tiny nook directly underneath the footpath above our heads. The steam from our soup wafted up to street level through the pavement grill. It was a welcome sight coming back to the office on a cold day.

As assistant national director of Simon my report was my main focus, but I was also the liaison person for Simon hostels in Belfast and Cork. Alongside the report, which took up most of my time and energy, I interviewed workers who wanted to join Simon. I travelled to Spode in England for a conference run by the Cyrenians, bringing together different groups working with homeless people. All of it fed into my thinking about the strength that grows by bringing separate groups and organisations together to talk to one another.

I gave a radio interview to RTÉ presenter Andy O'Mahony about the Simon soup run. It was such a unique and special service and still to me today it's the best example of what a soup run should be about. In Simon the soup run had a philosophy. Its people were as important as the hot soup they delivered. It was very organised and very little time or food was wasted. Now this work is commonplace but that idea of going to meet people where they were in doorways or skippers, as they were called, was relatively new then. Skippers were makeshift shelters made by people as refuge from the weather or the world. That outreach idea was something for which Simon will always be remembered. The emphasis wasn't on the food it was on the human contact.

Our history of soup kitchens goes back at least to famine times, when wealthy households and the Government established soup kitchens as part of famine relief efforts. There was often a very strong Christian influence. You 'took the soup' and sometimes when you took the soup you changed your 'colours'. Charity came with strings attached. That's what made the Simon soup run different; you didn't have to change your allegiances.

An extraordinary group of people met and became friends through the soup run and they would have a huge impact on my life and the direction I took. One of them was a young newly qualified doctor called David Magee. Like me, he had been a fulltime worker in Simon, and, as a medical student, he had lived with the people I had come to know during my time on Sarsfield Quay, although our paths had not crossed in the Simon Shelter. When Dick Shannon introduced us one day, we recognised something in each other, a common drive, which was to take us down the road together in a partnership that would lead directly to the setting up of Trust.

My radio interview about the Simon soup run wasn't my first. Journalist Fred Desmond had interviewed me years earlier for a radio programme called *Down the Country* about my guinea pig project when I was a teenager. I remember listening back to it and hearing myself talking at the rate of knots, remembering how my heart pounded the whole time as if I was running as fast as I could. When I talked about the soup

Fethard-Killusty Newsletter DEC. 1976

CHURCH OF IRELAND NEWS

A Flower Festival with a difference in Holy Trinity Church.

Alice Leahy, RGN. RM. - a Pioneer for the Vagrant: I was in Dublin on a cold wet day in early spring, and I noticed an elderly woman lying probably drunk on the steps of the Bank of Ireland. That evening hurrying across O'Connell Bridge in the bitter weather, I noticed a young man lying on the pavement. I felt I ought to do something, but I could not think what to do, and everyone else was passing by, so I too "passed by". Also during a cold spell travelling to Wicklow and putting in time between trains, I went into a waiting room which had some stoves in it. The whole room was filled with ragged men huddling near to the stoves. I had "passed by", but at least one Fethard girl, with top nursing training, had felt called to give up a good job, to work for the Vagrant. She joined the Simon Community and then made a thorough study of the treatment of the vagrant and the numbers involved in Dublin, Cork, Limerick, Dundalk and Killarney.

O. Hughes.

Olivia Huges wrote this piece about me in 1976 for her local Church of Ireland newsletter, describing how I started to work with people who were homeless in the city. Those who knew me from back home continued to follow and support my progress through the years.

run I was older, dealing with a specific subject. Knowing and believing what I was talking about was the skill that got me through that second interview more easily. This opened up a new world of dealing with the media, journalists and politicians. I didn't feel I needed any training to deal with any of them.

Before an interview I always remind myself that people are there to hear what you say and I plan the points I want to convey. I'm always very careful to think before I answer a question. I'm there to share my experience rather than lecture people as an expert, and I'm conscious that my words could hurt people, especially when I talk about individual cases.

In the nineties I saw an advertisement in *The Irish Times* for a public-speaking course.

'Fintan, do you think I should do that course?' I asked journalist Fintan O'Toole, wondering if he could give me a feel for what the course might be like.

'No, Alice. You could give it,' he said.

Getting out of the Simon office and going to those hostels brought me through the doors of many of Dublin's hidden places. I realised quickly that each hostel had its personality. Each was a self-contained kingdom, with its own quirks and hierarchies, characters and power struggles. If I was going to be able to do more than ask questions, if I was actually going to be able to call to the hostels and treat people, then I would have to get to know how each place really worked and have the right people on my side.

I also called to hospital emergency departments, GPs' clinics, the offices of medical social workers, the ambulance service and soup run volunteers. I talked to the homeless people themselves about how they were treated by the medical services and any difficulties they had. In 1974 the homeless population of Dublin consisted of around 1,000 people in hostels or sleeping rough. The figure in 2018 for people in emergency accommodation or sleeping rough in the city is almost six times that number.

We finished the report towards the end of 1974. Nancy typed the name: THE SIMON IRELAND REPORT ON MEDICAL CARE FOR THE VAGRANT – in capitals on the front cover. Vagrant was a word of its time, consigned to history now.

Every day I still encounter the physical health problems associated with a life of homelessness. Those conditions haven't changed in almost half a century. The human body reacts the same way now to malnutrition, smoking, alcohol, exposure and poor hygiene as it did then. What was changing in the early seventies was a dramatic transformation in how the authorities were treating mental health. This huge shift would have repercussions for decades to come.

In 1966 the Commission of Inquiry on Mental Illness reported to the then Minister for Health. The report presented a shocking picture of the extent of mental illness in Ireland. One in every seventy people over the age of twenty-four was, at any given time, a patient in a psychiatric hospital, giving Ireland the highest rate of hospitalisation for mental illness in the western world.

The bulk of patients were housed in the 18,000 beds provided by the district asylums, most of them nineteenth-century buildings looming on the outskirts of towns and cities. Add to this the number of people in industrial schools and Magdalene laundries and we had an institutionalised culture of control that involved locking people away. The world of the asylum was threaded into the life of some towns. In Ballinasloe, Co Galway, in the early fifties the local mental hospital held 2,000 patients, almost half the town's population of 5,600, with much of the remaining population employed in the asylum or working in businesses supplying the hospital.

The Irish weren't any more insane than any other nationality. Our high incidence of incarceration for mental illness was a legacy of poverty, rural isolation, the religious culture of shame around children born outside marriage and the institutionalised care of many of these children who grew into broken adults after spending their early lives in industrial schools and orphanages.

The district mental hospitals, 'the madhouses', were described by the Commission on Mental Health in the sixties as 'barrack like structures, characterised by large wards, gloomy corridors and stone stairways'. In 1966 the Commission said the aim should be to reduce 10,000 long-stay places by half to 5,000 places over the next fifteen years. It marked the beginning of the end for psychiatric hospitals like St Brendan's in Grangegorman, where so many of the men and women I would deal with in the coming years went for help and medication.

The psychiatric hospitals had hellish histories. At their most benign, they were warehouses for people deemed unfit for general society, a blunt instrument of social control. At their worst, they were places where basic human rights were ignored and 'troublesome' people, many of them women, were committed against their will.

The 1966 report was the start of a positive modernisation. It had all kinds of wonderful recommendations for team work involving doctors, nurses, psychiatrists and general practitioners, exactly the kind of cross-disciplinary co-operation and open discussion that I had seen as a beacon of hope during my brief stay in London. That 1966 report recommended positive public education, community services with out-patient clinics, day hospitals, hostels and support for family care. At its heart, the report was about tearing down the walls of the asylums and integrating psychiatry into general hospital care.

But the institutions housed a huge population of long-stay patients who could not cope with life outside hospital. As the system began to be wound down, staff, who were often very caring, grew weary from the struggle. Patients were released into a changing Ireland, where the system that was supposed to be supporting them was still being worked out.

Over the seventies and eighties the authorities emptied the psychiatric wards, releasing people onto the streets, many of them bewildered and lost. If the positive spirit and recommendations of the report had been implemented, the patients would have been released into a kind and caring safety net of community professionals, all working together to help them. But the sad reality was that a properly integrated care-in-the-community system has never been put in place. The safety net was full of gaping holes and many people fell through onto the streets, homeless hostels and prisons.

In 1957 the two largest Dublin psychiatric hospitals St Brendan's in Grangegorman and St Ita's in Portrane housed 3,750 patients. By June 1973 that population had fallen to 2,700, half of whom were geriatric patients and mentally disabled people. The bulk of the 1,000 patients who were no longer being cared for inside the walls of those two institutions were navigating a new disjointed reality. The Eastern Health Board divided Dublin city and county into seven catchment areas, with adjoining counties of Kildare and Wicklow adding another two catchment areas.

Each catchment area was served by an area psychiatric team. 'It should be clearly understood that once a patient leaves hospital to take up residence in a hostel or elsewhere, his psychiatric supervision, in so far as this is required, will be provided by the area psychiatric team,' an Eastern Health Board report for the staff of St Brendan's in 1973 by Ivor Browne stated. These catchment areas would become the bane of our lives in years ahead. The lines on the map made for a bureaucratic nightmare, the first of many barriers thrown up between the person who needed care and the people trying to give it to them.

A 1974 report for Simon Ireland found that 489 people classified as homeless were admitted to psychiatric hospitals that year, the majority of them men. Two thirds of those 489 admissions were former psychiatric patients. Almost 80 per cent of all the homeless people admitted to psychiatric hospitals in 1974 were discharged after less than a month.

The former psychiatric nurse, Dr Damien Brennan, now Assistant Professor at the School of Nursing and Midwifery in TCD, charted the history of the Irish asylum system in his recent book *Irish Insanity 1800–2000.* Irish mental hospitals 'became a major repository for social problems', he wrote. 'It is good that the large mental hospitals are almost a thing of the past. However, it would be unwise to assume that Irish communities have become more sensitive and tolerant to individuals who "challenge" social expectations. The tenfold decrease in mental hospital residency since 1950 has been mirrored by a tenfold increase in the prison population,' he said. In effect these 'problem' people were being shifted from one system to another.

The institutions were not entirely closed to the outside world. Patients had contact with volunteers in a way that today's label-based approach would never permit. They were wonderful people, like Miriam McCarthy from Cork, who I had met when I worked in Simon. Miriam was a big strong woman. She always wore a cape and she was constantly in a hurry. She was firmly on the side of people nobody else wanted to know.

'Why is this man barred?' she'd demand to know, arriving at the door of the Simon Shelter, with the man in question in tow behind her.

'Well he was fighting,' someone said, peering nervously out from a crack in the door.

'That's not good enough. Did you find out who started the fight?' Miriam would say. 'I'm not leaving until you let him in.'

On the soup run she met people who were living in dire circumstances.

'They'll never come in,' she said when Simon workers puzzled over how to get them indoors.

'It's simple,' she said. 'Those people are out-and-out people,' meaning people who lived outside. 'They'll never come in, so we'll have to bring the houses to them.'

And she did. She persuaded Simon to buy a number of wooden huts and delivered them to places around the city, on a dump in Ringsend, under a bridge, behind a wall or on a beach. If it was private property, she visited the owner and persuaded them to turn a blind eye to a hut on the corner of their land.

Miriam and I went together to visit patients in the Central Mental Hospital in Dundrum. She had a written a list of people she wanted to see. Beside each name she would note the things they liked: humbugs or apple drops, Woodbines or another cigarette brand. She found out the idiosyncratic things that appealed to them, noted it all down and made sure to include whatever it was on her next visit.

She was less organised in her own domestic affairs. 'God, Alice, I forgot he's coming home for his dinner this evening,' she'd say as she drove back in a tearing hurry from Dundrum, the 'him' being her husband. 'I have to stop off and get a head of cabbage.' Sometimes her husband would arrive home to find a homeless person sitting in his house. Miriam took people in. One woman set fire to her sofa. Miriam had no boundaries. That's what made her special, and made me so fond of her.

It was a time when the media had begun to open doors on the country's institutions. In a groundbreaking piece of journalism, in 1966, Michael Viney of *The Irish Times* wrote about the reformatory system, interviewing a former inmate of Daingeain, the reformatory school in County Offaly. The seventeen-year-old boy had been released from Daingean, only to find a different family living in his old home, his mother having left for England. Just like that, he was left homeless in Dublin, wandering the streets until a night shelter opened. 'The people in that shelter, they've given up. They're no-hopers. But me, I'm only seventeen,' the boy said. Michael's piece ended with the boy being put on the boat to try to find his mother.

In another 1966 piece headlined 'The Dismal World of Daingean', Michael wrote about the annual Christmas holidays when the boys were released to go home. 'Others had to stay behind because their parents did not return the holiday form and Daingean had to assume the boys would not be welcome. One of these children cried for three days.' Many of these boys would grow up to be the men that we saw in the Simon Shelter, lost people finding consolation in drink.

In 1971 Athlone writer Hanna Greally's *Bird's Nest Soup* was published by Riverrun Press. In a crystal clear voice Hanna recounted her twenty years in St Loman's Hospital in Mullingar, in the forties and fifites, after she was committed, as a nineteen-year-old, by her mother. Hanna had been training as a nurse in Guys Hospital in London during the Blitz. Committed by her mother to Loman's for 'a rest' after the trauma of wartime London, she described two decades of spirit-crushing loneliness, brutality and occasional violence during tedious hours of unpaid work spent sewing and laundering.

When I read the book, I was shocked by her portrayal of the powerlessness of people like her and the other women she befriended in the institution. Hanna was given insulin shock therapy, a debilitating treatment where patients were injected with insulin to induce a coma and then brought around with glucose. She was held down by nurses and subjected to electroconvulsive therapy. Any attempt to rebel or escape led to her being sent deeper into another layer of the hospital system, where the regime was more brutal. Her book was a sensation and she appeared on *The Late Late Show*. Then Hanna and her story disappeared from view again. She died in 1987. In 2009 journalist Mary Owens made a radio documentary about her life.

In *Bird's Nest Soup* Hanna wrote about how some of the people who came out of that system lost their personalities and became so withdrawn that they stepped away from reality. 'I often think sometimes sadly of the friends I made there – the outcasts, the unloved, the incurably embittered and the spirited still fighting for their liberty. Some may be insane, in the psychiatric acceptance of that word, but I feel certain that many hundreds would be more normal if they were rehabilitated by charitable people or organisations. It would take understanding, patience, but more often a sense of humour, to assist and re-educate them to make the best of themselves,' she wrote. 'Some patients lived twenty, thirty, forty years in the Big House. In their day work was not plentiful and families were only too glad to shift their responsibilities on to the State, in some cases permanently.'

In 1975 the Oscar-winning film *One Flew over the Cuckoo's Nest* brought people like those I was meeting every day to the big screen for the first time. It was a film that got people looking at the psychiatric services and moved discussions around that closed world out into the open.

'Did you see that great film,' I heard a woman in a Dublin pub ask her friend, '*Two Flew over The Eagle's Nest*?' The name mightn't have stuck in her head but the story had.

As a nurse, I wondered why Nurse Ratched was such a heartless bully. Was she just as institutionalised as her patients? And did working in those extreme conditions have a terrible effect on some of the caregivers. It's a film that could still be used today for discussion around the issues that are still current. It made me think about the them-and-us roles we all take on when we work in 'caring' professions.

On one level my report for Simon was a simple fact-finding mission about the common chronic diseases and ailments a homeless community suffers. Those conditions – bronchitis and emphysema, acute respiratory tract infections, foot problems, malnutrition and alcoholism – are still with us today, with drug addiction added to the list. But I was going deeper than listing medical complaints in isolation from the systems and institutions people were encountering. I was also connecting up the separate entities: the hostels and drop-in centres, and accident and emergency departments, who all dealt with this population of people in their own way. I was trying to draw all the strings together, to weave a more solid support structure for vulnerable people, who were then (and are still now) navigating a splintered and haphazard world.

As part of the study, I had started visiting the Simon Shelter with various doctors, all known to me from Baggot Street. There was Alec Hipwell, Philip Kennedy and Bill Fagan (Bill became a GP on the northside), Kieran Daly from Vincent's Hospital, and of course David Magee. An American medical student Bill Kleypack, who worked in Simon as a fulltime worker, was very interested in casework. I contacted him in America and we wrote to each other in the early days about ideas of working with the kind of people I had met in Simon.

'A doctor shouldn't have the goal of curing people for at that I believe he would undoubtedly fail,' Bill wrote in a long letter, teasing out the difficulties of treating patients like the Simon residents. 'Instead his goal would have to be the more ancient one of medicine: to relieve persons from the stresses of disease and to "comfort" (in a very broad sense of the word) his/her patients.'

Meeting David Magee was the beginning of a powerful partnership that would continue for more than a decade. David is a tall, kind man. When we met, he had a beard and very little hair on top. Back then, he dressed in jeans and Jesus sandals, the uniform of young men of the time, and he had a great rapport with the people he met. Most people took an instant liking to him. He was very quiet, but I always got a sense of a wise head on young shoulders, and that he was somebody who thought very creatively about life. He was a newly qualified doctor

Tea and a chat. Dr David Magee, John Doyle, EHB, Fred Donohoe, EHB, Bishop Des Williams marking ten years of TRUST in 1985.

with real experience of working with homeless people.

As a child his mother had helped him to look out at the world and try to understand people who were having difficulties, involving him in the local St Vincent de Paul. He describes himself as having had a potent combination of social conscience and a 'profound elephant-catching addiction'.

'The elephant catchers are a vast movement,' he explained as we chatted over mugs of coffee recently, 'and our motto is very simple: It is noble to assist a stricken elephant in rising, foolhardy to catch him or her while they're falling down.' When we met back in the seventies, his way of existing in the world was to spend his time trying to save others, getting squashed several times along the way by those proverbial falling elephants.

We shared the same freedom of not being hemmed in by ideas of class, religion or status. We were both people who didn't really fit into conventional roles and that meant we could explore and go down laneways and darker alleys that others avoided. We were, what David calls, shoreline people. He had been inspired to become a GP by his godfather, a GP based in Banbridge with whom he spent summers as a child. I didn't see David as a doctor and he didn't see me as a nurse. The spark between us gave us an almost frightening energy.

Very quickly my research visits to the hostels turned into medical visits with David, starting the work that would lead to the setting up of Trust. We kept notes on the people we met in a brown ledger that I carried with me. Several people stand out in my memories.

The first was Nellie a woman listed on the first page of the brown book, in June 1974, along with six other people in the Simon Shelter at Numbers 9 and 10 Sarsfield Quay.

In my notes I described how Nellie had fallen out of bed the previous evening and had been taken to the Mater by one of the part-time workers, 'who said the doctor on duty refused to examine her'. I took her back to the Mater, noting that 'doctors and nurses couldn't have been more co-operative,' and she was given pain medication. In July 1975 she had a catastrophic accident and this was the second-last entry about Nellie:

'In National Rehabilitation Centre Dún Laoghaire for past four days. She fell through floor boards in a derelict house. Contacted the medical social worker on July 8th.' Less than a week later, she was transferred to ICU in the Richmond Hospital with a brain haemorrhage. Her husband visited her. 'Prognosis very poor,' I noted in the last entry. Nellie died shortly afterwards. Her short medical history was typical of the minor common complaints that we could see and treat and the chaos and danger that we couldn't.

There were happier cases. I met Christopher in the Simon Shelter in May 1975. He was aged just twenty and had had the flu for weeks. He had been under the care of the Eastern Health Board and was out of work. We applied for a medical card for him. In recent years I encountered him again. 'You won't remember me, Alice,' he said. As he talked, I realized who he was, Christopher, the young man I'd met all those years ago in Simon. He told me how he had found work, a home and a stable job.

David Magee and I were becoming advocates for the people we were meeting, working to break down barriers with the doctors and nurses people, to try to ensure 'existing goodwill developed rather than wilt[ed] in frustration,' we noted at the time. There were several talented doctors who were interested in devising a model for medical care for homeless people as a special community with very specific needs rather than a set of illnesses to be dealt with by the book.

Child psychiatrist Jerry O'Neill worked with people in the Simon Shelter, and I wrote to him to ask him about his thoughts on dealing with homeless people. He said he was frustrated that residents seemed to be lumped together as 'alcoholics, down and outs and no-goods'. 'Their disturbed, aggressive behavior was seen as something to be tolerated by workers rather than a cause for them to be referred for psychiatric help,' he said.

We could see the gap between the health services and a vulnerable population of people, whose illnesses, both mental and physical, were often ignored or pushed aside because of the difficulties of dealing with them. A bridge between this group of people and the medical services was badly needed.

I wanted to present my report to the Eastern Health Board, the health authority for Dublin which has since been replaced by the Health Service Executive. Fred Donohoe was the programme manager in community care, second in command to the chief executive. I knew Fred from my work in Benburb Street, when I was with VSI. He would have been a face around the table at community meetings with the authorities that I attended.

Philip Kennedy, the doctor from Baggot Street who had so impressed me with his compassion for Bernie the night she needed hospital care, and his colleague Kieran Daly were supposed to come with me to present the report. But they were both tied up in St Vincent's Hospital when the time came so our delegation was reduced to two: myself and David Magee.

On 16 December 1974 we walked in to the offices, with copies of the report under our arms. I wasn't intimidated by the idea of presenting the report to such senior people. I knew it was an important piece of work and I had a hunch that Fred Donohoe would understand exactly what we described. The Health Board offices were tiny cramped spaces inside the gate of St James's Hospital. No one at that level in a health authority, or a voluntary body, would work in those conditions now. It was a time before brass plates on doors, polished desks and expensive suites of offices kept clean by an army of contract cleaners. But there was a great sense of community in the then health board. It was a young organisation with a sense of purpose and energy. They could laugh and they all worked way beyond the call of duty.

Medical staff were also compassionate and caring but that humanity had its limits when faced with the challenge of dealing with difficult people. One of the key lines in my short report crystalised the moment when compassion soured into frustration. The medical administrator in St James's Hospital summed up the challenge: 'Vagrant patients tend to leave hospital before their treatment has been completed. Sometimes

Never without support. Fred Donohoe, EHB, me and Joe Robbins, Assistant Secretary of Department of Health, with Adelaide nursing sister Janet Smyth, behind us.

they return in an inebriated condition and the whole process has to be recommenced.' It's a description of a depressing cycle that anyone working in a hospital today would recognise.

That meeting with Fred Donohoe went well. We walked out into the cold December evening feeling that we had met someone who was on our side, a person in power who got what we were saying. Fred was bright, compassionate and entrepreneurial. He nodded enthusiastically at our ideas, even though there was no existing box or system into which this new way of working could fit. One of our recommendations was for a central co-ordinating body to take on the medical needs of homeless people and to co-ordinate the efforts of hostels, GPs, social workers, ambulance staff and emergency medical staff. The Homeless Initiative set up by Liz McManus in 1996, more than twenty years later, was along the lines of what we wanted to see put in place back then. The Homeless Initiative was replaced by the Homeless Agency in 2001 and that agency morphed into the Dublin Region Homeless Executive, a decade later, in 2011.

One of our recommendations was to involve GPs, medical students and nurses in preventative medicine for homeless people by regular visits to homeless hostels. We wanted a network of people to carry out the kind of outreach medical work that David and I had been doing.

Like the Simon soup run, the idea was to bring medical care to where people were, rather than set ourselves up behind glass doors with a brass plate and wait for them to come to us. Like the soup run volunteers, these professionals could learn from the homeless people how to be around them and what to do. The cogs started turning, and Fred went about putting things in place to make something happen.

It didn't take long. Early in 1975 I met him at a show in the RDS, where Simon Ireland had a stand. He said he was thinking of employing someone to provide medical care for homeless people.

'Well if you are, why don't you employ me?' I asked quietly, with a smile.

And he did.

Under the wing of Fred Donohoe, I became the health board's most unusual employee. I was free to carry on my visits to hostels, shelters, alleyways and skippers. I was an advocate and carer for homeless people, doing the practical work of washing feet, cutting toenails, tending to wounds as well as helping people navigate the medical card system or find a bed. I can't imagine the same thing happening today in the rigid world of job descriptions and tightly prescribed roles. I didn't have a base and I didn't know where my money was going to come from. The wage was a first year nurse's pay and I was technically expected to work forty hours a week. I would typically clock up nearly twice that many hours in a week.

Fred's colleague Brendan Garvey, whose office I shared on the rare occasions I visited the Health Board offices, once suggested I clocked in to keep track of my forty hours. I refused. 'Homeless people don't clock in,' I told him. There was no question of insuring us against any injury. I never worried anything bad was going to happen.

I subsequently discovered I was on the payroll of Brú Caoimhín, the home for the elderly in Cork Street. I would get to know it well when I started bringing Willie, an older homeless man who had chronic psoriasis, there for a bath to relieve the awful itch and discomfort that plagued him. Again it's something that would never be allowed to happen now, a lone woman nurse left bathing an elderly man through grace and favour of a place where he wasn't a resident.

One night I was going home from a St Vincent de Paul function with a friend and a man who worked in the Department of Health. We saw a homeless woman lying crying on Mount Street and we took her up to Brú Caoimhín. Her name was Kathleen. When I got to the door, the nurses said they couldn't admit her. Kathleen started to scream and cry. The night man brought her in to comfort her and I confronted the nurses.

They wouldn't believe me that I was on the payroll and wouldn't let the woman in, saying she would disturb the other residents. Eventually they called the guards.

'Alice, just move down the road and we'll give you a lift where you want to go,' one of the guards who knew me said when he came and saw the situation.

I can understand the nurses' hostility. To them, I seemed like this mad woman arriving up to them with a homeless woman. That's how completely outside the loop I was. I stood my ground but eventually I gave up and took Kathleen in a taxi to St Brendan's Hospital, arriving just after 2am. The doctor who was called to see her questioned Kathleen, 'Why did you come here? When I intervened, the doctor told me she had sent Kathleen from St Brendan's psychiatric hospital to live in the Regina Coeli hostel. Kathleen was finally escorted to a corridor beside the waiting room.

You couldn't have seen more vividly how a lone former psychiatric patients like Kathleen were when they were released onto the streets, bounced like pinballs between services that were not able or willing to deal with them. I don't know where she ended up.

My desk, such as it was, was in Brendan Garvey's office in the Health Board offices, which by now had moved to Emmet House on Thomas Street. They had more room than in the cramped offices in St James's but they were still basic compared to today's standard. Fred Donohoe took me around the building and introduced me to everyone.

Nora Greene was one of the most impressive people I met from that time. She could run the HSE single handed today. She did a brilliant job of getting to know everyone. Nothing was a major problem, much less impossible. Everything was something that could be dealt with calmly and efficiently.

Patricia Podesta could read my writing and did all my typing for me. She was wonderful. Three or four of the Health Board staff often came with me to the night shelters, as did Fred Donohoe.

Homelessness was a more fluid state then. It did not necessarily mean you were jobless or without resources. I knew one pair of men who were entrepreneurial in their own way. They would go around at night and break the glass in the footpath gratings outside pubs. Then they'd arrive up the next day and offer to fix them.

A lot of men had casual jobs, gardening and repair work. The Spring Show and the Horse Show were always good opportunities to get jobs doing casual farm labouring. One man grew potatoes where he lived on the bank of the river Liffey.

Fred Donohoe went down to the Back Lane Hostel one night a week as a volunteer. He was a man who always knew what he was talking about. People liked and admired him and did things for him. He could wrap them around his little finger. It was a big compliment when he said about me: 'Alice is someone you could never say no to.'

He came out with me looking for people in the fields, too, one day, and I got drenched. He brought me back to his house and his wife Kitty lent me some clothes. There was a brown blouse with little green dots on it. 'Now you keep that. It suits you,' she said.

Fred's flexibility gave me the freedom to work as I needed to, but he also protected me so that no one could rope me back into a more orthodox nursing role. I remember him talking about Miss Mattimoe, the senior public health nurse, as a force to be reckoned with. She was great at her job but he warned me not to let her take me under her wing. There was no give there. Miss Mattimoe was supportive and good but I wasn't operating under anyone else's stewardship.

Some time after Trust was set up, I fell out with Fred when I annoyed him by going to Bertie Ahern, who was then Lord Mayor, to complain about the Health Board decision to move the Community Welfare Service from Lord Edward Street over the river to Benburb Street. A lot of people we knew in the hostels on the southside were dependent on the Community Welfare Service, a safety net that provided the only income to people who couldn't claim the dole. The move out of Lord Edward Street left some of the people who needed the service completely at sea. Fred took a dim view of my going to a politician, breaking rank with my employer, the Health Board. I realized that I wasn't being invited to certain meetings and was suddenly out in the cold.

I wrote to Fred, telling him how much I valued his work and friendship over the years. 'Even if we have different ways of looking at problems at times, I do hope we can continue to do so without causing any more pain,' I said. I think he knew what he was getting into when he took me on. He had bent the rules to get me the job and I was not one to sit and wait for someone else to fix something when I could try to do it myself.

I didn't lose sleep over our row. We mended our differences in the end. I had support from all kinds of people. I was a complete outsider and yet I had an inside track to Fred Donohoe and others of his seniority. I could ring him at home at any time and I don't think that went down very well with some people I met, especially Health Board staff.

I was living in Ranelagh in those months, but was rarely at home in my bedsit. My life was my work, and the energy and excitement were addictive. There were relentless challenges and I was meeting new people all the time, building a service from scratch and identifying my allies and those who would put obstacles in my way.

I was idealistic and ambitious. Under Fred Donohoe's wing, I had started to establish the first co-ordinated medical system for a neglected group of people. I was convinced this was the first step to solving the problem and that it was a problem that could be solved. I was young but experienced. I had passionate and talented people around me supporting me. It was thrilling and empowering to have a group of like-minded people on my side. Between us we were going to make the world of homelessness in Dublin a better place. I had to think like that. Otherwise, I would have given up and might never have taken the next step.

CHAPTER SEVEN

Trust
The Gift from a Dying Woman

'If I can help somebody as I pass along ...
then my living shall not be in vain.'
Lyrics by Alma Bazel Androzzo, 1945
(made famous by Martin Luther King in 1968)

It was a row that stopped traffic. David and I were cycling through Dublin when it started. We cycled all over the city, all hours of the day or night, over and back across the river. In the early days we could leave our bikes anywhere, unlocked. It was the most efficient way to get around.

We stopped to catch our breath, at the top of the hill near Christ Church Cathedral, and the row flared. In a rage, we stood shouting at each other in the middle of the road, ignoring the cars stopped behind us. Then one of us ripped off a shoe and flung it at the other. The other flung their shoe back, and we stood there throwing words and shoes at each other, in what I'm sure the drivers in the cars behind us assumed it was a couple's blazing row.

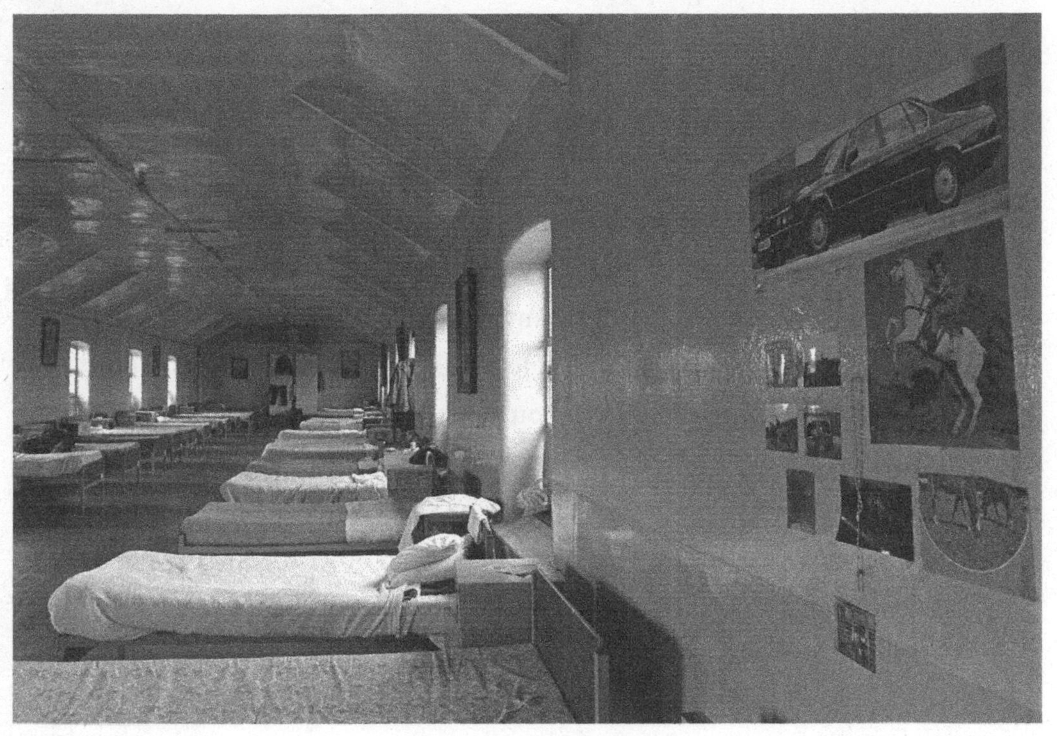

Morning Star hostel, 1980s.

David Magee and I weren't a couple. We were friends and colleagues, equals in a way that was unusual in the seventies when the doctor and nurse roles had a definite hierarchy. I can't remember now why the row started and neither can David. It quickly burned itself out. Our arguments were rarely about our work. They usually centred on trivial things, something in the news or a sporting event or politics. We both believed in airing our disagreements and moving on. Rows weren't allowed to fester. After that spectacular blow up, we calmed down, mumbled apologies, handed each other back our shoes, and pedalled on, much to the relief of those drivers.

It was the kind of fight that could have broken our partnership, but we didn't have the luxury of going our separate ways. People depended on us. We had a service to provide and that meant swallowing our differences and getting on with things.

In those months of summer and autumn 1975 we were making it up as we went along. I had come to the Health Board with my report the previous December, and David had the sense that there was more he could do. I was on the Health Board payroll as a nurse and he was working as a volunteer doctor by my side. It was a meeting of minds and we had the support of senior Health Board official Fred Donohoe as a wind at our backs. We went out into the streets and hostels and started putting my report into action.

Exhaustion was probably a factor in the row. We were both working day and night. We did our rounds of hostels and other haunts and filled up my brown book with the medical notes of the people we met.

In those early days we had no clinic or base for our service. We were a homeless service for the homeless. We moved around the city with bags of medical supplies.

Like the people we were seeing, we had nowhere other than the streets to have a blazing row. But lacking a clinic or base was a strange help when we started out.

It set the tone for everything that followed. We had to meet people where they were – in a hostel, or a doorway, or a makeshift shelter. It changed the power balance. David and I made ourselves vulnerable by being the guests of the people we were helping, whether it was sitting in an abandoned car or pulling up a chair beside a bed in a hostel. Like my visits to families with district nurse Biddy Butler during my training as a midwife, we were taking a health service to the person's place, making a more equal connection possible. It shifted the balance of power. We were guests in their place, wherever that happened to be.

Ideas challenging the rigid structures of medical practice were bubbling up in the seventies. From China came the idea of the barefoot doctors. These were farmers who were given basic medical training and sent to work in rural parts of China, bringing healthcare to people with no access to a doctor. Many of these farmer-doctors worked barefoot in rice paddies.

We were not farmers with basic training; we were health professionals, but we were taking our expertise out 'into the fields', parts of the city a world away from consulting rooms and hospital departments.

The other difference was how we communicated with people. David never used medical jargon. We always called people by their first names and he always used simple English to explain to people how they could do something for themselves.

'Look at the colour of your spit' was his regular advice. We also explained how important it was for people to keep taking any medicine they had been prescribed. These were invitations to the person to become part of their own treatment, to see themselves as people for whom it was worth caring. It's difficult to keep yourself clean on the streets and there's the added problem with some homeless people that they do not value themselves enough to take care of their own bodies. They have never learned to be comfortable in their own skin. They believe, in a reverse of the L'Oréal slogan: they're not worth it.

We knew that the lines between carer and cared-for had blurred when people began giving us advice. There was a lovely man who lived on the canal who used to come up to David pat his balding head protectively and say 'Cover your head, cover your head. You'll lose the heat out of your head.'

My enamel basin, scissors, Dettol and a bag of salt were always part of my kit. Feet are the first part of the body to get into terrible condition on the streets. People can go back onto the streets with a lighter step when their feet are in good condition. If they stop maintaining them, they go back to square one again very quickly.

Administering those first foot baths was a shock. In my decade of nursing I had never seen or smelled anything like the feet of people sleeping out. They lived in the same shoes day and night for a week or longer, afraid to take them off when they slept in case they were stolen. When you're homeless your shoes are everything. Without them you can't get around.

When I took off those stiff leather shoes in the seventies, the feet were often rubbed raw and sore. Today the foot conditions are every bit as bad as people tend to wear soft runners that make their feet sweat more. The smell of rotting skin came at me from feet that were white and wrinkled, a different colour from their legs, after days spent in sodden wet socks. Sometimes tight socks would cut off the circulation and feet would be painfully bloated and swollen. I would fill my enamel basin with warm water and add a good helping of salt to try and harden the jelly soft skin.

Most of the work of doctors and nurses is done standing over someone who's lying in a bed. Even physically you are higher than them and more physically in control of the situation. It is the opposite when you kneel in front of someone, remove their shoes and socks and bathe their feet.

People love this. Even today they would stay in the basin all day if they could, relaxing and wriggling their toes in the warm water. Some hostels, like the Iveagh Hostel, had a room of foot baths, like Belfast sinks, lined up on the ground, where people could come and wash their own feet.

Foot washing wasn't just about making people feel better and dealing with the stink of athlete's foot and sweat. It was also about keeping people from getting more serious problems with their feet like ingrown toenails, circulation problems, leg ulcers and even sepsis.

Jim was a Wicklow man who stayed in the Iveagh Hostel. In the later years when we had moved into the basement of the Iveagh, where we are today, Fred Donohoe brought him to our notice. Jim was a big man and he used to stand across the road from our gate. It turned out he wasn't able to sit down because his hips were so painful. His feet were in an appalling state. The first time we took off his shoes the sole of one shoe stuck, melded to the bottom of his foot like an extra layer of thick skin. He was an independent, proud man and when he went to his local health centre he had never mentioned his feet.

We eventually got him into Cappagh Hospital, where he had two hip replacements, and a social worker arranged accommodation in a nursing home near Wicklow, where he was from.

Another man came into us with a thick wad of banknotes rolled up and put into his sock. They were crinkled and damp. He had nowhere else he felt he could keep the money safely. We took him to a bank and they were very kind to him and organised an account for his cash.

In those months of 1975 we really got to know the hostels and day centres around the city. I called to nine of them and had built up a routine of weekly visits to the six main hostels. They weren't a widely-spread group of locations. You could easily walk or cycle between the network of hostels in a short time, crisscrossing the river between the Christ Church district and the area behind the north quays.

The Salvation Army hostel was on York Street just off St Stephen's Green, facing the College of Surgeons. In Tara Street, opposite the new *Irish Times* building today, the Dublin Shelter for Men was set up by a group of businessmen in an old building. It was small, badly ventilated, hemmed in by the city and had the smell of bodies about it. It was run by men for men. The conditions were basic and the men who stayed there tended to drift onto the streets during the day. The building has since been demolished and houses a bar now with apartments above.

Shelter Referral was based further out of the city, at Merrion Gates. It was a hostel set up by Martin McHale in 1973. McHale was a senior executive at the Irish Glass Bottle Company, who had worked on the Simon soup run in the sixties. The shelter ran along the lines of the Simon Shelter and had an emphasis on work, with residents paid to work recycling bottles.

The Back Lane Hostel, opposite Christ Church Cathedral, was run by the St Vincent de Paul Society back then. Sean Hoare was the supervisor there when I first started visiting. He was a former guard and lived with his wife in a staff house. 'Here she is again,' he used to say when he saw me coming. We had our rows, some of them serious, but Sean was kind. The kettle would be put on when I arrived, and once he gave me a bicycle. He had a terrible job, on call twenty-four hours a day. One of the hardest parts of his job was dealing with the volunteers. It was very easy to be a volunteer, to be nice to people when you were doing it one night a week. Sean lived it every day.

The residents were very fond of him. It was a strange mutual reliance. They needed him and he needed them because they made him feel he was doing a good job. I stepped on Sean's toes badly when I pleaded on behalf of the residents for a change to the breakfast regime. They wanted brown bread. Sean was not happy with my intervention and I felt he didn't believe me. I took exception to that and got him to apologise. Both of us were passionate people.

Another Back Lane resident, Paddy L, was a big man from Cork. When I heard where he was from I mentioned the Munster finals between Cork and Tipperary. Only those of us who have been reared in

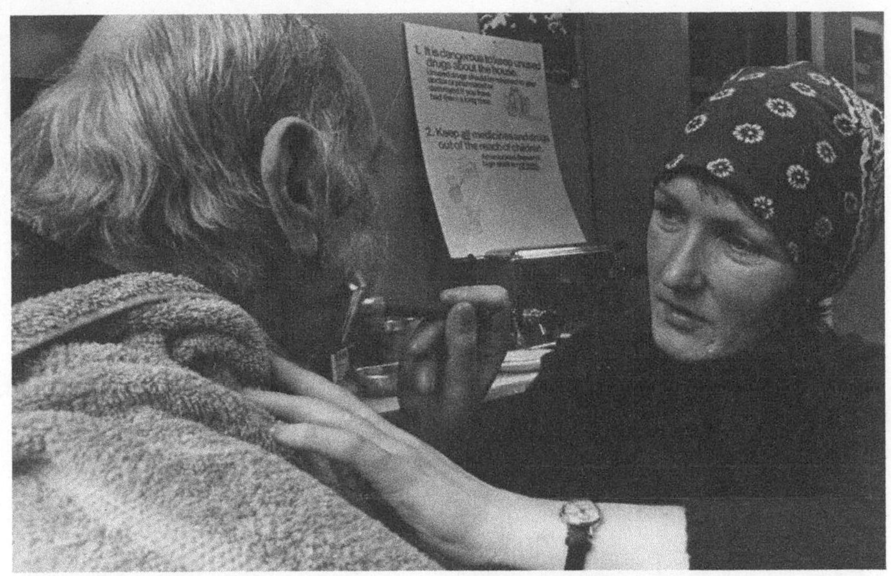

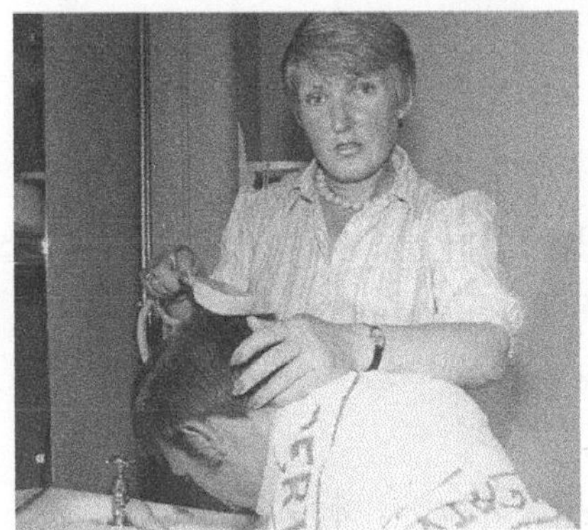

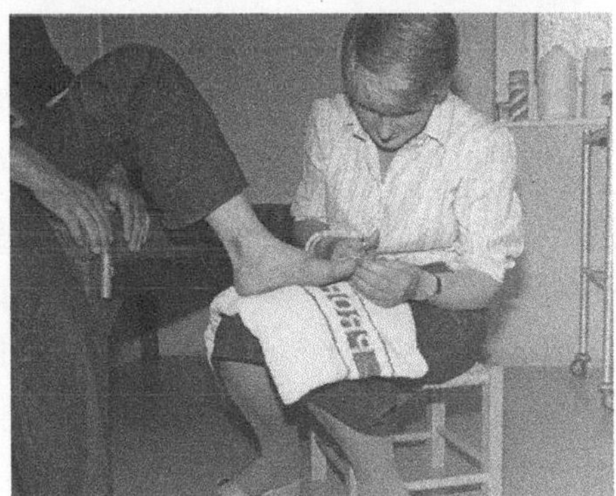

Lending a helping hand with practical health care and personal hygiene – all to help people feel human and face the day – continues to be a huge part of our work

Cork or Tipperary know the fizz of excitement a Munster final generates. If either team is playing anyone else you support each other but when we're in competition against each other it's all guns blazing. Cork and Tipp have a fan rivalry going back generations. I love football, but hurling has a special place in my heart. Its skill and dexterity make my heart pound with excitement watching a match.

Talk of sport was usually enough to spark a connection with anyone from that part of the world, but Paddy's face was blank. He wasn't part of that sporting rivalry culture. He had been reared in a children's home and spent his early working life working with a farmer and sleeping in a shed. His life had been cut off from everything else that was happening outside, even sport, which seemed such a leveler, with the power to bring everyone together.

Sean gave Paddy a job getting up early in the morning and putting on the kettles to boil for the breakfast. As part of the job Paddy was given a brown coat to wear. It was a delicate balance between involving someone in the work of a place without overwhelming them with responsibility and avoiding a situation where the other residents resented someone for their elevation.

One day Paddy got very annoyed with another man and he picked up a knife and stabbed him. I spoke to Sean and we contacted the guards in Kevin Street and solicitor Garrett Sheehan, a wonderful legal brain and human being. Between us, we agreed that both men needed the hostel. The injury was a superficial one. The knife was mercifully blunt. We couldn't have managed to smooth over the situation alone. We had to bring other people with us.

A number of years later we got a call from local GP, Dr Connolly. Paddy had been standing outside his surgery in the Cornmarket, gazing into space. I often saw people standing on corners looking into the distance then. They didn't have screens or phones to gaze into. I often wondered if they were looking into themselves trying to figure out how life had swept them to this point.

Paddy ended up in the Meath Hospital and we got him into the hospice in Harold's Cross at the end of his life. This may have been the only time in his life he had a degree of comfort, a lovely warm bed, with people looking after him, and pictures and flowers around him. He had that little window of happiness at the end of his days.

Like a lot of the hostels, Back Lane had very little money, but they had huge human resources in someone like Sean. It was one of the places where David and I were given a dedicated time in a room to meet people, with hot water, towels and carbolic soap.

Another regular spot on our rounds was Brother Sebastian's Franciscan tea centre in Merchant's Quay. A Franciscan monk Brother Sebastian, or Sab as we all called him. He worked with a lot of the more volatile younger homeless people. If you believe in saints, Sab was one. He wasn't very tall but he had a lovely contented smile that was never far from his face, and a gentleness that masked great strength. His warmth and serenity calmed people, even the ones who came into him from the streets jangling with stress or rage.

He had a way of encouraging young people away from crime, without any structured system or jargon. He would talk to them and give them a small job to do, like picking up the cups after a tea break, something that made them feel valued and responsible. He made everyone, even people who had little experience of being nurtured, feel that someone cared for them, by taking an interest in them and listening to what they had to say. He did Trojan work that couldn't be put into a report or pinned down like bullet points. He loved dogs, and I think people who love dogs are truly human. Anyone who came in with a dog was made to feel very welcome.

He was moved out of working in the tea centre and back into his monastery on Merchant's Quay after it was felt that he was surplus to requirements. I used to visit him there and talk about his work, which he missed very much. I've met people with strong faith which brings a confidence and people with buckets of energy who are in a rush to do things. He had both faith and that energetic personality, and I learned from him how important it is for people who have very little stability in their lives to have someone around as calm and stable as he was.

'Isn't it cruel how you've been moved?' I asked him on one of those visits, wondering how he could put up with being separated from the work he loved.

'Oh well, Alice. It's God's will, I suppose,' he said.

Across the river, on Church Street, we had Brother Kevin. I first met him in Benburb Street, where he was working with the families that we were helping. He was a little older than me but we got on. Because he was from Cork and I was from Tipperary, we always had a special relationship, going back to our counties' sporting rivalry. I felt the brothers were very much the poor relations of the church. The priests were seen as the higher-ups who preached and pontificated, while the brothers rolled up their sleeves and got on with the work. Brother Kevin designated a special place behind the kitchen, where we could see people, and we always enjoyed going to the Capuchin centre.

He and I would often bounce off each other, disagreeing about how to deal with people, giving things to them and what to expect from them. As the years went on, I became wary of how much the kindness of people could be exploited. Brother Kevin is compassion personified. But could agencies become stopgaps for people with problems and let the State out of its responsibilities?

'Alice we are getting so many families here now with small children who need everything, even down to basics like nappies,' he explained to me recently when I visited.

'Look, Kevin, why don't you get onto the HSE or social workers so you don't find yourselves carrying all those problems that aren't your responsibility?' I queried.

Nearby, in a lane off Henrietta Street, Sister Vincent Devlin ran the St Vincent's Trust, a food and day centre. She was another strong woman with great faith, a mother figure to many of the young men she helped. They still talk about her today.

David and I felt there were enough food centres in the city and little or no services to train homeless people for work. Having approached the nuns and Father Murphy, a Jesuit involved at the food centre, we were all agreed on a change of direction. We helped to develop the food centre into St Vincent's Community Training Centre for younger homeless men and women. It began to mushroom into a real community. A lot of local women worked there and a down-to-earth commonsense group held it all together. The buzz of noise and activity in the workshop replaced the relative silence that had been there when it was a food centre. People attending the day centre could sign up for skills training with the State training agency AnCo and go onto a job or further training. There was a busyness and a structure to it. They started a soccer team. It was a great hub of youthful energy and enthusiasm.

On Morning Star Avenue, just off North Brunswick Street, the Regina Coeli and The Morning Star hostels were run by the Legion of Mary, Frank Duff's lay religious organisation. I met Frank Duff and was struck by how much of a man before his time he seemed. He was a very tall, quiet man, almost aloof. He came from a firmly middle-class background and had been privately educated in Blackrock College. Through the Vincent de Paul he had come to know the slums of the city. He had turned part of the North Dublin Union building on Morning Star Avenue into The Morning Star Hostel. Later, the Legion opened a women's hostel nearby, the Regina Coeli. Between the two hostels was the Legion of Mary headquarters.

The Morning Star is a men-only hostel that provides evening meals bed and breakfast. When I first started calling there they insisted people had to pay a little something for their accommodation. If they couldn't pay, they could do small jobs, like cutting wood for kindling. Frank Duff lived in a house on his own on the right-hand side of the Regina Coeli. Mrs Jessop, who ran the women's hostel, would give him breakfast in the morning.

The supervisor in The Morning Star was a man called Tom Doyle. Like Brother Sebastian, he was the most serene man, an amazing presence. He never judged people. He dealt with everyone with the same gentle kindness. To get a job as a social worker now you need to have a third-level degree. I was surrounded by people like Tom who didn't have degrees but instead had an in-depth knowledge of what it was like to be poor and homeless. He saw goodness in everyone and yet he was nobody's fool.

David was always intrigued by The Morning Star hostel. He felt we always had to be careful what we said and how we said it, resident or visiting doctor, or nurse it didn't matter, because it was a hostel with a strong religious ethos. And we respected that.

They could also be uncompromising in the women's hostel. In the spring of 1975, when I called to the Regina Coeli, I was told there was no need to visit as they had 'too many do-gooders calling who will not join the legion'.

Later, that attitude softened and I got to know the women's refuge very well. I remember going up to the Regina, as we called it, early in the morning and seeing a woman resident sitting up in bed smoking a pipe. The hostel was always spotless. My respect for them has grown over the years after witnessing their enormous dedication and years of hard unpaid work that they have put into helping people, without looking for recognition.

Mrs Jessop was in charge in the Regina back then, helped by lots of other volunteer women. All of them were exceptionally helpful, and women of great faith. They would regularly tell me about the problems they were having, in the hope that I could lobby on their behalf and get someone to deal with it. I think they were under orders not to get involved in politics. Their lack of voice in the public sphere was a big absence and continues to be.

One of their residents of the Regina in the eighties was Maureen. She was under psychiatric care and very withdrawn. One morning I watched her in the hostel as she was talking to a pigeon that had landed on the table in front of her. She turned to me with eyes sparkling and started to tell me about the pigeon. I thought that this was healthy; here she was using the pigeon as a means connecting, however tentatively, with the wider world. I was so impressed with the effect the bird had on her that I wrote to the Health Board to say how wonderful the incident was. Big mistake. The Health Board responded by sending over people to get rid of the pigeons. For Maureen, the bird was a resource; for the bureaucrats, it was a health hazard.

Rosaleen was another woman who came into us in Trust in later years. Like so many women we see, she was expressionless and was forever rushing, as if she was afraid someone was following her. She rushed down the back of our offices and told us she wanted to get away from the man she was living with in a shed at the back of St James's Hospital.

But she had a cat that she didn't want to leave behind.

A week later she came back with her little kitten. We got onto the Regina and they said they didn't take pets. Doris Hansard, one of volunteers from Regina Coeli, came over to Trust on her bicycle and she took the cat and got it into the cats' home. Rosaleen was settled into Regina Coeli and she discovered they had a choir up there, which she joined.

She really blossomed. Her whole life changed. She looked younger. She was well dressed. You could see her skin glowing and she felt she was part of something. They brought her regularly to see her cat. Eventually she got a room near Croke Park. One Saturday morning I heard on the radio there'd been a fire over there and a woman had died. I felt sure it was Rosaleen, and sadly it was. Her funeral was one of the smallest funerals I'd ever seen. The only people there were myself, a guard and a nun, Sister Catherine Prendergast, one of the many Daughters of Charity I met and befriended over the years. She was from Galway, a dynamic community worker who ran a social work agency called the Open Door that became Centre Care at the Pro-Cathedral. Later, she was made Provincial of her order. Education meant everything to her and its power to help people succeed in life.

We got to know these people and places more effectively than we would ever have managed had we set ourselves up with a clinic and sat waiting for people to come to us. The only base we could call ours was when we used my desk in Emmet House, the Health Board office on Thomas Street. We went there to write up our figures, often staying till the rest of the building was empty and in darkness, to record the details of the people and problems we had seen.

'I feel by visiting all hostels regularly we might in some way get the spread of scabies under control,' I wrote optimistically in an early report handwritten at that desk. More than forty years later we still see cases of scabies in Trust

'My job is very time consuming due to the nature of the people I am dealing with,' I wrote. 'A day can be spent with one person alone, going from hospital to shelter. Apart from nursing I have dealt with queries of all kinds: accommodation, jobs, AA advice, seeking relations, filling in forms for medical cards. Many people are illiterate and are ashamed to admit this to people in charge of the hostels. I see my role mainly as working at the grass roots, making people more aware of their problems, and encouraging them to seek help. By regular contact with them the barriers can be broken down.'

It was slow and painstaking but we were seeing progress and figuring out a way of dealing with the kinds of people on which almost everyone else had given up.

By the end of 1975 we got a home. And it was a pretty strange one.

* * *

I had met Dr Maurice Davin-Power, father of the former RTÉ political correspondent David Davin-Power, when I was doing my research on the needs of homeless people. He was a GP based in a ramshackle premises on Lord Edward Street in the city centre. Everyone knew him in the area and he knew the hostels. His surgery's official address was The Health Centre or Dispensary on Lord Edward Street. We called it The Hut.

'I've got a place for you Alice,' Fred Donohoe said during a phone call in 1975.

'Dr Davin-Power is retiring and I'm going to arrange for you to work from his surgery.'

There was nothing warm or welcoming about The Hut when we

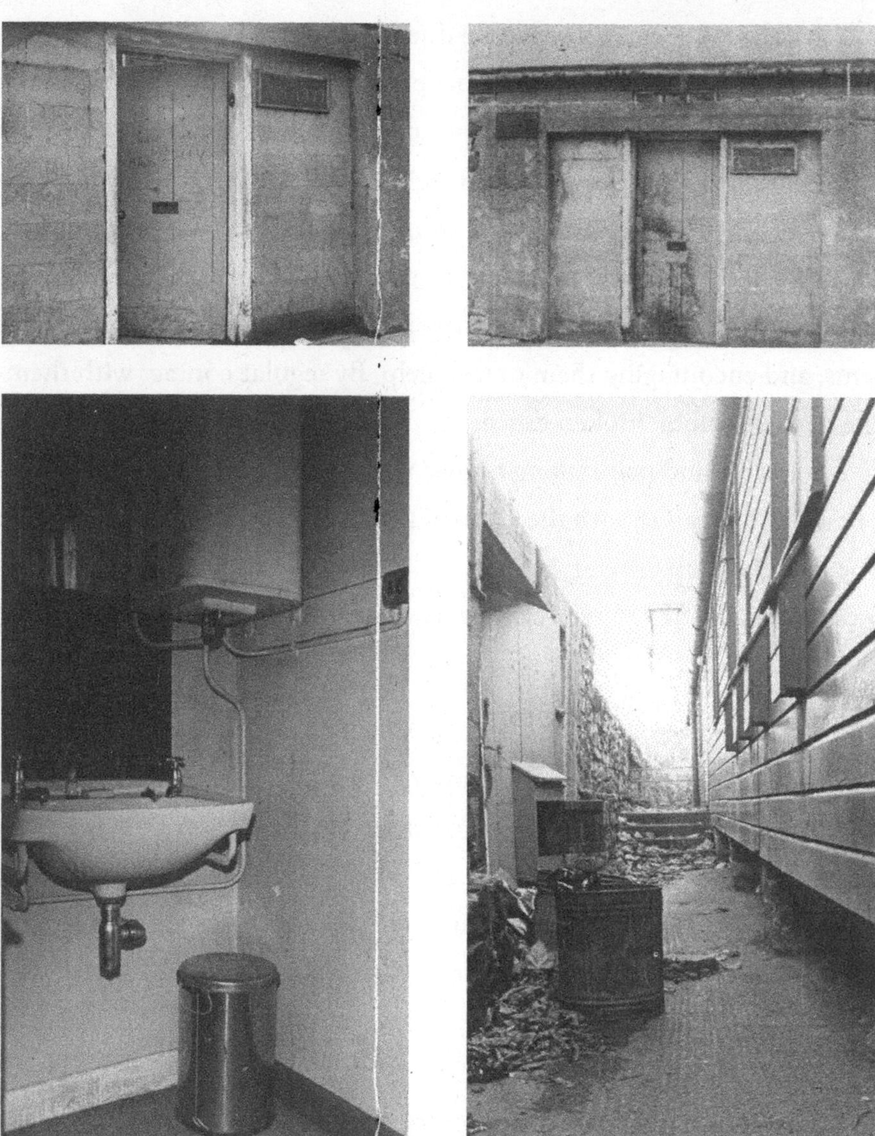

This was our first centre in Lord Edward Street. You can see the front door, the alleyway entrance and our washing facilities. The Irish Medical Times *featured the centre in an article, 1980.*

first walked into it on the day we got the keys. You shouldered open the battered wooden door into what felt like a forgotten drab place. We weren't put off. Having worked in the squalor and chaos of Simon, we knew you could ignore your surroundings in order to get on with helping people. David and I were excited about this as a first step, even though the place was an absolute dump.

There were two entranceways into The Hut, battered old wooden doors set into a blank wall on Lord Edward Street. Leaves and rubbish collected between the blank wall and the front of the building. A set of steps brought us up into the building. The fact that it was walled in made it feel cut off, like a separate world to the street outside. Lord Edward Street was a street of contrasts then, and now. When you work in homelessness you see all the power struggles. You still have it now in this area, the tussle between drugs and dirt, tourists and powerful institutions. In the seventies it was a district of pubs and churches, set against the handsome redbrick buildings of the Iveagh Trust flats and the Iveagh Hostel, where The Alice Leahy Trust lives now.

The Hut lay at the centre of an odd mixture of business, power, deprivation and philanthropic efforts to alleviate poverty. We were on the southside, the supposedly better heeled side of the city, yet around us there was a network of large Victorian and Edwardian buildings, built by charities to help the poorer people of Dublin who lived in such numbers in that part of the city. Across from The Hut lay the Dublin Working Boys' Club and Harding Technical School. It's a tourist hostel now but was built as a lodging house for Protestant boys. Like the façade of Baggot Street Hospital, it was designed by architect Albert E Murray using the same yellow and red brick combination.

An *Irish Times* small ad in 1893 advertised places in the home available to 'protestants who are earning small wages as apprentices or otherwise in Dublin and who are, from any cause, without a suitable home in the city. Each boy on admission to the Home must produce a certificate of good character from a clergyman, from his Employer or from some other person worthy of credit.' The age for admission was from twelve to sixteen years old.

Just down from the Dublin Working Boys' Club was the MRCB paint shop named after the two Frenchmen Marcel Regent (MR) and Charlie Bigoud (CB) who first opened it in the thirties. It has since moved up the hill to Cornmarket.

We were cocooned in our ramshackle building, but it felt like the whole city and the wonder of it opened up to us once we had a base, with an address and, most importantly, a phone. We got to know the network of social workers attached to the hospitals. They were all women, capable and hardworking. There was Margaret Horn in the Adelaide, Josephine Glynn in Jervis Street, Mary Lahiffe and Michelle Hart in the Meath, Mary Kennedy in St James's, Rosemary McCarthy in the Coombe, and many others. They were great people. We could pick up the phone and talk to them to find help for someone.

A lot went on in our near-derelict new home. The Hut had three separate sections. The first room housed the relieving officer. This was the title that used to be given to the people we now know as community welfare officers. A relieving officer was a much more descriptive term. They gave people relief when they were in dire need. Des Kelleher was the relieving officer and his chilly room often held a queue of people waiting to have soft well-worn notes, counted out to them by Des. These were destitute people who weren't able to work but were unable to claim unemployment benefit or the Labour, as we all knew it. Some of these were people without papers; their birth certificates had been destroyed in the fire in the Public Records Office in the Four Courts in 1922.

Things sometimes need explaining. Going through his medication with Paddy M from the Iveagh Hostel.

The middle section of The Hut was ours. The former GP surgery was a bare space with a couch and small desk, both of which we now have in The Alice Leahy Trust. I always think of where the desk came from when I lean on it now. There was a tiny steriliser, an electric kettle and a sink which sometimes worked and sometimes didn't. Two filing cabinets completed the equipment in the room. The glass roof had been painted green or had grown green from moss and mould over the years. There was a small window but it was covered in grime so we worked in a mix of murky green light and stark artificial light, regardless of the daylight outside. The only view of the outside world was when the door opened and somebody blew in with the leaves off the street.

The third section housed administration staff who dealt with a lot of visits from women looking for milk vouchers and other requests for help. Gerry O'Leary was the porter there, and a trade union man to his fingertips. Gerry was a permanent fixture in the place and he could have made life difficult for us. He and I had lots of constructive arguments. He knew that we were genuine about what we were trying to do, but he had a strong belief in working regulation hours and doing things by the union book.

'Well you know, Alice, I'll have to be there as a porter,' he said one night when I wanted to host a group of people who were carol-singing for us.

'Ah now, Gerry,' I said. Like all union problems, we solved it with a lot of dialogue.

David Magee and I were both outside any job description the Health Board might give us. If Gerry had stuck rigidly to the rules, he'd have objected to us working there, but he didn't.

An electric fire was the only heat source in each of the three rooms in The Hut. It would grill those closest to it, steaming the damp from their clothes, while the rest of the room remained icy.

The Health Board used the Carnegie Centre next door as an administration office. It was where the public health nurses were based, under the all-seeing eye of Miss Mattimoe. Fred Donohoe asked me to go and talk to them, in a large ballroom-type space at the centre, about the work David and I were doing. The Carnegie Centre is now a headquarters for Tusla, the child and family agency, set up in 2014. That big room has been partitioned into cubicle offices.

It was my first time addressing a large group of nurses, but I didn't feel nervous. I knew exactly what I was talking about and that made all the difference, facing the audience of listening women. I was talking to them about our work. All the public-speaking courses in the world are no substitute for believing in what you're saying and knowing your subject first hand and inside out.

It went well, and there was a great buzz in the room afterwards, as I talked to the public health nurses about how we could work together. They got what we were about because they were a group of medical professionals that were very much part of the community.

Along with The Hut, Fred obtained a general medical services (GMS) prescription pad for David, even though he was working voluntarily at the time. I was being paid by the Health Board but we were two outsiders who were deep inside the system, with access to its resources, but not bound by its usual conventions.

Now that we had a base we sought volunteer doctors. A well-known retired consultant arrived in to help. When he met his first patient he was sitting down behind the desk and barked out to thin air, 'Chart nurse', holding his hand up for the chart to be delivered in to it as if by magic. I walked the other way thinking, 'Well, that's the end of you,' and left him sitting there empty-handed. He meant well, but it was clear that he was used to an institutionalised way of working, supported by a large administration, and that wasn't going to work for us.

Even though we had a base, we never barricaded ourselves in behind the wall. We continued with our rounds, our visits to the hostels and food centres. We knew that lots of the people we were meeting wouldn't be happy going up to The Hut. It was a step too far. But they made sure to meet us on our rounds. People would position themselves in the right place and wait for us to arrive.

In spite of the chaos we were encountering we made sure to stick to a structured week. If there was a crisis, we could change things, but there were set days and nights when we were out on our rounds and set days when we were in the clinic in The Hut. You have to be very organised to work with very chaotic people.

Privacy was one thing you lost when you became homeless. It wasn't possible to keep your homelessness a secret from anyone, even strangers on the street. You could spot a psychiatric patient released from hospitals from the state of their clothes. A man might be wearing a pair of trousers with one leg shorter than the other. People were often dressed in clothes that were patched, or too large or too small for them, as if looking smart didn't matter. Nobody seemed to care that this marked them out as strange and out of step with the world.

We often saw people talking to themselves, completely cut off from the world around them. It's not unusual to see people by themselves today, having animated conversations on the streets, but you'll usually find they're on a mobile phone, and maybe just as cut off from what's going on around them, but for a different reason.

One of David's favourite health complaints to encounter was psoriasis. It wasn't that he was glad that someone was suffering from the skin complaint. But it gave us the opportunity to get someone back on their feet in all kinds of ways. In a bad case a person's skin became a source of torment and the only way to ease it was if they became involved in the care of their skin. They would have to take a coal tar bath. Then they would have to be dressed in reasonably fresh clothes. They had to come off the street in order to care for their skin and this meant they could not go drinking until later in the day, helping them to stay sober for longer. At least three men took our advice. Once they began to stay off the streets more, they managed to detox a little and feel the relief as their skin, which had been killing them with itch and soreness, began to feel pleasant and warm.

Christy, the man I knew from Simon, gave up the spirits on our advice at one stage, and someone in Guinness would give him Triple X, their extra-strong bottled stout, leaving it somewhere for him to pick up so the brewery wouldn't be seen to be encouraging an alcoholic to drink. Compared to his usual drink, Triple X had a bit of nourishment in it, and acted as a slight detox.

We got to know the casualty departments all over Dublin. The people going into the departments were known by the staff, as they tended to come from the area. The hospitals were under different pressures than they are now and they also had very experienced older social workers, nurses and support staff who were good at dealing with difficulties. In recent times, younger social workers are under appalling pressure, given great responsibilities when they arrive from college, with the academic knowledge but without the hands-on experience.

The homeless people were our teachers. We took our tone from them, learning how to ask questions or whether to ask questions at all. They showed us, or told us, the kind of approach that worked best. Listening was something we had time to do, and in the hospitals there was more time to listen. They would regularly criticise or complain if they weren't happy with something. They felt freer to talk to us than complain to a hostel or a hospital. We weren't going to turn them away. For us, criticism was a step up from outright hostility or silent indifference. Like me, David was never frightened of the people we were meeting. He remembers standing his ground in the Simon Shelter when one of the more disturbed men would barrel in over the wall, snarling and raving, sending everyone else scattering.

It wasn't always easy to make a connection, to get someone to come out of themselves and relate to us so that we could encourage them to take better care of themselves. But as the months went on and we became regular visitors to their places, there seemed to build a sense of pride that we were taking an interest in them.

People like Christy had been shunned for most of their lives. Their typical visit to a casualty department was when they were in bits, often bleeding, unwashed and smelly, so they were dealt with as swiftly as possible, if at all. They had no notion, or experience, of a medical professional sitting down to have a conversation with them.

We learned to be careful with people's clothes. Even today, clothes can be filled with all of someone's earthly possessions: documents, photographs, mementoes, miraculous medals were all pinned or pocketed in their clothes, however shabby and out of shape they were. Their lives were in those pockets, and it was important if we were giving someone a new set of clothes that those possessions were transferred intact.

People often seemed to be almost held together by their own clothes. We worried that if you tried to bathe someone they would simply collapse, end up in hospital and then be dumped out on the streets again in an even more fragile state. We had a base for what was now an informal medical centre for homeless people. It was a real start, but very quickly we began to question the point in giving someone a prescription, cleaning and dressing their wounds if the rest of their body was still dirty or their clothes and hair were lice-infested?

The Hut needed a bath.

David heard someone mention that there might be an old bath in the basement of the Iveagh Hostel, where The Alice Leahy Trust is now. We went scavenging, and there in the middle of rubble and rubbish we found this magnificent huge cast-iron bath. It was ridiculously large and eyebrows were raised the day the bath came to Lord Edward Street. We needed a team effort to manhandle it through the door and up the steps and into The Hut. The porter, Gerry, didn't object, even though there was no official sanction to upgrade our facilities with a bath.

Everyone lent a hand, even though they had no responsibility for that kind of thing. We didn't waste our energy wondering whose job it was. We just did it together. Our whole focus was on the people who would be able to come here and wash, leave clean and smelling good with a new spring in their step.

A gas boiler was rigged up to heat the water and we had a working bath. Health and safety would not have approved.

Once we had a bath, we needed towels, and then we needed clothes that we could give to people. It was the beginning of the simple service of providing people with a place where they could peel off layers of wet or dirty clothes, wash themselves with hot water and soap, and dress themselves in clean dry clothes again, and begin afresh. It sounds like such a basic thing, but I still see people getting their dignity back in a small way when we provide the same service in our centre every morning. They are transformed, their humanity restored, and they walk up our steps back into an unfriendly world, with their heads a little higher.

Public washing facilities are not a glamorous high-powered idea but they can have so much positive impact for people living rough. In 2006

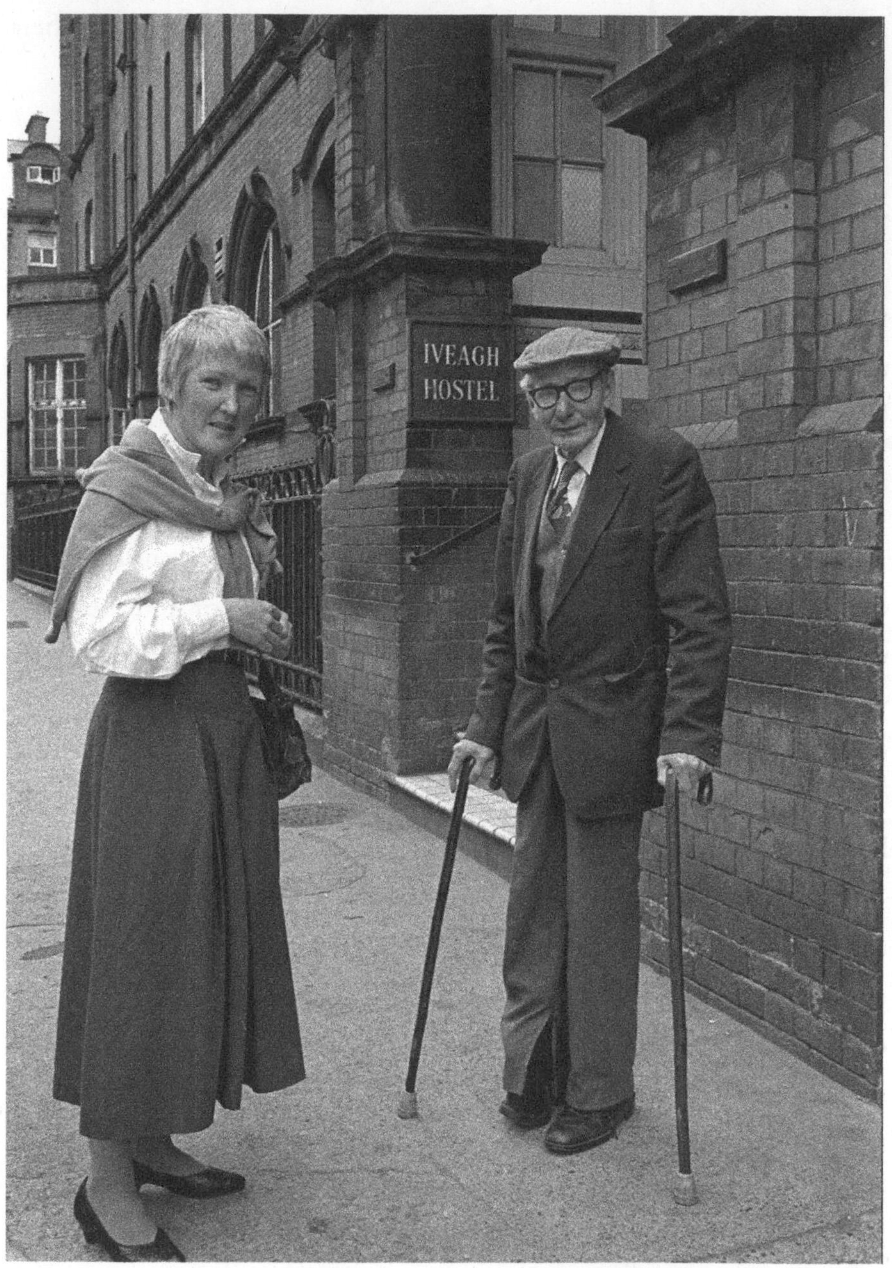

Freddie from the Iveagh Hostel once gave me money to send to Sligo Rovers Soccer Club who were struggling at the time. Many years later, I read about this donation in a book by Eamonn Sweeney, There's Only One Red Army.

we got an architectural student to draw up plans for public showers in Dublin, pointing out possible sites. We sent it to all the city councillors. We resubmitted the plan after the latest election in 2014. No one took it up as an issue. People don't seem to get it – the importance of public washing facilities.

The old Iveagh Baths were still open to the public in the seventies. They were built by the Iveagh Trust and then loaned to Dublin Corporation in 1943, before being sold to the Corporation in 1951 and run as a swimming a pool and public bath and shower facility. The poor of Dublin went there routinely to have a bath or shower. The Corporation closed the baths in the eighties, and it was left derelict until it was bought by a private gym operator.

Even after we got a bath in The Hut, I would still regularly go to the Adelaide Hospital, where nursing Sister Denise Barkman would let me bring women in for a bath. It was a superb hospital. The women I brought up would be able to bathe in a spotless bathroom and come out to clean towels and warm dry clothes. Sister Janet Smyth always ensured there was a tray with tea in a china cup and hot toast ready to be enjoyed. It was really like taking someone into a four star hotel. Sister Barkman made sure I could always go in quietly and we got to know them so well.

On the wider scene people began to notice us, ask us, 'What are ye up to?'

We were a bit of a novelty. A senior official from the Department of Health remarked tartly that we would be gone in six months. More than forty years later, I think I proved them wrong. There should be no need for us now, but the gaps we fill are still there all those decades on, and sometimes they're even bigger.

They were hectic exciting days, every moment packed with a new challenge and a new idea. I had had a dream that has stayed with me over the decades. I was in Annesgift, dressed like a Russian peasant woman with leather boots. I was walking through a golden corn field touching the ears of corn with my fingers as they swayed in a light breeze and the smell of wheat wafted up in the warm air. I crossed a flooded river with great difficulty stepping on a fallen tree to get over and everything changed.

The land was withered, trees felled and crops failed and blackened. Philip Kennedy, the doctor from Baggot Street who had been so inspiring, was with me. I walked away from him and reached down to lift a heavy dead branch of a tree. Underneath was a glowing blaze of colour – tiny green shoots and the beginnings of thick stemmed bluebells. And I could hear the voices of the plants saying, 'We're alive. We're alive.'

I woke up, gripped with that idea of life and voices in a wasteland, the sense that I couldn't give up on people, however small or forgotten their lives were. The dream, which I had while researching the needs of homeless people, pointed me in the direction of setting up our own agency. The dream and a legacy from the Dublin woman Anne Rush combined to make it happen.

Anne was a housewife and mother living in Shankill, in South Dublin. She worked on the Simon soup run with David Magee. It was on the soup run that Anne met Kitty.

A lifer on the streets Kitty was the homeless woman I first encountered in Baggot Street Hospital. She used the hospital bathroom to wash her voluminous knickers and hang them up to dry in Baggot Street and other hospitals around the city. She used to call me Miss Alice. Later, I would bathe her feet and cut her toenails. Kitty and Anne struck up a friendship based around one simple act of kindness. Kitty loved to go to the Phoenix Park to watch the deer and Anne would take her there, at any hour of the day or night.

Kitty had a pattern, places she would always be at set times. Anne would drive to find her, pull up on the street in her car and bundle Kitty and all her belongings in plastic bags into the car. Then Anne drove to the Phoenix Park, driving around the park to find the deer. The two women got out in the rain, the sunshine or the moonlight, to watch the deer. Often, they were the only people for miles around, looking at the deer, each thinking their own thoughts or maybe sharing them with each other in quiet voices so as not to startle the animals. It was one of the lovely things that used to happen, a quiet kindness from one human being to another.

They were both beautiful women. Anne Rush was small and blonde. Her kindness shone out of her lovely face. Kitty's beauty was strong and raw. Kitty ended up living in the Debtors Prison on Green Street, the only person living in the building. I remember visiting her there and seeing a small pile of Christmas presents. They were all still wrapped, never opened, never used, as if Kitty wanted to preserve the joy of getting the gift rather than use what was inside. They were probably small things like gloves or slippers. After that, she moved to a Simon house. Kitty was one of the characters of the city in a time when there was no rush to change people. They were allowed to be different. They weren't seen as a problem or a resource to be researched or moved on.

Anne and her husband Brian were a couple committed to doing good. He had worked as an engineer in Lesotho building wells. Around the middle of 1975 Anne discovered she had cancer. She knew she was very sick. She wanted to leave something to help people like Kitty and help put our informal work on a more formal basis. She decided to leave a legacy to fund a doctor's position putting David's volunteer role on a professional footing.

It was she who came up with the name Trust.

Over several months, in 1975, David and I met in the St Vincent de Paul headquarters, in Nicholas Street, with Anne and Brian and Trust's first solicitor Owen Mulholland, and others. Owen was a great fan of the theatre and we often stayed with him in the Abbey, long after the curtain came down, with the theatre's front-of-house manager Lily Shanley. Bob Cashman, a senior civil servant in the Department of the Environment also joined us. He would later become national president of the St Vincent de Paul Society and he was a treasurer of Trust. I loved the theatre: the Abbey, the Gaiety, the Project Arts Centre, and the Focus. I never felt it was a place for the wealthy, and as I get older it seems just more of a reflection of real life. Plays can be a wonderful way to focus our minds on the stories we need to hear. Walking home from the Abbey in the eighties, I would pass *The Irish Times* on Fleet Street and get a copy of the newspaper still warm from the printing press.

In that Nicholas Street office we talked at length over how to set up Trust. The room held the most experienced group of committed people who had worked with homeless people and for months we teased out the best way to set up a new service. We had Health Board people, Simon workers John Long and Justin O'Brien, and people from St Vincent de Paul, bringing voluntary sector, medical professionals and a senior civil servant together. The question we debated long and late was whether we tuck ourselves in under the umbrella of an existing organisation, like Simon, or the St Vincent de Paul. I always argued against this idea. We drew up a list of reasons we should and reasons we shouldn't. The reasons not to join another organisation far outweighed the pros. We were going to stand on our own.

Anne Rush grew gravely ill in the spring less than four months after

Trust was set up. David and I nursed her at home, where she died in March 1976.

The courage to set up our own organisation with limited resources but lots of ideas and energy came from people around me but was also a legacy of the strong women I grew up around. Some of my earliest memories are of women making brave and empowering decisions. In Fethard in the 1940s Olivia Hughes had seen the potential for a local co-operative market in the town to give rural women their own incomes. The management of the creameries was firmly in the hands of men, and the creamery cheque was always made out to the man of the farm. Mrs Hughes wanted to set up a co-operative market run mostly by women in her home town.

On Friday 17 January, in the freezing winter of 1947 Mammy went to Fethard in darkness in the early morning to open the first Country Market in the former Town Hall. The seventeenth-century Tholsel building was being used to store a fire engine and packing cases. Today it has been restored and is home to a new centre, the Fethard Horse Country Experience. That first year, in 1947, vegetables were scarce after the viciously cold winter and bread rationing had just been introduced.

The old walls had holes which let draughts whistle through. The iron-cold winter wouldn't thaw out for another two months after that first market. Some broken-down furniture was fashioned into counters and covered in hessian cloth. A chicken run was used to display cakes and bread. They started with a borrowed weighing scales and an electric fire, and hired chairs and tables, a new electric kettle and an old Victorian workbox that had been fashioned into a moneybox by a local craftsman.

On that first morning in 1947 they sold out all the produce in ninety minutes and took £9 in takings. Friday was pension day and a religious fast day so it was the perfect day for a market selling eggs and vegetables as alternatives to meat.

The work of the market, the farm and our own household gave me a sense of being part of something, a big effort in which everyone had a role. Mammy worked as the Country Market secretary and treasurer for more than thirty years, keeping track of the producers and the costs and making sure everything was organised properly. She became part of a network of women running Country Markets. Letters came to our house from towns and villages all over Ireland, through the hub of The Country Shop in Dublin. We got to know the handwriting of these women, and were able to guess their identity when the postman came on his bicycle, often not just with letters but with news from the town, a daily link to the gossip and goings on.

As much as she loved her family, Mammy loved the independence of her work with the Country Markets and valued her national network of friends and colleagues – other women, many of them mothers fitting work into family life. She was dedicated to the project, so much so that when we were adults we learned not to buy her certain kinds of presents.

'Don't give Mammy anything like a pot plant,' my sister Eileen used to say. 'It'll just go into the market.'

There was a great 'can-do' spirit around the women who ran the market. They took a big risk and they succeeded. They were working for themselves, and the success of their idea and effort was a huge lift to their confidence.

Growing up surrounded by that spirit, I absorbed the idea that you could see a problem or a challenge and try to fix it with something that had not been tried before. This was one of the strongest threads I brought with me to later in life. In another time Olivia Hughes, Muriel Gahan (who founded the Country Shop) and my mother, Hannie Leahy, would have been called social entrepreneurs.

We were learning every day from the people we were meeting how to do what it was that we wanted to do. But we couldn't have managed it without Anne Rush and Fred Donohoe, and legions of others. There was a network of them, these wonderful people who popped into my life, delightfully alive and challenging. I didn't gravitate to the pompous and the self-important types who believe they have it all worked out. They left me cold and still do. The people who were still wondering where they fitted into the world were the ones that resonated with me. Self-belief is seen as such an important quality. But self-doubt can be a positive and creative force. The people who helped me keep going were the humane and compassionate individuals who questioned things and, most importantly, questioned themselves all the time.

Even as we were setting up Trust we wondered if we weren't in danger of Sellotaping a problem, letting the State off the hook, feeding our own egos, like the 'do-gooders' the Legion of Mary dismissed. But we had a community of people that relied on us and a network of strong individuals who supported and inspired us. We were empowering ourselves, breaking rules and not doing what we were told all over the place. If I had been depending only on people working in nursing, they would have made me feel I was even madder than I thought I was. But I knew what needed to be done and we were going to do it.

CHAPTER EIGHT

Restaurant Revolutionaries

'Truth is likely to hurt, to be uncomfortable, and could conceivably threaten our livelihood and our place in society,'
From a lecture by my mentor,
the late Professor James McCormick

There was no music in Gaj's Restaurant on Baggot Street in the seventies. It would have been drowned out by voices. You walked upstairs to the first floor and turned into a warm wall of chat and the steamy smell of good food. On a busy lunchtime you could share a table with an aristocrat, an outcast, or both. Gaj's was like a cross section of the city, with all its layers. Movers and shakers ate alongside the immoveable and shaken, all under the shrewd motherly gaze of a large Scottish woman called Margaret Gaj.

Gaj's Restaurant (pronounced Guy's) had a way of pulling people like me and David Magee to its heart. I don't remember how we first found it, joining the regulars who sat at Margaret's dark wooden tables to talk for hours as the light faded into darkness outside the two first-floor windows on Baggot Street. It was a busy room, crammed with tables, with few frills apart from fresh flowers in a jar on every table and a marble fireplace. The food was cooked and eaten on the same floor so the restaurant filled with steam, the view from both windows obliterated by condensation on all but the warmest days when the windows could be thrown open to the breeze outside.

There was an earthy comfort here, the earthiness that comes from creativity and openness. It was not far from my first Dublin home, in Baggot Street Hospital. Gaj's was closer to town at the corner of Baggot Street and Pembroke Street. In the seventies Wigmore Opticians was on the ground floor where Café Boulevard is now. Gaj's was upstairs. Today it's an office run by a trucking company. Around the corner, on Pembroke Street, Florrie Carthy had a boutique, a tiny place full of beautiful clothes. When I was a student nurse, I had saved up to buy

Good food in a solid place. Gaj's on Baggot Street was more than just a restaurant; it was an institution.

a brown tweed suit. I've always loved tweed, not only for the look of it but for all the work and pride that goes into making it, from shearing the sheep to designing the patterns.

Margaret Gaj was born in Edinburgh in 1919. She declared herself a conscientious objector when the Second World War broke out. Like me, she worked as a nurse and she was highly critical of how patients were treated. I think that was our bond. We shared a past life as nurses and a healthy skeptical attitude to the medical world. She married a patient, Polish soldier Boleslaw Gaj who had escaped the Nazis and come to Britain to work for the RAF. The Gajs moved to Ireland in the forties to run a farm and restaurant in Baltinglass, County Wicklow. That business failed and they moved the restaurant to Dublin, first to Molesworth Street and then to Baggot Street, where I first met her.

Margaret was a woman who cared deeply about people. Everyone was welcome in her restaurant. It was both a refuge from a harsh world and a place where people discussed ideas of how to alleviate that harshness. Radicals and revolutionaries shared ideas over Margaret's burgers and sauerkraut, plates of hot goulash, macaroni and cheese or wedges of tomato pie with a thick pastry crust.

Typically the first person you saw when you arrived at Gaj's Restaurant was Margaret. She stood behind the counter, wearing a shawl over her broad shoulders. She wore her dark mid-length hair scraped back from her open face. She was a big woman, very strong and one look from her could quell any rowdy behaviour. I think she was a woman of great faith but she didn't wear that on her sleeve. She had beautiful handwriting and wrote her menus by hand. At night she played poker, driving to poker games around the city in her own car. She was a great poker player and easily won. She could play all night and still put in a day's work at the restaurant the following day. Not drinking or smoking helped her stamina.

When she wasn't in Gaj's Margaret held court in Bewley's on Grafton Street, where Tattens the senior waitress was her wing woman. Tattens' name was Kathleen Toomey but everyone knew her as Tattens. She looked ageless, elfin in her Bewley's uniform and was as much a Dublin institution as the cafe where she worked. She had the air of a duchess welcoming guests into her home.

'There you are now, Alice. How are you?' Tattens used to say in her grand voice. 'She's over there,' and she would point to where Margaret was sitting in her usual seat. Margaret was in residence regularly and people knew when she was there so they could come to her with a problem. Tattens always knew what Margaret wanted. She didn't go for cream cakes or buns. Her staple snack was macaroni cheese.

Gaj's was a proper melting pot, where ideas and movements swirled

Tattens and me in Bewley's, a waitress known and loved by many.

around the room along with the smell of food. The Irish Women's Liberation Movement, a group comprised mainly of women journalists campaigning for women's equality, met in an upstairs room. I wasn't part of the women's movement, at least not under that banner. I was ploughing my own furrow. Women in extreme poverty, often from rural backgrounds seemed to be excluded from everything, including the new women's movement.

The extraordinary atmosphere in Gaj's started with Margaret's personality. She was one of the few people I could talk to about my work. I used to climb the stairs on bad days weighed down by the dirt and misery I had encountered and always feel lighter for sitting down with Margaret and talking things out.

There were regulars who seemed to be part of the furniture. I often sat at a table with the actress and writer Christine Lady Longford, who was in her seventies by then. With her husband the Earl of Longford, she had worked with Hilton Edwards and Micheál Mac Liammóir at the Gate Theatre in the thirties. She managed the Gate for four years in the sixties, wrote plays and four novels. I met the brilliant barrister Paddy McEntee there. I could listen to him forever. His charisma, command of language and knowledge made him mesmerising in court. I found the courts a sobering experience and would also see him in action later in life when we were on the same committee looking at crime in Dublin. I'm glad I've never needed his professional services as one of the best defence barristers in Irish legal history.

In Gaj's in the seventies you might see a high-ranking civil servant lost in their *Irish Times* at one table and then someone would come up the stairs in a flurry: a traveller or a prostitute looking for Margaret's help, or just a hot meal, which she would happily give them free of charge. David used the toilets of Gaj's to treat the wounds of men who had sustained injuries while in Garda custody. These were the days of the 'Heavy Gang', a term used by *The Irish Times* to describe a group of gardaí who used brutal methods to interrogate serious crime suspects. David's help was noted by the people who kept a close eye on Gaj's (all the best spies go to Gaj's was a saying from the time). One night David was threatened and told he needed to watch himself.

I could ring Margaret and she would come out with me to meet people in difficulties. Twice we went out to bonfires on traveller camps, where a wake was being held for a traveller. It was always the women in the travelling communities that she and I could relate to, their strength and resilience. We would stand alongside them in the light of a bonfire and pay our respects to their dead. We might bring some food to the bonfire, but never cigarettes. Margaret didn't approve of smoking. There was a sternness to her alongside her broad streak of kindness.

We brought a woman who needed advice on contraception to Paddy Leahy, a Ballyfermot-based GP who, despite the same surname, was no relation, although he was from Thurles and played minor hurling for Tipperary. Paddy was one of the few doctors who would give a woman contraceptives at a time when it was still illegal.

One night when I was sitting alone at a table, a man came into Gaj's with a gun, looking for someone. I looked down and lifted up a copy of *The Evening Press*, pretending to read, to avoid catching his eye, as he stared wildly around the room. It was only when he left, I realised the newspaper had been upside down in my quaking hands all the time.

Among the many causes that Margaret fostered and fed was the setting up of the Prisoners' Rights Organisation (PRO), bringing legal students, solicitors, academics, would-be politicians and friends and family of prisoners together to fight for prisoners' rights. It was formed in 1973 to try to reform the prison system and get education, training and recreation for prisoners. It was the nearest thing I had seen to the Simon Community spirit, that sense of everyone in it together. It also brought home the idea that prisoners had rights no matter what they had done. The group reported to the Commission of Enquiry into the Irish Penal System in 1979. It was chaired by Seán McBride, the son of Maud Gonne, who served as IRA director of intelligence in the twenties, set up the political party Clann na Poblachta in the forties, became a barrister and a Minister and founded Amnesty International. The Commission also included two members, Michael D Higgins and Mary McAleese, who would go on to become presidents of Ireland. Trust also made a submission to the Commission and its report was published in 1980 with 68 recommendations for reform of the Irish prison system.

The PRO took the view that it was not necessary to know every prisoner's story. You could advocate for prisoners without condoning their crimes. The PRO were very clear that there were many people who ended up in prison who would not have been there if they'd been given a chance.

Early in the eighties I travelled with Margaret and law student Mary Ellen Ring, who's now a High Court judge, to Glasgow. We met Kay Carmichael there, a good friend of Margaret's. Kay was a well-known social campaigner in Britain, and one of the forces who helped put liberal values at the heart of Scottish public life. Kay had contracted polio when she was a baby and the disease left her with a weakened left arm for the rest of her life. She used her tough start to inspire others and always took the side of marginalised people. Kay embodied the difference between those who preach something and those who live it. I immediately liked her calm spirit and confidence; it almost gave her the air of a prophet, a word we usually only use to describe men.

When I met her she had been invited into Barlinnie Prison in Glasgow after clashing with a politician in a television debate. A special project unit had been set up for prisoners deemed too dangerous to be integrated into mainstream prisons.

The Barlinnie unit opened in February 1973, when five long-term prisoners were transferred to a newly converted wing in the grounds of the main prison. The unit was run as a therapeutic community rather than along the command and control lines of regular prison units. Prisoners and prison officers all had equal decision-making rights in the running of the unit. They made their own rules and any member of the unit, prisoner or prison officer, could call a meeting of the community if there was a dispute. Art became central to life in the special unit: writing, painting, sculpture and crafts.

It wasn't the first time I would meet people imprisoned for long sentences. I was always struck by how handsome they were. These men living a predominantly alcohol-free regime with exercise and good food had a common pale-skinned but lean and healthy look about them. You didn't see the crime; you just saw the effect on these men of a life of relative comfort compared to the streets. The prisoner we were there to visit was at that time Britain's most famous prisoner, Scottish man Jimmy Boyle. He was due to be married to psychiatrist Sarah Trevelyan shortly after our visit.

Jimmy was charismatic and charming. People with charisma can influence things but they can also control things. They can become heroes in a community because they robbed or murdered. Charisma is a powerful tool in all walks of life. Celebrity comes and goes and deep down you're struggling with your own feelings, whether you're a TV star or a serious criminal.

I felt that someone like Jimmy who likes the limelight, and maybe needs it, can set the agenda, and then we forget about the people who are in prison for very small things. There was always a danger of hero-worshipping.

Jimmy was handsome, athletic-looking and trim from prison. He had pale skin and lovely black hair. Mary Ellen and I stayed with Sarah before her wedding. The media camped on her doorstep, hoping to get shots of the infamous criminal on his wedding day.

Jimmy Boyle's book, *A Sense of Freedom*, published in 1977, told of a life started in a Gorbals tenement and ending with a murder conviction when he was twenty-one. At the time, it was described as the most controversial social document since Ken Loach's powerful film *Cathy Come Home,* broadcast eleven years earlier. In the introduction Jimmy said he owed his survival to the many people who had reached out to help him. His life sentence, he wrote, 'started the day he left his mother's womb'. Today when I see the name of someone involved in crime it is often a familiar name from my Rotunda days as a midwife. When that happens it always prompts the same questions: Did I listen to their heartbeat in their mother's womb and did they have a chance?

One of the people who reached out to Jimmy was Margaret Gaj. 'Dear Margaret,' Jimmy wrote to her from Barlinnie, including a cutting on his case from the *Observer* newspaper. 'I hope this finds you well, and making progress in your struggle for a better world.'

In the Prisoners' Rights Organisation we strongly believed in prison reform and the potential of prison to be a positive influence in someone's life. The special unit in Barlinnie was an example of people in authority working with people who hadn't been given a chance, who'd been born into bad luck, fates mapped out from birth.

Ken Murray, a Scottish prison officer from Lewis, was the campaigning, compassionate man who put together the unit. The move faced huge public hostility.

I was interested to see how it worked, how the people achieved such a progressive unit and remained so hopeful. The unit was fascinating. People were able to mix freely, rather than being confined in separate cells. The prisoners could talk to us and the prison officers were part of that open sense of community. The prisoners were probably more aware of the background they had come from and the possibilities that lay ahead, aware of where their lives fitted into the picture of society. This was revolutionary compared to our prisons in its effort to create a better understanding on both sides. My prison visits in Dublin had been to people who just inquired about day-to-day practical things. The level of discussion in Barlinnie was different. Both prisoners and prison officers were questioning things and informing themselves about the system. They knew they had support out there. You didn't know their crimes, but you were aware they were people serving life sentences, and they weren't in there because they had stolen a shirt.

Scotland has always struck me as a great model for social services. In September 1986 I spent a week on the tiny island of Iona in the Scottish Hebrides at a healthcare workshop, organised by the Iona Community. At the time Iona had a population of just eighty people. The ecumenical community was set up in 1938 by Scottish minister George MacLeod, who was appalled at the lack of impact that the church had in poor communities. An Oxford-educated veteran of Flanders, MacLeod had become a pacifist and a committed social campaigner after the war. He brought unemployed skilled craftsmen and young trainee clergymen to Iona to rebuild the medieval monastery. A writer and broadcaster, he was another strong voice on the left in Scotland until his death in 1991.

My stay on Iona in the eighties was one of those mind-opening weeks, sitting down with all kinds of professionals and the people who use the healthcare services to talk about what we were doing. Lots of us worked in, or lived in, difficult urban settings so it felt like there was room to breathe and think in the spectacular remoteness of the island. I left feeling full of hope and energy and convinced again of the need to involve people in their own health care and to demystify medicine.

There was also the great feeling of not being alone that I got from meeting others doing similar work to ourselves. 'There were no easy answers,' I wrote when I returned to Dublin, 'apart from not giving up.' Our work in Trust was very different and it was important to try to encourage others in the healthcare system to do things differently.

They had great visionaries in Scotland. We're inclined to look to mainland Europe, but I think Scotland is a better model. I remember visiting a night shelter in Glasgow. It was absolutely chaotic and reminded me of the Simon Community, where the chaos made sense because everyone was pitching in together. Kay Carmichael came to Dublin a few years later and wrote a piece for social work magazine *New Society* about our work. All of that came about from our visits to Gaj's Restaurant. It was so much more than just going in and having a solid lunch. We made links with thinkers like Kay Carmichael and her partner David Donnison, who became professor of urban studies at the University of Glasgow. These connections validated our work and made us feel we weren't wasting our time.

* * *

Lunch at Gaj's connected me with the wider world of Dublin activism. Now that Trust had a home in Lord Edward Street, David and I were able to look up from the day-to-day slog of our work and plug into some of the energy there was in the city around social change. A new generation seemed to be taking control. We felt part of something bigger, a generation of baby boomers in a world that felt vibrant and full of possibility and hope.

Great agencies were set up. There was Contact, an agency for young people between fifteen and twenty-five, set up in 1972 by the Sisters of Our Lady of Charity. There was also Hope, set up by German student Winfried Schickle and ex-Simon workers. Hope had its first public meeting in 1976 and went on to open a night shelter for children sleeping rough, filling a gap that was not being met by Simon. Cherish, which is now One Family, was also set up in 1972, to support single mothers. Later in the seventies the Dublin fireman Willie Bermingham would set up Alone, an agency to help elderly people. He was prompted by a number of fatal fires where people had lived in appalling conditions. When you're touched by experiences like that you feel that you must act. I got to know him through our work. He was clearly committed to helping elderly people and upset at how little was being done for them. Today's agencies sometimes give the impression that they broke new ground, but there has been a long history of people who set up powerful organisations before the newer names existed. No one had much money. It was in the days before technology and the corporate structures that are now imposed on voluntary agencies. There was a vibrancy and a lack of demarcation lines. The media were interested in social affairs. Margaret introduced me to *Irish Times* journalist Eileen O'Brien, who gave a voice to the voiceless in her regular 'Social Sort of Column'. Eileen had been the journalist who had gone to the flats on Benburb Street in 1970 to report on life there. Fellow *Irish Times* journalists like Paul Murray, Padraig O'Morain, Kathy Sheridan, Nell

McCafferty, Elgy Gillespie and the late Nuala O'Faolain took the time to look long and hard at homelessness and interview people on the streets as well as come to talk to me about the issue. In the *Irish Press* there was Patsy McGarry, who's now in *The Irish Times*, and the late Liam Ó'Cuanaig. In *The Evening Press* I knew the late Michael O'Toole, Alison O'Connor and Kate Shanahan, Anne Dempsey from *The Independent* and many others. Con Houlihan's commentary on a match wasn't just about the match. It was a wise take on where we were at.

The *Sunday Tribune* gave us social commentary like we had never seen before. Journalists like Michael Clifford, Richard Oakley, Justine McCarthy, photographer Derek Speirs, and editors Vincent Browne and Matt Cooper made poverty a big part of their coverage of Irish life. I always enjoyed working with *Irish Independent* photographer Mark Condren, and inequality continues to be talked about by Gene Kerrigan with great insight in *The Sunday Independent.*

The *Sunday Tribune* was a newspaper with real heart and a social conscience which put homelessness into the minds of readers in a sensitive and professional way. I feel its absence in recent years when those deeper questions about society and how it operates needed so much to be asked. The loss of *Magill*, the current affairs magazine, also left a large hole in the Irish media landscape.

Through Gaj's I met campaigner Deirdre Kelly, who set up the Living City organisation and *Irish Times* journalist Frank McDonald. Frank was a news reporter with *The Irish Press* at the time. Later on in the eighties I'd go along to the Dublin Crisis Conference at the Old Synod Hall on Christchurch Place, where the talk was about trying to wrest back control of the city from a golden circle of developers and public officials.

Journalists were people you met on the street or in cafes, their notebooks in their pockets, with the time to not only ask the questions but also listen to the answers. We valued each other's roles. Reporters were regularly dispatched to the streets, to see things and talk to people first hand. Dublin had a lively pool of journalists between its three main papers, the *Irish Press*, the *Irish Independent* and *The Irish Times*. The latter was often used as a badge of class. An *Irish Times* folded and tucked into a tweed jacket pocket seemed to be a statement about who you were or wanted to be.

Gaj's restaurant opened up a left-wing world of activists and radicals to us. They wanted to challenge the status quo, but I was also getting to know the other side through the various religious orders who helped the poor in Dublin. A lot of those were convents that opened their doors and always had breakfast or tea for someone who called. It's unfashionable to mention the good work of the religious orders because of the revelations about their treatment of women and children who came into their care. But I saw the good work they did.

We were conscious that we had a duty to the people we worked with. We were always careful not to align ourselves with any one side or the other, remaining interested but objective. It gave us a very clear-headed outlook in what were heady times. It's a culture that I continue in The Alice Leahy Trust today. We are non-denominational and entirely non-aligned. I am wary of anyone trying to use us or those we work with to push their own agenda.

As we set about putting Trust into operation, in the early days, we weren't hampered by a them-and-us culture dividing the voluntary and the statutory agencies. Authority wasn't seen as the enemy. We had Fred Donohoe and many of his senior colleagues on our side. We could see how things could be done differently and better, but we were working with the system rather than trying to smash or destroy it. Discussions, even heated ones, were friendly and had less of a blame culture and nastiness.

There wasn't the same rush to pry into people's affairs, to find out all the details of their stories. It was a time when people like the residents of the Simon Shelter were part of the fabric of the city. They were the characters of the street. One of them was a couple called Michael and Frank. They were known as Darby and Joan, an unspoken acknowledgement of the fact that they were a gay couple. They stayed in The Morning Star and sometimes in Back Lane. I got to know them through the years. Eventually Frank became too ill to stay in the hostel and we got him a place in Simpson's Hospital in Dundrum, a nursing home for men, which had been given a glorious original name by the Victorian philanthropists who set it up. It was called Simpson's Hospital for the Reception of Poor, Decayed, Blind and Gouty Men.

I was in a taxi with Frank one day when he started to talk about his life.

People tell me things on their own terms, slivers of information that sometimes explain how they have reached the point in their lives where they needed my help. Frank was looking out the window at the prosperous redbrick houses in Dartry as we drove along when he began to speak. Not making eye contact made it an easier for him to talk.

'My mother died in a fire, Alice,' he told me. 'A fire in the poorhouse.'

'Oh Frank. I'm sorry. That's awful,' I said quietly.

'I don't know where she's buried.'

I contacted the authorities and was able to discover his mother had been buried in Inchicore.

When Frank died, in the nineties, we had a Mass in Back Lane for him and I invited Mary Foster, the matron of Simpson's and one of her nursing colleagues back to Trust for a cup of tea. I told her we were looking for another nurse, and I said I needed someone who could be compassionate with difficult people.

They both said simultaneously. 'We know the nurse.'

Geraldine McAuliffe, or Gerri as I came to know her, was in Australia after the death of her father. She had been to a clairvoyant and had just been told she would be offered a most amazing job. Something told me she was the nurse for us.

She arrived for her interview beautifully dressed, as she always was, petite and blonde and oozing compassion. I spotted her for a kindred spirit as soon as I met her. She had trained in Dr Steevens' Hospital so she came from an old-school nursing background like my own. As she was leaving, she said: 'Alice can I come here?' Geraldine worked with us for years and remains a huge part of The Alice Leahy Trust, as a director.

As the work progressed, in those early days, we had the freedom to work with people without subjecting them to questionnaires. They could tell us as much about themselves as they wanted. David's GMS prescription pad, authorised by Fred O'Donohue, meant we were able to get medication for people who didn't exist as far as the system was concerned because they lived without medical cards or paperwork.

The district around Lord Edward Street was our village in the city and it contained the colour and character of a close-knit community. There was the Napper Tandy pub on Bride Street. Maura McHugh was the landlady in the Napper. It was a dark and dismal pub, but Maura gave customers drink on the slate, let them talk if they wanted to or stay silent if they wished. There were a lot of men living in hostels who didn't have the confidence to go anywhere else other than the Napper for a drink. Joe McDonald's was another local pub on Patrick Street. Corbett's pub was at the top of Werburgh Street. Donnelly's

Garage, a business run by two brothers, was at the other end of Patrick's Park, where the new Kevin Street Garda Station is now. It was always a place to pop in and have a chat en route to work and buy the papers.

We are coming down with churches in our current location, sandwiched between Christ Church and St Patrick's Cathedrals. Then we have a further scattering of smaller churches: Werburgh Street, facing Burdocks. Whitefriar Street, Francis Street, Meath Street and John's Lane churches.

Deirdre Eustace's shop sat on the corner of Bride Street. It was a tiny, solid room, with a big counter and a large window. Just a handful of people could make it feel packed. The groceries were stacked on shelves, floor to ceiling. She always had Lyons Tea, sold loose from a tea chest. Fresh rock buns and cigarettes were a big part of her trade. She kept notes on bills given 'on tick', where somebody didn't have the money that day to pay her. She was part shopkeeper, part social worker and was trusted by the men in the Iveagh hostel. Deirdre's shop was a great meeting place, even though it was tiny.

At the other end of the row was Billy's shop, equally tiny and just as much a social hub, where he was known for his turnovers, crispy puffed-up white loaves of bread. We knew them as 'grinders' down the country. Customers called in on Thursdays to pay their shop bills, and there was an honesty about settling a debt. The site where Jury's Inn hotel now sits was a car pound run by the Corporation, with huts and prefabs surrounded by cars. The whole area was a hub of manufacturing despite its location in the city centre. Shoes were made in the Winstanley Shoe factory on Back Lane. There was a Glen Abbey factory down opposite St Patrick's Park.

Frances, one of the women I know well from the area around the

Iveagh flats, described that sense of community when I met her recently. Small, slim and energetic Frances lived in a couple of properties on the Rosser, or Ross Road. She was always interested in helping other people, and still is. There was a very old lady who lived in the flat below. She would not let Frances pass her door every day until she gave her home-made bread because they were neighbours and Frances was raising her family on her own.

To an outsider the Lord Edward Street area down to Werburgh Street and Bride Street might look unfriendly, full of imposing anonymous buildings, but we knew every corner and character. On a walk around, it often felt like everyone knew me and still today I rarely walk around there without meeting one or more people and stopping to chat.

Outside the Werburgh Street Labour Exchange I used to meet journalist and trade union activist Pádraig Yeates selling *The Irish People*. With his beard, glasses and gentle voice, Pádraig was one of the people I felt I could chat with about the wider world and issues of the day. He was a a journalist who looked in depth at the poor housing conditions in the city in flat complexes like Allingham Street. Burdocks, the chipper on Werburgh Street, the pubs The Lord Edward facing Castle Street and The Oak facing City Hall are some of the landmarks still standing in that area from those days. The chipper, two pubs and me.

The Iveagh Markets lay a short distance up the hill from The Hut on Francis Street. It was opened in 1906 as a new home for the street traders who used to trade on the streets around where the Iveagh Buildings are now. The markets building on Francis Street was given to the Corporation by the Iveagh Trust as a market for old clothes, vegetables and fish. To one side, they built a disinfecting chamber to clean the old clothes before they were sold.

By the seventies the disinfecting chamber was a delousing centre run

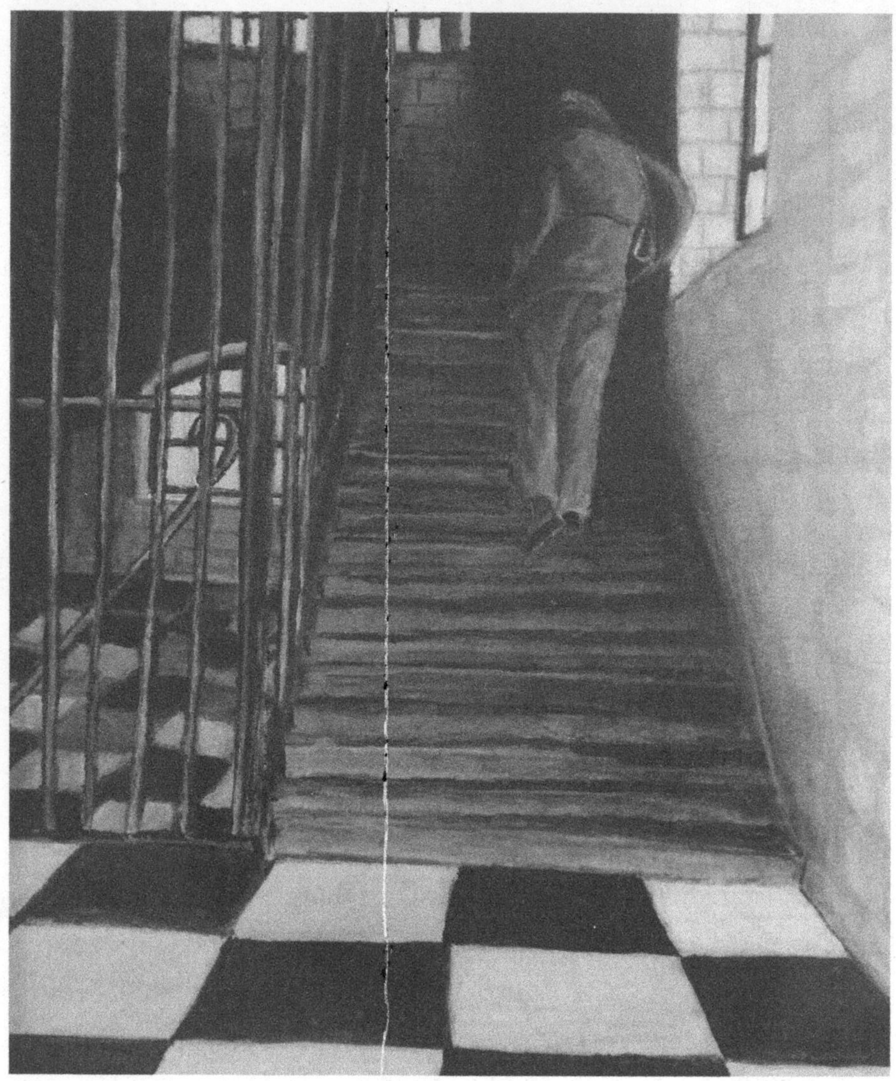

Photograph of a painting by Paddy Gallagher showing Michael making his way up the stairs of the Iveagh Hostel. The painting hangs at the Alice Leahy Trust.

by the health board. It was a bleak place where people were washed and had their clothes steamed to kill the lice. The clothes always came out shrunken and wrinkled so you could tell instantly by looking at someone that they had recently been in the Francis Street delousing centre. They wore those wrinkled clothes like an identifying uniform.

Michael was a man we came across first in those early days. He wore a short tweed coat, was thin to the point of gauntness and carried a little bag on one shoulder. He sometimes stood outside the Iveagh Hostel with a child's soother in his mouth. He embodied all of the complexities of someone who ends up homeless. He was disconnected from almost everyone when we first met him, his history like a story locked away inside. Michael seemed like a man clinging on, just surviving. He was louse ridden and malnourished. We worried that if he got into the bath he was going to fall apart. He seemed held together just by his grimy set of clothes. We didn't want to have him collapse and see him sent to hospital. When that happened with someone like Michael we had to connect with the hospital to make them aware of how fragile they were. They were not patients that could be just pointed to the door and pushed out once they were over their immediate health crisis.

David used to visit Michael in the Iveagh Hostel. The staff were worried that they couldn't keep him there because of the lice. Michael was incredibly private and didn't seem to want anything other than to be left alone. We slowly drew him out and David got him to come into us in The Hut where we were able to help him. We managed to get him a room in the new purpose-built Dublin Social Aid Centre run by the Methodists on Marlborough Street by reassuring both them and Michael that we would keep in touch, and support him. I was on the board of the Social Aid Centre when it was first set up.

It all nearly came off the rails when Michael barricaded himself in a locked room, securing the door from the inside with chains and a padlock and refusing to come out. We went up and talked to him and the staff, mediating a solution that allowed him to remain there despite the outburst. He benefited so much from having a home there, growing from a brittle, silent figure into someone living in relative comfort, with access to meals and contact with fellow residents and staff. He had a living, breathing life rather than existing like a husk.

Michael was full of schemes and notions. He had all his Iveagh receipts, kept neatly in a pile for years. He believed he was going to be able to cash in these receipts for a fortune at some unknown point in the future. He'd talk about going to Leahy's estate agents (no relation) and keeping an eye on his property empire, tutting loudly that his properties weren't selling. There was space for him to live like that without anyone trying to shoehorn him back into a grimmer reality.

David and Michael used to meet up at Christmas every year in the bar of Wynns Hotel so that Michael could buy David a drink. One year on Christmas Eve David arrived into Wynns to find Michael looking smart. He had pressed his trousers by putting them under his mattress as he slept the night before and he had a high polish on his shoes. He did not look out of place among the other men in the bar. Michael insisted on paying for the first round with his own money, fishing carefully folded notes out of the pocket of his pressed tweeds. David would buy them both another drink. That year David had to leave after two drinks and Michael stayed on.

Then a call came through that Michael had gone missing.

'Where the hell has he gone?' David wondered. It was just a short walk from Wynns to Marlborough Street so David had assumed he'd have no difficulty getting home. We were more puzzled than worried about him.

It turned out that Michael had taken the ferry to England and when he tried to come home the ferries had stopped for Christmas. He slept in the terminus in Wales for two days. David believed it was a trial run for a later trip that he made where he made it out of the terminus and to a town in England where he believed he might be able to find his family.

In those early days we saw many former patients of the mental institutions who had become helpless because of their years inside. Many were let out into the world with little or no ability to look after themselves. Those we encountered were all different but some of them shared common traits. They sat quiet and withdrawn, very unsure and isolated and often unable to say what they needed. I didn't see them laughing often. They were lifeless and grey, some on long-term medication, anti-psychotics, tranquilisers or anti-depressants as well as street drugs sometimes. They had very little sense of being in their bodies or pride in their appearance. We often knew very little about them. People regularly disappeared. Sometimes we would discover after they had died that they had given us a false name, and that they had also used other services. We could give them help in the short term, in the hope that things would work out, but often we were just a very small part of their lives.

The whole process of closing down the big wards and moving people into hostels was a disaster. A big institution was just replaced with several smaller institutions. Former patients went from an institutionalised life in hospital to an institutionalised life in a hostel. But hostel staff had no training or funds to deal with their problems. Former patients could disappear and be lost. They had no home, no place to anchor and define them. Often they were defined only by their illness, their only identity a diagnosis on a file in a deserted hospital office.

In our first eighteen months in Trust we met 749 people. Most of these became regulars; more than four out of five of them were seen several times. One hundred and forty eight people we saw in that first year and a half had been in prison or psychiatric hospitals. Twenty-three men and thirteen women had spent their childhoods in institutions. Eight people had been discharged to no fixed abode and with no follow up services from the Central Mental Hospital in Dundrum, the secure hospital where patients are referred by the courts, prisons and hospitals.

We could see where the cracks could be sealed up, with simple changes to bureaucratic routines. Prisons often discharged prisoners late on Fridays, especially before a bank holiday weekend when social services who might have been able to get the prisoner a hostel place were off duty. This still happens today.

In those early days John Long was one of our founding trustees. John who was a social worker had been a founding member of Simon in Dublin. John was solid-looking and wore his brown hair long when I met him. He was serious and professional and always open to a discussion and, like any good social worker, you knew you could tell him things and they wouldn't go any further. Simon released John to work with us a few hours a week and he played a crucial part in helping us to find places for people where they could be safe and comfortable. He went on to work as an advisor to Labour Minister Ruairi Quinn much later. Sadly he died in 2014.

The Simon Shelter moved from Sarsfield Quay to the old fire station in Buckingham Street. Anne Daly from RTÉ spent a morning with us when I was visiting the shelter and made a very powerful radio programme about the place which was nominated for an award. It was

Deep in conversation with social worker John Long.
Dialogue was not confined to boardrooms.

around that time that I met RTÉ reporter Paddy O'Gorman, who has spent his career opening his microphone to people on the margins. Both Anne and Paddy did Trojan work in highlighting social issues in a way that appealed to the average listener, getting across the concerns of the day on national radio. Joe Duffy is another journalist who has a unique rapport with people and an ability to ask the right questions and ruffle feathers. These journalists allowed listeners to hear the voices of some of Ireland's most marginalised people, encouraging them to tell their stories.

We worked closely with senior officials in charge of psychiatric services. The key person in the late seventies with an interest in homeless services was Dr Joe Fernandez, who was employed by the Eastern Health Board. Joe was a compassionate and very good man with a monumental task. His job was to set up dedicated services for people with no fixed abode who were being discharged from psychiatric hospitals. He was wise enough always to remind his superiors that such a task required huge resources. He was also wise enough to remind campaigners that the task wasn't a simple one for which somebody could be blamed. He always seemed close to the edge of being overwhelmed but he never said it and he battled on. In his younger days he told me he had played in a band. One of his venues was the Crystal Ballroom in South Anne Street. I may well have danced to his tunes in the Crystal, although I didn't always dance to them when we worked together as colleagues.

Later in the nineties I went to Brussels with Joe Fernandez for a conference on psychiatry and social exclusion. He arranged for the Health Board to pay for my trip. We both worked very well together. It was as far from a junket as you can imagine. We stayed in a hostel and in the evenings our meal consisted of ham rolls eaten in the hostel dining room.

As an academic as well as a practising psychiatrist, he wrote medical papers that linked him to wider ideas about psychiatry. One of his key supporters was Bill Breakey, a senior psychiatrist based in Johns Hopkins Medical Institution in Baltimore in the US. Bill visited Ireland and came down to us in Trust in the early nineties to talk to Joe about the services in place for homeless people with mental health problems.

I provided Joe with the link to people on the ground and he connected us into the wider thinking around mental illness. Many years later Joe rang me at home late one night. He was asking me to talk to someone about an issue around homelessness. I felt there was more to our conversation. He had something he wanted to tell me but he couldn't get the words out. We talked about meeting up, but sadly he died before that happened. I think now that he knew he was dying when we spoke but couldn't find a way to talk about it. Doctors are often the worst at expressing their own emotions, as they are so used to bottling things up and dealing with other people. A bit like the religious, we don't allow them to be human.

We both shared the frustration of seeing little progress in services provided to homeless people with mental health problems. Joe was this well-meaning psychiatrist dealing with a group of what David likes to call 'the most wonderfully impossible human beings', each side trying to make sense of one another.

One former St Brendan's patient, Frank, was typical of the kind of man we saw a lot. He'd come in to us in Trust and sit there and ask for a blue shirt, always a blue shirt. He'd ask to be shaved and we got him to the stage where he was able to shave himself. He slept under a table in a snooker hall on O'Connell Street and he began to get attached to the attention he got in Trust. He could get quite jealous and would kick the shins of one woman if she was sitting next to him and he thought no one was looking. For a number of weeks he brought me in a copy of *The Irish Times* until we realised he was stealing it from a letterbox. Then he got sick and spent a fairly long time in hospital. When he came back to us he was right back at square one again, not able to do anything for himself and as dependent as a young child.

Ned Butler and Ted Keyes (father of the author Marian Keyes) were programme managers based in St Brendan's who made heroic efforts to patch up the broken system. They controlled the purse strings and they were accessible to people like me. I could knock on their doors and they knew me. Today I wouldn't know whose door to knock on and they wouldn't know me. Over the years I have moved from being part of the system to being very much outside it.

In 1977 Ted told us he had spoken to Dr Ivor Browne, the Eastern Health Board's chief psychiatrist, and there were plans to convert Dr Fernandez's unit in St Brendan's Hospital to a 'vagrants' unit' with staff, including a doctor and two floating nurses. Until that happened David, John and I were the safety net for people being released from psychiatric hospitals into the community, which was an enormous responsibility. St Brendan's Hospital issued a circular in February 1977 stating that homeless patients from the hostels were being looked after by us in Lord Edward Street or at the various hostels where we did our rounds. We were to be notified when any patient without a home was being discharged.

By September that year little progress had been made in setting up a psychiatric service for homeless people. In October David said he felt the plans had been shelved and homeless people or (NFAs – No Fixed Abodes – as they were referred to) were no longer a top priority.

In November 1977 there was finally a plan to hold pre-discharge meetings, an outpatients' clinic and visits by psychiatric staff to the

Two inspirational human beings — Joe Robbins, Assistant Secretary Department of Health with Chairman of TRUST Professor James McCormick.

hostels. But the plan remained just that a plan. We were caught in the middle of a bureaucratic tangle. The State could point to our service as plugging up a gap for discharged psychiatric patients, while delaying the much needed setting up of a proper service.

In May 1978 Professor James McCormick, Trust chairman said he would raise the issue with Ivor Browne. James McCormick was a hero of mine, a deep thinker about how doctors and medicine should operate. He was the first professor of community health in Trinity, a former chairman of the Eastern Health Board and a powerful mentor. When it came to setting up Trust he was the obvious choice to be our chairman. He was the most human of doctors. 'Ill people are not just disordered machinery,' he wrote in his 1979 book *The Doctor, Father Figure or Plumber*. James's party trick during a lecture was to bamboozle a room of medical students by talking about love.

'If therapy always promised cure, if aging and death were not a fact. If human beings were not dependent on others, a mechanistic approach would answer their needs,' he wrote. 'In reality they need love as much as they need therapy, particularly as so much therapy is needless or ineffective.' His ideas were inspiring and countered all the conservative instincts that tend to make Irish doctors so convinced of their god-like abilities.

Consultant psychiatrist Aidan McGennis was appointed in St Brendan's and set up an emergency twenty-four-hour clinic in 1979, which could be used by homeless people living in hostels. Aidan McGennis later held a psychiatric clinic in the Iveagh hostel and worked very closely with us in the basement in Bride Road. He was approachable and a great support and always very understanding of the people on the margins. Aidan had been inspired to become a psychiatrist after working as a medical student with psychiatrist Dr Noël Browne.

The aim of integrating psychiatry into general hospitals took much longer to take effect in Dublin than elsewhere in the country. St Brendan's continued to provide outpatient services until 1993, more than a quarter of a century after the Commission of Inquiry on Mental Illness report recommended closing the institutions and putting care into mainstream hospitals.

For years afterwards, the ball continued to be bounced around. When a separate NFA unit was finally set up in St Brendan's Hospital it was far from the service I, or indeed Joe Fernandez, would have wished it to be. Like many of the structures put in place since, the emphasis was on medication and statistics: the cheapest solutions to mental health issues, prescribing pills and ticking boxes, without ever getting to the root of issues. Because the deeper approach is a process that takes time, resources and a level of training, we are still struggling at a political level to see as being worth the investment.

* * *

In those early months of Trust my days were crammed with work. I noted an average week as follows:

On a Monday night at 6.30pm in Back Lane I saw an average of twelve people. Then down to Sarsfield Quay. I always meet two or three people along the way. Lots stop me to chat, but taking time with these people is important. I leave Simon any time between 9.30pm and midnight. Sometimes Simon soup runners contact me to go and see someone they had encountered on the soup run who needed medical attention.

On a Thursday the day started at 9.30am in the Iveagh Hostel with 'numerous queries, medical card application forms etc. One man – foot bath, one man – nail cutting, one man – letter for opticians. While there, a phone call from St James's Hospital: patient wanted to see me before an operation. I called to the hospital.'

Sometimes the hours between 3pm and 6pm were free time.

'Then at 6.30pm to The Morning Star, where there were three to four foot baths and a range of chiropody appointments, glasses, medical card forms and medication queries.'

'8pm left Morning Star,' I noted. 'On the way met two young people sleeping out. One woman wished to see a doctor. Nearing home met a man from Bray with no place to stay referred him to Simon Soup runners.'

There have always been fewer women living on the streets. Women seem better able to cope in a room or maybe even in an institution. The one thing they all had in common was that they had their secrets. It really wasn't up to any of us to pry unless they told us. Mary in Simon was a very big strong-looking woman. She had greying hair and wore her sadness on her face. She always carried a small string bag. She kept her whole history to herself and often drank 4711, eau de cologne, which was cheaper than spirits and easier to nick as it came in a smaller bottle. Alcohol was the only outlet many homeless women had to deal with their hurt. Then, of course, they were labelled alcoholic. Institutions of the State, including the courts, were very kind to them. The judges were kind to them, as were many prison officers, psychiatric nurses and doctors.

Mary came down with me to Cashel when I brought another homeless man Harry to St Patrick's Hospital, the former County Home. I brought her to my family home at Annesgift and I remember how uncomfortable she was, sitting down to a meal in my home, how out of place she seemed to feel. I never knew Mary's story. I never felt I had the right to ask.

Later I came across a woman staying in the Regina Coeli, who described her mother to me and told me her mother had lived in the Simon Shelter. I just got snatches of conversation, with long silences in between as the woman dredged her memory about the mother she hardly knew.

'Mammy was from Cavan,' she said. 'She was called Mary.'

I think it must have been the Mary I knew. She never told me she had a daughter.

Privacy was the last shred of personhood you lost when you became homeless. It wasn't possible to keep your homelessness a secret from anyone, even strangers on the street. So if people didn't want to tell me why they were homeless, that was their right.

* * *

In September 1979 I got on a plane to Amsterdam for a two-week visit to the Dutch city to assess their services for homeless people, prisoners, prostitutes and addicts. I was travelling on a social fellowship scheme, with funding from the Council of Europe.

I asked for directions outside Amsterdam train station to the Salvation Army Goodwill Centre. The young clerk looked at me wide-eyed and said, 'You know it is the red-light area and a little dangerous.' I must have looked odd, carrying my new suitcase, with a smart tweed suit skirt and jacket walking up the narrow lanes, but I arrived safely.

The Salvation Army Goodwill Centre was lovely and bright, and staff were welcoming and cheerful. I stayed across the road in the women's hostel and shared a tiny attic room with a woman from Eritrea who had come to Amsterdam as a refugee. We were both complete strangers in a strange place. 'How lucky I am to even have a passport,' I wrote in my diary. It was noisy outside my window, and my thoughts kept me awake long into the night. In the morning I was struck by how quiet the district was.

I visited the main hostel where that 'hostel smell' was noticeably absent. There were twenty-five residents, a cat and six kittens there that first night. They had a colour TV, a relative luxury, and coffee and tea and refreshments were paid for.

In a workshop fifty men were working on woodwork projects, printing and sorting through recycled clothes. The scheme worked like our youth training scheme in the St Vincent's Day Centre in Henrietta Street, where AnCo, the State training agency, paid the homeless workers a training wage. That afternoon I met lots of prostitutes on the streets and many sitting in windows. Being with the Salvation Army workers opened up whole facets of the city that I never would have seen without them.

One afternoon I visited a prostitute to take her to see a doctor, a commitment she had made to avoid going to prison. We had coffee together and I found her warm and friendly. She gave me a present of a bottle of Oil of Ulay and paid for our coffee and cake.

One night in a strip club with a member of the Salvation Army, I was walking along a narrow corridor a woman rushed out and put her arms around me and said, 'you speak Irish' and she pushed me into something like an old wardrobe, with the smell of musty clothes, and she started to cry.

She said she was from the south-east of Ireland. Her parents had been killed in a car crash. She had been put into care and gone to London, where she started taking drugs. She had black hair, sunken cheekbones and her teeth were rotting, her beauty faded and lost over the course of a hard life. She asked me to pray for her. The memory of our intense encounter stayed with me. Any time I'm giving a lecture I always feel her presence, as if she's standing at my shoulder. She captured how easy it is for somebody to take a path. If life had been different for her, she might have been in my shoes, and vice versa.

Those strange things that happen along the way colour your view of the world and sense of who is voiceless and who has power. By the end of my time in the city I was exhausted. 'Too much drugs, abuse of women, too oppressive in many ways,' I wrote.

I visited the Jellinek clinic outside Amsterdam, an addiction centre staffed by general nurses, social workers, and a doctor specialising in treatment for alcoholism. I liked the spirit of the place. They didn't see alcoholism as a disease.

At the Opohoso, or Open House Centre, I got a glimpse of Dublin's future. We had yet to see a huge influx of heroin into the country. But Hol land had 15,000 heroin addicts, Opohoso was a therapeutic community, which was very like Simon in its philosophy and work. They accepted people for who they were and operated on the humane rather than the medical model. A methadone bus was used to dispense methadone to 160 clients a day. The house did not forbid residents from using heroin. Dealing was forbidden, along with selling stolen goods. Verbal aggression was allowed but the use of weapons was forbidden. The group had just opened a new centre for girls, some as young as thirteen, who were being used by pimps who were also drug dealers. They had good relations with the police. They didn't work with the drug squad but with neighbourhood police who were seen as father figures in neighbourhoods.

At the Ministry of Justice in The Hague I was given a briefing on the Dutch prison system and then I visited Scheveningen Prison. 'Do you know a man called Paddy Gallagher?' the governor asked me. Paddy was an Irish man who had been on hunger strike in the prison two years earlier? I didn't recognise the name, but later when I asked Margaret Gaj about him she said, 'Yes. I know Paddy. I pray for him regularly.'

* * *

I came home from that trip to Holland with a sense that Ireland could learn a lot from the Dutch approach. It came without the baggage of religion or class. So much of how we were dealing with poverty came from a hangover of Victorian philanthropy, the upper classes looking down from their high positions and dispensing charity, to fulfill their good deeds obligation. The system let the State off the hook and left the recipients of the charity feeling like a class of subhumans, less entitled to comfort and care than anyone else.

We wanted to recreate that clean, efficient space where anyone was welcome to visit and get help and comfort. Within two years of returning from Amsterdam we got a chance to open exactly that kind of place.

Working with the Salvation Army in Amsterdam's red-light district (see the street above), living in their hostel and working from their wonderful Goodwill Centre was very encouraging and rewarding.

Our association with the Iveagh Hostel on Bride Road had been going on for almost a decade. It was the largest and nearest hostel to us in The Hut. Mr Scanlon, we always knew him as Mr Scanlon, was in charge of the hostel when we first started visiting, and then Michael Monaghan took over from him. Michael had been in the Irish army, and had served in the Congo. He was a very nice man, with that decent streak that army people often have. Staff were very understanding about our visits to see people. A lot of the residents were workmen who were paying their own way and were very independent. We were always conscious that the Iveagh was the home of the people who lived there, many of them for decades.

We loved the building and began to ask if there was any possibility of getting a space in it for Trust. The Hut was disintegrating around us, and there were signs that the parcels of dereliction like ours were going to be redeveloped soon. We knew we were not in a position to buy a building and we didn't want to go into a Health Board office and become just another anonymous clinic. The Iveagh seemed to be somewhere that would suit us so much better.

We met Fred Stephens, the secretary manager of the Iveagh Trust, and put our proposal to him. He pulled out all the stops and helped it to happen, giving us the foundation that has endured all these decades. One of their London buildings housed a health clinic, so they could see that we would fit well in their ethos. Dunwoody and Dobson were the long-established builders who were chosen to do up the premises, the unused basement at the western end of the building. They built the steps down to our new basement entrance and put in a new gate in the old railings.

We ended up getting an office, a small sit-in bath and two toilets, our main room with its fireplace, where it was safe to light a fire in those days. Later we began to light it just at Christmastime. One room had lovely old wooden shelves and was entirely covered in old white tiles and you're conscious when you touch it of the age and worth of it. The old strongroom, where valuables were once kept, was changed into a washroom. We installed a tiny bath and shower, along with the couch from Lord Edward Street, a good sturdy doctor's couch that we still have. We saw the value of old things. We are often dealing with people who are seen as wasted bodies, but they're not, and we take a similar approach to things, always seeing the value in them. We brought chairs down from the hostel. We've always used recycled furniture. The chairs in our front room today came from AIB. Other chairs came from the Credit Union. We've always had pictures and flowers. A painting of racehorse *Desert Orchid*, painted for us because of my interest in horses and a St Brigid's Cross have disappeared over the years, probably sold for a bottle of wine. In the eighties we had two budgies but it was difficult to get people to look after them when we weren't there.

When we made the move to the Iveagh the people we helped were part of the effort, shifting things and sorting out the rooms. We feel very safe under the umbrella of the Iveagh Trust. It has meant that we can say no when we're asked to do something outside our remit. Pressure has been put on us to have psychiatric or dental clinics. Any time we were asked to do this, we knew it was because the State was planning to close down a State service and offload it onto us. We refused so as not to allow the State off the hook. We were also offered a very large sum of money to offer a total healthcare service, and we said no. We didn't want to ghetto-ise services for homeless people and allow the State to shirk its responsibilities. We have also refused to become a methadone clinic, a psychiatric clinic or a dental centre out of respect for our neighbours in the hostel and the Iveagh flats.

In a funny coincidence our move to a permanent home happened the same year that my parents became home owners for the first time in their lives. At a moving ceremony in the RDS my father received the RDS long service medal for fifty years working on the farm at Annesgift. His father, my grandfather, had been among the first farm stewards in the country to receive the same medal in 1927. My father's medal marked more than a century of Leahy family service.

The directors of the Hulseboch estate presented my father with the keys of the house where I was born and raised and where he had been born and raised. A letter was read at the presentation of the medal breaking the news that he now owned his home. It came out of the blue and my father described it as a 'very pleasant surprise'. The home that had always felt like home was now officially our family home, earned by long years of hard work.

Later the Hulsebosch family made Trust a beneficiary of the Tobias Trust, giving us a generous regular donation.

At Trust our partnership with the Iveagh has been wonderful in the decades since we moved here. We can feel the history in the building. I'm convinced we have at least one ghost, but she's a friendly presence, like most of the people who come through our door.

Photograph of painting by Paddy Gallagher of a man who used our service – name unknown.

CHAPTER NINE

Partners and a Sort of Homecoming

'Today I spoke to no-one,
And nobody spoke to me,
Am I dead?'
Tony Gill, street poet

'Sorry for the trouble.' This was the short message scrawled on the front page of my recently returned diary on a warm summer's day in July 1982 – just four words written in red ink. I wonder now what happened to the young man who wrote those words. Did he stop bringing trouble into people's lives?

The odd thing was I had asked for a message that morning. Walking to work that morning I'd asked God for some sign that I was doing the right thing in our work in Trust. It wasn't the first time I had done this and it wouldn't be the last. But I never expected the answer to jump out of the blue at me so dramatically.

I had finished my morning's work in Trust and had got the bus out to Finglas, on my way to Cappagh Hospital to visit a friend of my mother's from Tipperary.

As the bus pulled up at the green in Finglas the conductor asked me to keep an eye on a frail-looking, older woman getting out at the same stop. She was dressed in black and had a young girl with her. The woman looked like she had stepped out of a different era. She was carrying an old-fashioned suitcase on her way to the hospital. It was the time before the wheelie cases that let us trundle along more comfortably.

She was making slow progress and I fell into step with her and the girl and asked her if she had somewhere to stay that night. I was in my know-it-all nurse mode. I advised her to make sure to see the social worker and one of the nuns. If she was stuck, I said, the Legion of Mary would give her a bed. I felt she was a bit lost. It was business as usual. I was the one in control of the world, the strong one, the minder.

Until very suddenly I wasn't.

Someone jumped out over a gate beside the footpath and threw his arm around my neck, pulling me off balance and holding me in a strong grip. A second man grabbed my bag. It was a roomy canvas bag with my usual stash: a scissors, tweezers, cotton wool, a small bottle of Dettol, lipstick, a folder of photographs, my purse, a pager (in the time before mobile phones), my address book, a notebook and my diary. The woman and the girl carried on walking, totally ignoring what was happening, as if they hadn't noticed something was wrong. I was alone, outnumbered and couldn't even look my attackers in the face to try to reason with them. I struggled to hold onto my bag but lost the fight. My left arm was bruised in the tussle but that was my only injury. The two young men ran away.

'I work with people like you,' I shouted after them, my heart pounding and my lungs burning as I screamed after them. 'I work with people who've been in prison,' I know they heard me, but they kept running.

They had been waiting for someone to come along. If they hadn't mugged me, they would have attacked the old woman. She was fragile and vulnerable and was probably carrying all her belongings in that battered, old cardboard case.

That thought and some kind of inner strength that kicked in, when I was put to the test, made me reasonably calm after the attack. I walked the rest of the way to Cappagh and rang the taxi company to take me to Finglas garda station. A guard at the desk stood there picking his teeth and ignored me for a while, using his power as the one in a uniform behind a desk to avoid my gaze and appearing to be engaged in something much more important than whatever had brought me in. Eventually I got them to come to the gates of Cappagh. 'They went that way,' I said pointing up the hill where the men had run. The guards shrugged, turned the steering wheel and drove away in the other direction.

I was furious. It was obvious that I wasn't going to get any official help in my attempts to get back my bag. I didn't care about the money, but the bag had a contacts book with the addresses of the relatives of homeless people I'd been working with. It was vital information for use in emergencies.

I took another taxi down to Sean McDermott Street, to put the word out about my bag. Then I went back to Trust and rang the *Irish Press* journalist Denis McClean. He was one of many journalists that I had come to know. In 2000 he left journalism to work with the Red Cross. He put a short piece in the *Irish Press* the following day.

'Trust nurse appeals to bag-snatchers,' the headline read above four paragraphs outlining what had happened and asking whoever had taken my bag to return it to any health centre in the Dublin area. A few hours after the paper hit the shops my bag was handed in to the reception at Cappagh Hospital. Everything I had had in my bag was still there, including my money. The only thing that had been tampered with was a plastic folder of photographs of homeless people. Someone had taken out each of the pictures, maybe looking at all the faces for someone they recognised, and they were stacked in a bunch together. On the inside cover of my diary someone had left the short message in red ink: 'Sorry for the trouble.'

I felt it was an answer to my prayer for a sign. There was something powerful about it and something unexpected. These men had grabbed me and held me in an iron grip, close enough that I could feel their ragged, panicky breath on me. I had appealed to their better nature. And here was my bag returned, an apology for the mugging, and an acknowledgement that my work was important. I wonder still whether that apology led to anything stronger or more lasting than four words scrawled in red biro on my diary.

The day I got my bag back, I went out to RTÉ to do an interview with Pat Kenny on his radio show. I described my frustration at the attitude of the guards. What I had needed when I walked into the station was someone to say 'it's alright' or 'here's a cup of tea or a glass of water.'

I felt Pat understood what I was describing. As a young student, he had gone to hostels and places like Brother Sebastian's and The Morning Star, to educate himself about social issues. He knew the city. I left the studio feeling it had been an important interview. Over the years I continued to talk to Pat on air about my work. There's something special about him. He's interested in what you're saying and he has great empathy. Just before Christmas 2003 he came to Trust with his RTÉ team and broadcast a full radio show from our basement.

I felt a connection in that first interview, not knowing that decades later I would still be talking to him about the same problems and the newer ones. Although he is a serious journalist, he avoids negativity, and that's an important difference in approach.

A garda superintendent rang me later to ask if she could use the tape in the training of the guards. 'Alice, you said it so powerfully,' she said. 'Coming from someone like you it can really make people think.'

We later became involved in garda training, regularly taking in students from Templemore on placement so they could get experience of dealing with difficult people in a calm non-judgmental environment.

An organisation as big as the gardaí contains all kinds of personalities. Many of the guards I dealt with over the years were the opposite of those men in uniform who didn't seem to care. Joe Dowling was a junior liaison officer with the guards when I first met him and recognised him as someone I could call on for help. That occasion came in the shape of Robbie and his rabbit.

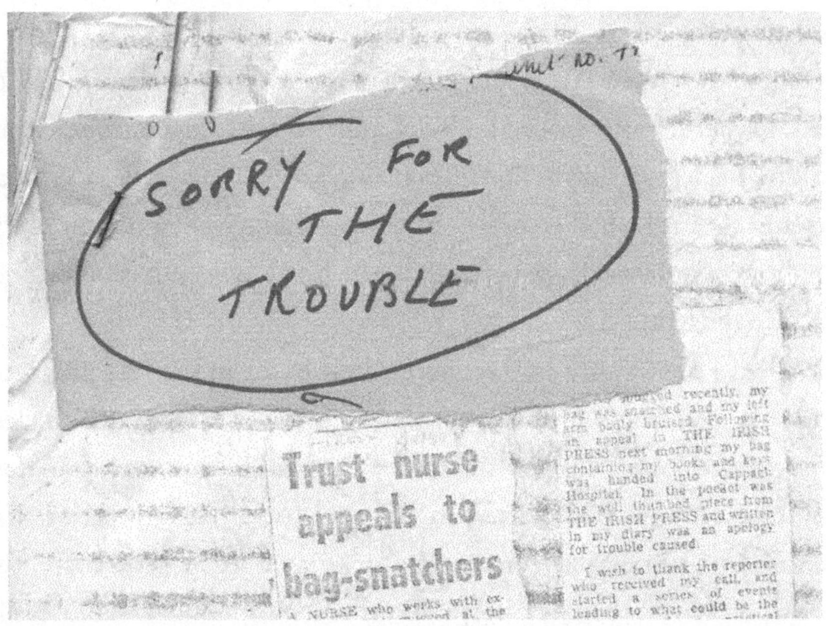

'Sorry for the Trouble' note confirmed my belief that there is good is everyone.

Robbie was a homeless man who slept in doorways around Grafton Street. He had been reared in Rathdrum and was well known on the streets. He busked for money, playing an accordion and kept a rabbit perched on his shoulder like a pirate's parrot. After years on the streets, he decided to go on hunger strike outside the GPO. The eighties was the era of the hunger strikers, after a long campaign by Republican prisoners in the north to get special status as political prisoners, and Robbie was very impressionable. He felt he wanted to make a protest, to be part of something bigger.

I rang Joe Dowling and asked him to go and have a chat with Robbie. He persuaded Robbie to go with him to Burdock's, the chipper on Werburgh Street, where they had fish and chips together. Joe brought Robbie down the hill to us in Trust with a blanket around him. We helped him to get cleaned up and dressed in warm clothes and chatted to him about the dangers of being out there on the streets in a weakened state.

Robbie moved to Galway in later years and rang Trust one day to speak to me. I wasn't in the building and I tried to make contact but couldn't track him down. Sometime later I spoke to a nun in Galway and she told me he had just died. There are often phone calls out of the blue from people we haven't seen in years. It's a sadness that I didn't get a chance to chat to him.

We had a strong base as Trust in our new home in the Iveagh Hostel in the eighties, but we were seeing other services on which homeless people relied being lopped off like dead wood. In a series of hospital closures that had started in the seventies, the city centre was becoming a tougher place for people to go and get medical help. The list of phone numbers for hospitals where we knew we could easily refer people grew shorter, another line drawn through another phone

Robbie sitting outside our entrance. He had been on 'hunger strike' outside the GPO in 1984 and here he is in the same attire he wore then.

number for a hospital that no longer existed.

The voluntary hospitals, with their experienced staff, were all phased out and the services they offered, along with some of the staff, were moved into the larger campus hospitals of St James's, Tallaght, Beaumont, St Vincent's and the Mater. Dr Steevens' Hospital, Sir Patrick Dun's Hospital, Mercer's Hospital and the Royal City of Dublin Hospital, Baggot Street (where I trained) all closed. The Meath, Adelaide and the National Children's Hospital in Harcourt Street were transferred to Tallaght and St Laurence's and Jervis Street Hospitals were moved to Beaumont. Jervis Street is a shopping centre now to a new generation; the hospital that once stood there gone but not forgotten by an older generation.

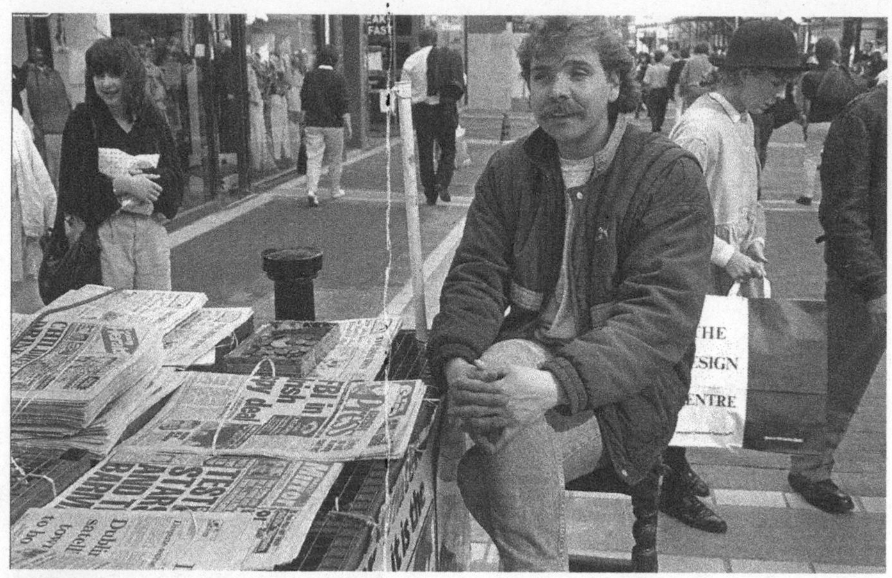

Thought for the day. Another great person who was always keen to help myself and Trust through the years was Michael Kavanagh, a paper seller in Grafton Street. Michael is still there to this day.

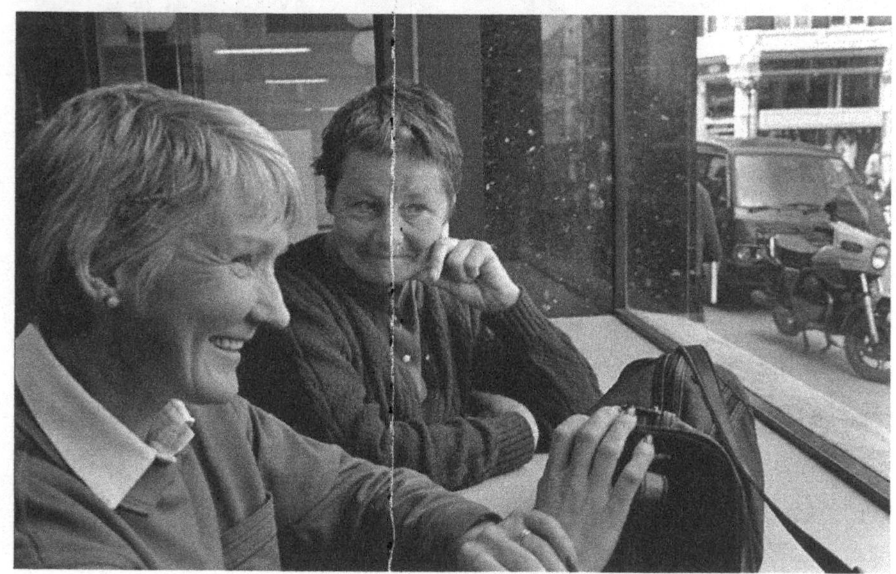

Me and Marese watching the world go by, looking out the window of Anne Street Post Office, 1995.

The eighties saw the dismantling of this part of the health system for the sick and vulnerable in the city centre, the part of the city where most homeless people were concentrated. A lot of people who end up homeless move to cities to find services. It's easier to be lost in a city. You are under less pressure to fit in than you might be in a small town. The dismantling of the voluntary hospitals freed up some prime city centre properties for sale to private developers.

But there remained in the heart of Dublin an unofficial web of kindness in public life. People whose jobs had nothing to do with healthcare or homelessness still involved themselves in helping people, bending the right rules and turning a well-judged blind eye when it mattered.

Michael Kavanagh, the paper seller in Grafton Street, who sells papers there to this day, kept a caring eye on vulnerable people. In the flow of shoppers and buskers and tourists up and down Grafton Street, Michael was a constant presence. He knew the homeless people who lived around the streets and would keep an eye out for someone if we were worried about them.

Marese was a homeless woman who slept in a cardboard box near the Dáil. The staff in the post office in South Anne Street, which is now gone, were very good to her. She could sit in there when the weather was miserable and they wouldn't ask her to move on. Photographer Derek Speirs took a beautiful photograph of us sitting in the window of the post office chatting.

Marese never asked people for money. She hid an electric kettle at the back of the side altar in the church in Clarendon Street. I met her one day and she brought me into the church to show me her kettle. It was such a simple thing that most of us take for granted: being the one able to make herself a hot cup rather than the person who always received it from other people. It gave Marese a dignity and private place even though she wasn't making tea in her own kitchen but at a side altar in a church, where they let her keep her kettle, some cups and spoons, tucked in out of sight.

Journalist Patsy McGarry wrote a piece about Marese and a line from it struck me as profound and true. She was, he said, 'living in a world of silence'. Once in biting cold snow we tried to persuade Marese to go into a hostel. I rang the sergeant in Pearse Street, Denis Corcoran, and they came up in a van to collect me to drive around to Marese so the snow wouldn't pile up on top of her cardboard box, like a lethal blanket.

She agreed to go in for two nights to be in out of the weather. With the help of Simon we helped her apply for a disabled person's maintenance allowance. We also helped her to open a bank account, knowing how frugal she was. There was a danger that she would not spend all

Sean Maher in St Stephen's Green was one of those who had the best interests of the lost and homeless at heart.

of the weekly allowance and start keeping money on her, which would make her a target for muggers.

Every so often she would visit us in Trust. She loved mini-skirts and if we got one in we'd keep it for her. She talked about herself in the plural, 'We are,' she'd say as if there was another person in her life. I always wondered if she was a twin. I met her once walking along Stephen's Street coming towards me carrying her cardboard box. 'Sorry, Marese I'm in a hurry,' I said to her. I was rushing home to get a delivery of home heating oil. 'The oil is coming for me.'

Afterwards I thought how two worlds collide with such different priorities and how you could say something without realising it. There was I rushing home to get home heating oil delivered while she was carrying her damp cardboard box to go and sleep out.

In 1993 Marese told the health board about her bank account during a routine interview. They told her she would have to be means tested and her disability allowance could be cut. Padraig O'Moráin wrote about it in *The Irish Times* after I got in touch with him. In the piece I raised the question of how much money someone like Marese could cost the State. If she decided to rent a flat wouldn't the Health Board have to pay for it? If she took up the drink she could cost them thousands in expensive hospital visits, court cases or trips to prison. She didn't even claim her free travel allowance. At 8.30am on the morning the piece appeared a very irate woman official in the Eastern Health Board rang me. 'Are you paid by the *The Irish Times*?' she snapped. Knowing a good journalist was the only way to get that kind of story out into the open and shine a light on the unfairness.

Another unsung champion of homeless people was Seán Maher, the park superintendent in St Stephen's Green. Seán was an ex-army man, and he knew everyone who went into the green. He had great pride in his uniform and respect for the elegance of the park. He could be very strict about its beautifully planted borders and manicured grass, but he also cared about the homeless people who slept in the park. I would go and sit with him in the staff shed over tea and swap stories of the different people we were worried about. Seán knew who was sleeping under the bushes. He was in his rights to throw them out at closing time, but he let them be.

Pat was one of these park sleepers. He was from rural Ireland and I first saw him when I was standing at a bus stop at the end of O'Connell Street. Pat was shuffling along with no shoes and the backside out of his trousers. He was so run down and out of step with everyone around him that there seemed to be no way to reach him. I felt embarrassed to try and approach him to help.

I went to Store Street Garda Station to ask about him and they didn't know him. Seán was my next port of call. We discovered that Pat was sleeping under a tree, facing the Shelbourne, one of the city's oldest and most luxurious hotels. Pat was tucked in so tightly under the tree, with cardboard and newspaper, that you could hardly see him.

I started calling into the Green and bringing him a boiled egg in the morning and he began to talk to me. I contacted Joe Fernandez, the psychiatrist, about him, and Joe organised a place in hospital and afterwards found him a place in a halfway house in Howth.

One morning I got a call from Joe to say that Pat had gone missing. Someone in the halfway house, who probably didn't mean any harm, had talked to Pat about tidying his room and Pat had left.

I was sure he was back in the Green. I couldn't find him in his usual spot, so I walked over to the public toilets, which sat where the Stephen's Green Luas stop is now. I went to the door of the gents and called in. I thought I could hear someone shuffling. I grabbed a man going by and asked him to come in with me. I don't know what he thought I was up to. We went in and I told the man I was trying to find someone. Pat was sitting upon the toilet with his feet on the seat so he couldn't be seen from under the door.

'Are you in there, Pat?' I called. 'I know you're in there.'

I talked him into coming out and I walked with him up to Trust. It was a time before mobile phones, so I couldn't ring to let anyone know I'd found him. He had a hot bath and a change of clothes, and we gave him some breakfast. Eventually, they took him into the Iveagh Hostel and he lived very comfortably there. We used to have an afternoon where the Iveagh residents would meet up and I showed Pat some simple exercises they could do together. We never spoke about mindfulness, but we talked about being quiet and relaxing. It got to the stage where Pat was able to lead the exercises. It was a very simple thing, but what appears to be simple had a complicated history.

People come in from the margins because you get to know them. You often have to do it in a very quiet and painstaking way. It's nearly always a stop-start process. You make some progress and then you fall back. In Pat's case we needed to keep trying to offer him an alternative to the isolation, and that lonely spot under a bush in a park that he retreated to when life challenged him.

People like Seán on the Green were the glue that held things together, the workers whose jobs bring them into contact with the public every day, who know so much about the anonymous streets and connect people's lives together. I often think our postmen and women have a huge role in keeping these kinds of social connections alive. It goes back to my childhood, where the visit from the postman meant getting the news from the town as well as the actual delivery of letters.

That kindness and connectedness is still evident in our postal workers,

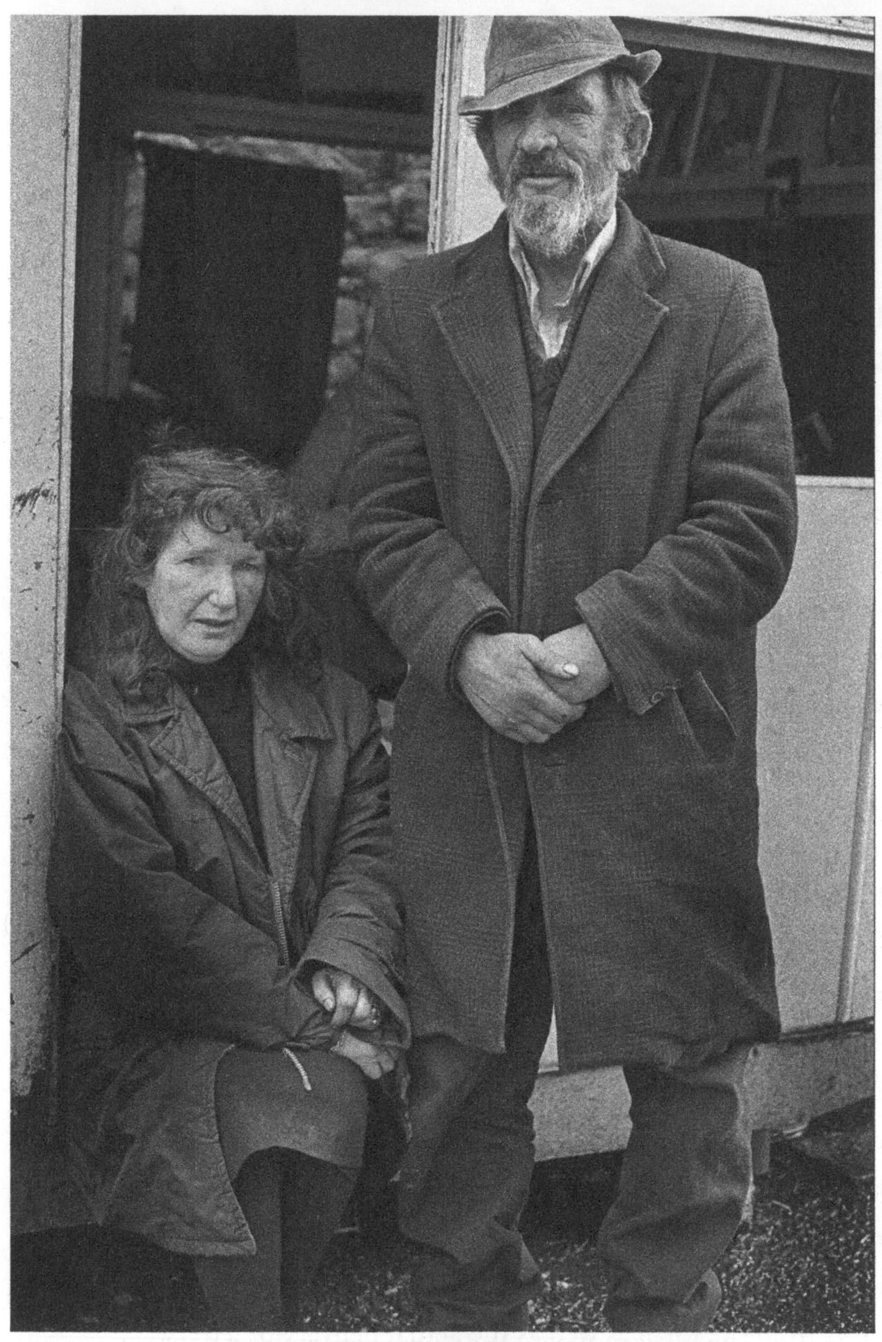

A strong couple, Traveller family Tom and Mary McCann.

despite the widespread closures of the rural post offices. Sometimes a letter will arrive for us with just 'Nurse Alice' written on the envelope. Someone in the sorting office has pulled it from the undeliverable pile and made sure it got to us.

Just as individuals can be marginalised, whole communities can too. In Exchange House, where Smock Alley is now, Bishop Des Williams had set up a centre for the travelling communities in the city. It was a warm place for people to gather. We didn't meet many homeless travellers in Trust, but I had plenty of contact with their community. I went canvassing for Nan Joyce when she ran for election in Tallaght. We got to know many of the families: the Cawleys and the McCanns. Mary McCann would call into us frequently. 'Alice I hate going to shops,' she'd say and she would ask us for clothes. She would try to insist on paying for them. She couldn't understand that we wouldn't take the money for them. She was a regular visitor to Lourdes so she would come in to Trust after a visit, telling us how she had lit a candle for us and bringing the gift of a medal for my mother.

David Roycroft lived in a caravan on a site at the corner of Bride Street and Golden Lane. He shared his caravan with his beloved dogs, four of which were killed when his caravan was set on fire after he was sent to prison for refusing to leave the site in 1980. The derelict land had been bought by property developers. The City Council eventually built a public-housing scheme on the site. When David died his funeral took place in St Patrick's Cathedral.

There were other times when people I helped gave me small things like flowers or plants or a bar of chocolate or brought me places. Once, I went down to Mullingar with a homeless man to a wedding. I think his mother thought I was his girlfriend. He wanted to go to this wedding to make contact with his family again but he felt he couldn't do it alone. We got him a suit and we both went down together. I was his plus one.

In the former Jury's Hotel in Ballsbridge staff used to put on an annual dinner for homeless people. They laid out the ballroom with silver service settings and there was a band. Dublin Bus helped to bring people to the dinner and the guards made sure that people were there. Brother Kevin used to have a big party in Malahide. And the Lions Club held Eric's Party, named after the man who first held the party every year. They celebrated their 59th party in the GPO as one of the first events in the 1916 commemorations. Brother Sebastian had a lovely Christmas dinner in Merchants' Quay, prepared by David Lancaster, who once worked as a chef in the Shelbourne Hotel. David is now with Carroll's Catering, and he brings us in a large pot of homemade soup on his way to work regularly.

The guards in Kevin Street and Pearse Street still hold great community parties. We try to keep Christmas as normal as possible. We put up a small crib. Half the time the figures disappear. We light a candle and get a nice floral display. Lyric provides us with Christmas carols. David Essex's 'A Winter's Tale' always reminds me of the people who've died.

It was a sign of the twisted nature of the times that while guards like Joe Dowling were our allies and friends, we were also watched at times by other members of the force. You could pick out the unmarked car a mile off. Even though they were plainclothes, the guards were easy to spot. Most of them were from rural Ireland and had that ruddy raw look to them. They wouldn't have been doing their job if they hadn't kept an eye on us. But it was also very clear that I wasn't involved in anything subversive and wouldn't allow myself to get involved. We were very careful from the start that we weren't going to be used by any particular group. But were also adamant we were not going to ignore the humanity of the people who came through our door and turn them away because of what they had done or the causes in which they believed.

One morning in the early eighties I was standing up in our front room. It's a clean welcoming place. We keep the old parquet floor sanded and lacquered so the pale wood shines brightly. In winter we used to light a fire in the grate. Now we keep a candle there. We had an open door back then and anyone was free to walk in off the street during our opening hours. Sadly increasing violence in recent years has meant we have had to lock our gate and only admit people after they rap on the gate with the padlock and we can be certain of the safety of us all.

But back then anyone could come through our door, and that morning it was a small slim man who came down the steps and into the warm room. He was angry.

'Alice, somebody told me to come down to you. I don't know can you help me with anything, but I've just been down to the Corpo to see about getting accommodation. And they told me to come to you.'

I didn't realise it until years later but this was Paddy Gallagher, the man that the Dutch official had asked me about on my trip to Holland a few years earlier and Margaret Gaj said she prayed for and knew.

That first morning we met Paddy told me he'd been in prison and his family was in Belfast. I didn't ask him what he'd been in prison for. In all the years that I knew him we never spoke about his life before prison and what led him there. We have a policy of never asking people about their background and it was something I never felt we needed to talk about.

By then Paddy was working in a restaurant part time and went to claim social welfare to supplement his income. He felt the woman in the social welfare office had taken gleeful pleasure in deducting his money because his hours crossed over from night to day. At the Corpo offices he was met with a blank wall when he went looking for accommodation, so he came into us that morning in a rage with the world.

Later he wrote a short piece for us, illustrated with one of his paintings: a cello with a broken string. 'For a short time I was a homeless person. I emphasise the word person for this in many people's eyes we cease to be, even to those who should know better, the ones who daily attend seminars and meetings and discuss case histories, etc. They speak only of 'the homeless'. The homeless what? Cat? Dog? Mouse? Jesus will you look at me. I'm a person.'

I sent him to Allingham Street. The flats there were in an appalling state, but I told him to get his head down and pay the rent. 'Because when you're in there they can't put you out.'

The flats were partly empty and crumbling but a solid shell at least. I got on to Willie Bermingham, the founder of the elder care charity Alone, and he organised a mattress, a table, a chair and a clock. Marie, Willie's wife, came down to me with the clock. Paddy needed to keep time because he was holding down a job with irregular shift hours. Paddy kept his place spotlessly clean. He reminded me of Jimmy Boyle, the lifer in Barlinnie Prison in Glasgow, with that lean look of someone who had been in prison for a long time.

Paddy had been charged with an attempted armed robbery at a Cabra post office in 1974. He left Ireland and was arrested in Amsterdam, where he was remanded to the high security Scheveningen prison in The Hague. He went on hunger strike, in protest at his extradition, but was sent home to Ireland in November 1977. In January 1978 he was sentenced to six years for his part in the robbery by the Special Criminal Court.

Paddy was from the south inner city, the son of a Glasgow man and the youngest of four brothers. His mother died when he was very small and he and his brothers were raised by an aunt. He had been in the British Army and served in Libya. He met his wife Teresa in north Wales, where she had travelled over with a crowd of young Belfast women to work in the Queen's Hotel, a big place owned by an Irish family.

Teresa had been working as a wet spinner in the Belfast mills since leaving school at the age of thirteen. It was punishing work, threading the wet linen onto bobbins as it came off the machines and inhaling the fibres and the damp. Theresa blames her lung condition now on those early years in the mills.

The two were married in Michael's and John's Church in Dublin. The couple had three children by the time I met him: Brendan, John and a daughter.

The family lived between Belfast and Dublin for years. They lived in a squat in Clarinda Park in Dún Laoghaire and became involved in the Dublin Housing Action Group, campaigning for better public housing. Teresa remembers how they squatted in Frascati House, where the Blackrock shopping centre is now, lifting the floorboards at the bottom of the grand staircase to try to stall a garda raid. Plenty of the well-off locals supported their protest with food and moral support. They were the first people to be arrested and charged under stringent new anti-squatter laws on forcible entry and occupation.

By the eighties, when I first met him, Paddy was homeless for a second time, this time as a lone man, coming to grips with the world after years in prison, his family still in Belfast. He got settled in Allingham Street, and one day he came in and said simply: 'You've been very good to me. Can I do anything to help you?'

I asked him to come in one morning a week, after discussing it with our trustees. It wasn't fashionable to take on a former prisoner. He came to meet the trustees. He told me he didn't want his involvement with Trust to damage us if he was on a committee or anything like that. I said, 'Well, you won't be on a committee but we can employ you.'

He came to work at Trust, first for one day a week and then every day. He was a great timekeeper, almost always the first to arrive in the morning and staying in the afternoon to help clean up the place. He used to make a salad for us at lunchtime and we'd sit down to eat together. Paddy became my right-hand man, coming with me on hostel visits and always providing an alternative view of how people were feeling about our services.

His brother Hughie was in the Irish army all his life and a great baker of apple tarts. He would drop them down to us in Trust regularly.

Paddy could talk to people he thought might be heading down the road to crime with an authority that I didn't have. I remember one young man coming in to us with a social worker; he was brandishing a set of keys to a car he boasted he'd just robbed. Paddy took him quietly to one side and asked him whether he wanted to end up in prison for the rest of his life or always linked up to a social worker. 'My advice to you is get out there. If you've done something wrong, admit it. Go to the courts and they will listen to you. But you're a young man. Get your life sorted.' Paddy had seen his own sons make choices that would lead to misery later.

The social worker was a bit taken aback. I don't know if Paddy's words did anything to steer the young man away from a career in crime. He would have been wise if he had taken the advice.

In the mornings, if we were going around to the hostels, I'd meet Paddy in town. We made an odd couple. I often thought if he had had different opportunities he could have been a great lawyer.

Paddy liked quiet places. Sometimes he'd sit and paint in Trust after the place had returned to itself and people had filed back out onto the streets. He painted a bridge once, which weirdly gave me the chills. It had a lonely feeling coming from it. When I looked at it I couldn't say anything about it. Something about it unsettled me and I'll never know why. His painting of two well-known race horses *Generous* and *Desert Orchid* hung in our front room in Trust. I had probably made a throwaway remark about my love of horses, and we always had a flutter on the Grand National. *Desert Orchid* disappeared off the wall one day. I suspect the man who took him for a walk is buried up in the Trust plot in Glasnevin.

People could be prejudiced against Paddy, even after he had become such a valued member of our team. Often if he answered the telephone, with the inner city Dublin accent of which he was proud, they wouldn't give him a message.

'Your greatest strength, Alice,' he once said to me, 'is that people think you're a greenhorn from the country.'

I knew Paddy had two sons and a daughter. He talked about her going through school and doing volunteer work up in the Hospice in Harold's Cross. His son Brendan also painted, like Paddy. He ended up in prison in the north and wrote to me from prison. Paddy would mention John to me occasionally.

I first met Paddy's son John in Trust one day when he came to visit and saw him again when Paddy's brother Hughie died. The funeral afters were in the Ballyfermot United Social Club. Like his father, John had that ex-prisoner demeanour and appearance. As we talked, I had the strange sense that I wasn't reaching him and he wasn't connecting with me. There was an intensity about him, a coldness that sealed him off from normal conversation.

I sat with him over a cup of tea at Hughie's funeral in Ballyfermot and tried again to reach him. 'Look, John, you're a young man. I don't want to know anything about what you're into but what I do know is that you're a young man and there are great educational opportunities up there in Northern Ireland.'

'At my age that wouldn't be the thing to do,' he said. 'Those courses are for younger people.'

I got this sense he had nothing in this life. There may have been people around him and he may have had a vision, but I felt he had no possessions. His mother Teresa remembers how he carried a toothbrush and toothpaste in his back pocket, a habit he picked up from Paddy. John had no watch. I had a watch in a drawer in a brown envelope. A man we knew, also called John, who had walked off the pier in Dún Laoghaire had owned the watch. The staff in St Brendan's Hospital, where he was a patient, had given it to me after he died. And I decided to give that watch to Paddy's son, the man I knew as John.

'From one John to another,' I said as I handed him the watch and explained where it came from. 'We've had that lying in a drawer for ages and I'm delighted that it can be of some use.'

John looked surprised. Something in the gesture seemed to crack his composure.

'Thanks, Alice, and thanks for giving my father a job. I know he loves working here.'

John wasn't called John in Belfast. He was called Gino. Paddy was helping someone to wash their feet in the washroom before he saw the chiropodist when a phone call came about Gino. It was January 1996 and Gino Gallagher, who was then the leader of the INLA in Belfast, had gone to the dole office on the Falls Road to sign on. He had just sat into the chair opposite the counter when a gunman walked up and shot him three times in the back of the head.

It was an awful day. I often think Paddy questioned for years later how different his children's lives might have been if his life had been different. Brendan, his other son, died six years after Gino.

Gino Gallagher's murder unleashed an INLA feud that would leave many more dead. I travelled up to the funeral with our solicitor Dudley Potter. We stopped for a cup of tea along the way. I was uncomfortable about going to the funeral, but felt that it was where I had to be, as a gesture of support to Paddy and Theresa.

Gino was laid out in the house surrounded by a sea of Mass cards. A young man stood beside his coffin, dressed in beret, belt and gloves – the full paramilitary rig-out. I got this mad mischievous urge to pinch this man in his strange garb. This was not a scene I ever imagined being in, but I needed to be here to help a colleague cope with his grief.

People were praying, weeping, smoking cigarettes, their tough lives etched on their faces. When I go to a funeral in a poor area I'm struck by how much the struggle in people's lives seem to come through in their grief at a funeral. I was conscious of the security and how everyone was playing a role, from the RUC outside to the young man in paramilitary garb. Yet the common denominator was a death, a human being, a son lost.

Paddy and Theresa also lost their other son, Brendan. On the positive side in all of this, their grandson has graduated with a degree, his future looking bright thanks to his hard work and education. I know how proud Paddy would have been.

I was glad to get back over the border and home. Later someone rang me up. 'Oh, Alice. I saw you at that funeral,' they said, a note of judgment in their voice.

I went to Gino's funeral because of my regard for Paddy. I never once heard Paddy use his life experience to turn people against the gardaí, the media or the church. I think that came from him but also from our ethos in Trust, that people were humans to be treated humanely when they came through our door, not to be politicised, labelled or preached at. I think Paddy saw in us, this motley bunch of people, that there was something that brought us all together and that maybe there was hope for the future. Teresa Gallagher told me recently that she believed Paddy might have taken his own life after prison had he not met me and come to work for us. It's extraordinary to think you can have had that effect on someone's life. He became less angry through his work with Trust. It gave him a positive outlet for his skills and a chance to relate to people who had been through crime and prison.

Sometimes people are too protective of their image to do anything unconventional, like taking on someone like Paddy. Yet, knowing and working with him was one of the very powerful experiences of my life, from which I have learned so much.

Not long after Gino's murder, Paddy fell into poor health and couldn't work. In 1998 we organised a gathering for him. He dictated a letter of thanks that Evelyn typed up. We got our first manual typewriter from the Rotary Club Dublin. It captured Paddy's voice.

'When I tell you it was such a shock, not to mention a few more feelings I can't describe, but when the initial surprise died down I was filled with what I can only explain as happiness and a sort of sadness that such a wonderful assortment of people care so much for me.

'I thank you all. I shall always treasure the good wishes, cards, presents etc. I received, the television with the remote control and all the mod cons, especially when I think of the one I had. It was a bit like a reject from *The Flintstones*.

'The only ones missing at the party were priests, nuns and politicians, but I know if Alice thought I wanted them there she would have arranged for Bertie and the Pope!'

When Paddy died, we knew he didn't want a religious service at his funeral. He was a spiritual person, but the hypocrisy of the church did not appeal to him. My nursing colleague Geraldine came with me to the flat in Chamber Court where he was laid out with flowers and Mass cards. It was a sobering sight, this tiny box of a room where he lived the final quiet years of his life.

His funeral in Mount Jerome was an extraordinary gathering of ex-gardaí, barristers, well-known solicitors, locals from the inner city, Belfast natives, Quakers, Protestants and Catholics. It was a service that captured what Trust was about.

* * *

David Magee, my GP friend and colleague, decided in the eighties to train as a psychiatrist. Our working relationship and friendship had developed to a point where we could talk to each other about anything. David had only qualified as a doctor when he started working with us and he felt that he had to move on. Our work had introduced him to people with serious mental health problems and the psychiatrists who were trying to help them. We were both fascinated by the mind, and his decision to train as a psychiatrist felt like the right road for someone as interested in human behaviour as David is. His calm presence would never provoke anger and his kindness made him a great listener. There's a thin veil between working with homeless people and working in psychiatry. There is the same search for a 'cure', although often a cure may not exist.

He remained on the board of Trust, and a friend an ally for years afterwards, but we needed a new GP. Laurence McGibben joined us. A Belfast man, he came from a background in psychiatry. His northern accent was often welcome to the people that came to us in the eighties, coming from the troubles in the north, to escape to more peaceful places.

One of these men, Michael, was well known around town and would always go up to Belfast to stay with his sister for Christmas. She would set him up in a comfortable bedroom with his own TV and he would spend all his time locked in his room watching it. I got the impression that he showed little or no gratitude to his sister. As he was leaving us one morning just before Christmas I called up the steps after him.

'Michael, will you buy a bar of chocolate for your sister for Christmas?'

He turned around and he spat at me. I was furious and I walked away, but the next time he came in that New Year I told him that was no way to behave. I don't know if he ever did buy the bar of chocolate. It was unpleasant, but at least it was a reaction to being challenged. I don't know had anyone every asked something like that of him before. And I was left wondering why my question had made him quite so angry.

Those were hectic days but I still had a life outside the basement on Bride Road and it was important to me. Three times a week I went to Enda Ryan's gym on Cope Street. She ran her gym in a big room with staff who gave you a series of exercises. Enda was always sitting there with her cat on a chair beside her. She'd watch you as you exercised and let you know if you needed to pick up the pace. After that I joined the gym on Abbey Street run by Dave and Francoise Hegarty. I had started doing transcendental meditation in the seventies, doing a course to learn how to sit with my breath and relax. There were days I felt I shouldn't go to the gym or yoga studio, but those were the very days I needed it.

I started and finished my days with twenty minutes meditation. If I had a meeting in the afternoon that was worrying me, I could take a ten-minute meditation break and ground myself in preparation for it. I could see things more clearly when I did that. Some people dismiss it because it's hard to quantify results, but for me it's when I stop doing it that I realise the benefits.

Tipperary was always very much home and I kept in constant contact and travelled down to visit for family occasions. Over the years all my siblings married and lived within a twenty-mile radius of Annesgift. I was the only one who went further afield. Eileen married a dairy farmer on the other side of the town. Donal worked on the estate and reared cattle on his farm alongside it. Martin was the only one of us to go to college. He went to the horticulture college in Kildalton and works today as the head gardener in Ballydoyle, home of world-famous horse trainer Aidan O'Brien. Mary is married and lives near Eileen. Like my mother, she has a great head for business and works with a long-established Irish company. The twins Mary and Martin are great card players, like Mammy was. It's a bug that I was never bitten by.

My nieces and nephews have all travelled around the world and most of them attended college. They brought with them a new wave of family events, christenings, First Communions, weddings and sports events.

As the only one of us not married or with a partner, I never felt lonely or experienced any stigma about being single in my thirties and early forties. I never felt that there was anything wrong with not being married. Work was fulfilling, sociable, challenging and exciting and had opened up the world of politics, business and media to me. I was married to my job, which is something a lot of men say, but not many women.

Growing up in Fethard I went to dances in my teenage years. One of the dances was held at the crossroads near Annesgift. It was a platform dance, where the makeshift floor was installed for the band and the dancers, with lights strung up to take the dancing into the half-bright darkness of a summer evening.

It was difficult to start a romance when you had to cycle home, but I met a young man who had a motorbike. He was handsome and wild. Early one morning he pulled up outside our house and started singing Sam Cooke's song 'Only Sixteen' outside in the darkness.

'You know you're not really good enough for my family, Alice,' he told me once, because he had an uncle who was a bishop in America.

After I left home and moved to Dublin to train as a nurse, I returned one weekend to be told that he had left. I think we might have passed each other out on trains going in opposite directions.

People could vanish then. There were no social media to allow you to track their progress and unravel the mystery of why they left without word or explanation. Years later, I was home one weekend and the singer Joe Dolan was playing in the ballroom in Fethard. We dressed up and headed into the hall. The men lined up on one side and the women on the other, like cattle waiting for someone to come over and pick us out of the lineup. This man came over. He was beautifully dressed.

'Hello Alice,' he said with a glint in his eye.

It was him, my wild disappearing act.

We just looked at each other and moved together onto the dance floor. We danced the night away in the town ballroom. He never explained where he had been, and I never asked. Leaving Fethard felt like something we both had in common, severing our connection to home. We were both outsiders now, belonging neither here nor there, and that felt like a kinship, a strengthening of the bond.

That weekend we went back up to Dublin together and had a meal in the Berni Inn, at the Grafton Street end of Nassau Street. When we parted that night, he said he'd ring me the following night. I never heard from him again. Later, I heard he had gone back to England. But my life was so busy I had very little time to mull over my loss.

He wasn't the only person who vanished. There was a beautiful nun, Sister Agnes, in my secondary convent school. She always smelled of perfume and spoke French with a native accent. She encouraged me to the go the Gaeltacht one year and set me up with a family in Ballferriter where I would do housekeeping in return for my keep. She too disappeared. I often wonder did she fall in love and leave. Fethard was a place where I felt a huge sense of belonging but small town Ireland was suffocating for some. The home where I felt I belonged could be a place where someone else felt trapped and desperately alone.

The intensity of the work of Trust and my network of friends and colleagues in Dublin meant I was far from being a lonely heart, looking for a partner. Then I met Charlie properly in my early forties. He was someone I'd known for years as Driver Four Five. He worked as a taxi driver with National Radio Cabs. The first time we met he walked into The Hut to pick me up as I was bringing a black sack full of bedding to a family in Crumlin. I liked him immediately. He opened the door to help me, didn't have the radio blaring and knew where he was going. I could talk to him if I wanted to, but I was also comfortable letting a silence fall. He had dark black hair and a moustache and kind brown eyes. I knew him as Driver Four Five. I didn't ask his name.

When I arrived into the house that day with the sheets and clothes the woman had the four gas rings on the cooker burning, to try to heat the house. I chatted with her young son. He seemed bright and interesting and I talked to him about school and the importance of going to school. I've been very sad to see his name in court reports since. And I just recently heard he had died in England.

When Trust was coming up to its tenth anniversary and we decided to have a get-together. And I rang National Radio Cabs and asked if they would let Driver Four Five know that we were inviting people to come and celebrate ten years.

'I was talking to that very nice taxi driver and he told me his wife had died,' our solicitor Dudley Potter told me afterwards.

'His name is Charlie, Charlie Best.'

It was only later that I remembered the prediction from the dying patient in Baggot Street that I would marry a widower with the initials CB. A short while after the tenth anniversary party, Charlie invited me to a dinner in the Glass Bottle Company social club. And that was the beginning of our beautiful friendship.

Charlie was born in Mount Pleasant Avenue in Rathmines and grew up in Drimnagh, a proud Dubliner all his life. When we started going out together marriage wasn't in my thinking. Children were definitely not. I had never felt the need to be a mother. I think it's something that's expected of women. Even today the pressure on women is worse, but I never felt there was anything wrong with me that I didn't have this urge to have children.

Charlie had three grown-up children. When I was younger my heart would have been pounding about someone like Charlie, but I had a much deeper kind of understanding of life. I liked him and was attracted to his quiet kindness and his sense of humour. He was someone who felt like a kindred spirit. We were both very different, but we became friends first and it was that friendship and understanding of each other that deepened into love.

The year I married Charlie I discovered I had a lump in my breast. I

1987 a gathering in Trust to discuss community services. Mary Frawley, trustees Dudley Potter and Sean Hogan, me in the front and Charlie, Driver Four Five, NRC and my future soul mate.

Our wedding day in St Kevin's Oratory, St Mary's Pro Cathedral, Dublin, November 1988.

got a jolt of pure terror when I found it. For a short time afterwards I went around in a daze, thinking it was the end. I went to see our chairman James McCormick to talk to him about it. The lump was moveable so I didn't think it was anything to really worry about.

The mammogram I had to investigate the lump was a dreadful experience. The woman stood over me and was moving pieces of my body around like they were lumps of steak. Her bedside manner was unfortunate and she had made no real connection with me. She was feeling me and prodding me like meat, all the while asking me all sorts of probing questions. The whole experience made me feel confrontational, and I challenged her as to why she wanted all this information. Afterwards, I was so appalled at the appointment that I rushed out and nearly walked under a car.

I wrote a strong letter of complaint to the hospital about my treatment. When I went to see my consultant I heard him saying to one of his colleagues that I had 'caused problems'. He gave me the all clear. The lump was a cyst and I have never looked back since.

My health scare had made me think of calling off my wedding. I didn't want Charlie going through the trauma of losing a second wife, but once I knew I was going to be okay we set about making plans.

Our wedding was not a conventional one. We decided we wanted something very simple. In different times we might have decided not to get married at all.

The ceremony was in the oratory in the Pro Cathedral. I wore a long brown leather skirt that I bought in Ronan's the Tannery in Tipperary. Looking for a blouse to go with it was a long search. I eventually found the perfect one – a cream blouse with a tan spot – in Switzer's, the department store on Grafton Street, which has gone now. The saleswoman who sold it to me just recently retired from Brown Thomas.

We asked Catherine Prendergast, the Daughter of Charity nun, if we could use their kitchen and have our family wedding meal there. We wanted to show that you don't have to spend a lot of money so we prepared our own meal. Paddy Gallagher's brother Hughie cooked us a batch of his delicious apple tarts.

It was a wonderful day. The wedding goers were made up of friends and family and lots of the people I worked with. Bishop Des Williams and Father Dermot McCarthy officiated at the wedding. Guests were a cross section of all walks of life, people of all religions and all political persuasions, and none.

Tom, an old man who lived in Back Lane, heard we were getting married and gave the caretaker money to buy a pink Tara tea set as a wedding present. Another Back Lane resident, Paddy L, the man who had stabbed another resident and who I had helped by intervening on his behalf, bought a suit and marched to the top of the church on the day. A few years later, a social worker in the Meath Hospital rang me worried that he was suffering from dementia.

'He's telling me he was at your wedding, Alice,' she said.

'He was. He marched right to the top of the church,' I told her.

We had a wave of good wishes from people we worked with the day we got married. The honeymoon was as simple as the ceremony. We drove down to the Glen of the Downs hotel in Wicklow and stayed there for a few nights.

Around the same time as the wedding I got a People of the Year award. It was my second time meeting Pat Kenny after the interview about my bag. That night I also met Jack Charlton and his wife Pat at the awards in November 1988. We became good friends and kept in touch for a long time afterwards.

I also met the extraordinary Fermanagh man, Gordon Wilson, whose daughter Marie had been killed in the Enniskillen bombing. I was in awe of the strength that he found to say that he forgave his daughter's killers. I find it hard to understand. It's similar to how I feel about the person who declares that they're a pacifist. How do they know until they're put to the test?

Stena gave us a trip by ferry to Wales after I appeared on the *Kenny Live* TV programme to talk about my work and getting the People of the Year award. Charlie and I drove around the beautiful Welsh countryside, meeting lovely people. Pat Kenny auctioned a collection of the books given to him to review for his show that year, raising thousands for Trust. We never knew who bought the books. I think it was a farmer from Cork. After that, we had no trouble raising money. Whenever I appear on radio or television, we always receive generous donations, even though I never ask for money.

Just before I got married, I talked to Paddy Gallagher about our plans.

'Ah, Alice, you'll give up the work once you're married and everything will change,' Paddy said.

'No, Paddy. That won't happen. I'm not going to let that stop me.'

Charlie has always encouraged me to work and he made my work easier. In many ways my marriage has been a homecoming for me. Charlie grows our vegetables in the back garden of our house in Rathmines and keeps a good compost heap, like Daddy did. He does all the cooking and makes great soup, which is always nice to come home to after a heavy morning at work. He's very involved in the community, like my family was when I was growing up. He is often seen with a blonde in McCoy's Bar, but I'm fine with that. It's part of his regular work as a television extra in the fictional pub in the RTÉ soap opera *Fair City*.

When we first got married Charlie's dog Holly was the only one whose nose was out of joint. If I sat beside Charlie on the couch and leaned over to him, she'd climb up and go between us, giving me a look that definitely said: 'I was here first.'

Holly was Charlie's mother's dog. She was grieving after my mother-in-law's death so Charlie decided to take her. She lived to the grand old age of nineteen and we were heartbroken when she died. Walking by the Dodder one day, someone offered me a rescue dog. I said I'd ask Charlie, but the woman got to him first. When I got home one day the dog came out to meet me. Even though she was a girl, we called her Viduka after the Australian soccer player who'd played for Leeds. She had been very badly treated and was a great gentle soul. When she died we cried our eyes out. It was so much of a wrench that we couldn't bear the thought of getting another dog.

Having Charlie by my side made it easier to say no to doing things that I didn't want to take on, to carve out time for ourselves, away from the demands of Trust. A decade on from setting up the service conditions on, the streets were showing no real sign of improving. Things were going to get a whole lot more challenging in the nineties. My long-held hope that Trust would be made redundant as the State took up the slack would look further off than ever.

CHAPTER TEN

Trials

'I'm worrying about what I'm going to do when I get out. It's not so bad sleeping out rough in the summer. The winter's the worst.'

Pauline Leonard in a letter to me from prison

Tony was a man whose life story chimed with so many others who came through our door in the first decade of Trust. In his late twenties, he was medium height, articulate and well-dressed. He had spent time in an orphanage and in foster homes. He'd been in the army, St Patrick's and Mountjoy prisons and hostels in London. We had known him for years when he began to tell us about his stroke of luck.

Tony was flush with money. He had been getting £33 a week in dole money, a pitiful amount that led a lot of people to beg or rob to get more. But now he could earn £20 a day. All he had to do was submit himself as a human guinea pig for drug testing.

'Did you hear about this business with the drug trials, Alice?' he asked me one day when he arrived in. He felt it was something he could handle but maybe more vulnerable people could be harmed by. Tony told us he had been recruited to the drug trials by a man in a hostel where he was staying. We later learned that the company behind the clinical trials was paying men to recruit homeless people like Tony.

My alarm bells rang as soon as he told us. He said he was volunteering for the drug trial. But how could he truly be a volunteer when £20 a day was a transformation of his life? He had met others like him on the drug trials: addicts, people with psychiatric problems, people on social welfare, students and young people from broken homes who needed money for rent and clothes. How much 'informed consent' could vulnerable people like these be giving to take part in a drug trial?

I began to hear about drug trials from other homeless people. It was 1983 and there was a huge gap in power between the humans being tested, the medical staff who were running the tests, and the drug companies who stood to make such vast profits from a successful drug. Our chairman James McCormick encouraged me to dig deeper into what we were hearing from the men and women on the street. It went to the heart of ethics and power in medicine, areas that he had been fascinated by all his professional life.

Later a solicitor was to warn me to watch my back. I could be knocked off my bicycle and it might not be an accident, he said. It sounded paranoid but who were we in a basement in Bride Road to take on the might of the pharmaceutical industry? I knew I couldn't do this on my own. We needed the help of others.

Sometime earlier I had been down to Bellinter in County Meath for a meeting of Partners in Mission. They were a group of religious and lay people that had been involved in missionary work overseas and met to discuss social policy. I got in touch with Sister Catherine Prendergast who was a key person in Partners in Mission and, with her help, we formed a new group.

We met in the back room in Trust around a table: social workers, community welfare officers, priests, nuns, a solicitor and a community activist. We called ourselves SPAG, the Social Policy Action Group. We were organised as a co-operative rather than using the traditional committee structure, which meant everyone had an equal voice around the table, and we met once a fortnight. We wanted to link up people involved in the day-to-day support of homeless people, to keep them informed, and to identify the gaps and concerns. We ended up with one single focus: lobbying the Government to regulate and oversee the dangerous world of human drug trials.

I was worried that a homeless person could die on a drug trial, without consequences. A death or serious illness might not be investigated because the homeless person didn't have family or friends to ask questions. There were at least three men whose deaths in separate incidents were rumoured to be linked to drug trials. I wrote to gardaí in Kilmainham, asking to be informed when an inquest into one man's death would take place as I wanted to have a solicitor present. The man had died in a night shelter. The letter was never acknowledged and the coroner's office told me to ring the hospital to find out the result of the post mortem. I got nowhere. I never found any evidence to link the three separate deaths to any drug trials. But the rumours on the street persisted.

We wrote to all our local TDs. It was a time of letter writing rather than email contact. TD Proinsias de Rossa raised the issue in the Dáil. Journalists began to take an interest, radio, the newspapers even the BBC.

It was heartening to see so many people more powerful than we were taking the trials seriously. I felt a great support from the SPAG group, made up of so many professionals working together.

In May 1984 the story exploded. Niall Rush was a thirty-one-year-old man living in Iona Road in Glasnevin. Niall's father Kevin was a diplomat. He had been Ireland's first ambassador to Portugal. In a truly small-world coincidence, Kevin was a brother of Brian Rush, husband of Anne whose legacy had allowed us to set up Trust. Niall was the nephew of our benefactor Anne Rush.

On 29 May Niall was taking part in a drug trial at the private drug-testing company called the Institute of Clinical Pharmacology (ICP) in the grounds of St James's Hospital.

Niall was the last of four volunteers to receive a dose of the test drug that morning. The drug being tested was eproxindine, a treatment for irregular heart rhythm. When Niall got his injection at 10.06am it had a catastrophic effect. He said he felt 'dizzy as a dog' and seconds later was in great distress. He died within minutes. It emerged later that a day before he took part in the drug trial Niall had received a long-acting injection of depixol, a drug used to treat psychiatric illness. At the inquest into his death the jury heard evidence that Niall died because of the interaction between the two drugs.

The death was exactly what we had feared could happen with poor regulation of clinical trials. At Niall Rush's inquest the Dublin City Coroner took the unusual step of telling the jury they could go further than just finding the cause of death. He said they could add a rider to alert the public and avoid a similar death in the future. The jury added a lengthy rider to their finding of death by heart attack, suggesting that testing bodies always obtain a full medical history, that test subjects be examined before and afterwards, and that an independent body be set up to examine recruitment, screening and safety procedures at the ICP where Niall Rush died.

The *Sunday Tribune* reported that the ICP had received a large grant from the Industrial Development Authority and had a nominal rent agreement with the Eastern Health Board, a total package worth almost £2 million in Government subsidies. Four months after Niall Rush died, RTÉ's *This Week* programme interviewed a man who said he had been paid extra money for recruiting other volunteers to the ICP testing programme. RTÉ sent an undercover reporter to the Iveagh Hostel who was offered paid drug-testing work by men who were not homeless and seemed to be staying in the hostel to work as recruiters.

Barry Desmond was Minister for Health and after Niall Rush's death he piloted legislation on the control of clinical trials through the Dáil. In the run up to the act, we pushed hard to make people accountable and, at one stage, I was worried that we might be sued. Journalist Colman Cassidy reassured me. 'Alice don't you worry Barry Desmond isn't going to sue any of you,' he said. The Minister was on our side. The Control of Clinical Trials Act became law in 1987 and was amended in 1990, the same year that ICP went into receivership.

Informed consent and the use of homeless people as subjects for research is still an issue today. I recently visited an emergency shelter where people were talking about a visit the night before by medical staff who had taken blood samples to test cholesterol. This is mind-boggling to me. If someone is homeless, their cholesterol level is the least of their problems. What is being done with that data and who is benefitting from that study?

After the law was passed to regulate clinical trials, our Social Policy Action Group dissolved. We had achieved what we were looking for, a tough regime around drug testing to make it safe for subjects and to protect vulnerable people from exploitation. Sometimes I wonder if the legislation would have been put in place so swiftly if the person who had died had been a homeless person. It brought home the importance of my role as an advocate. The people I worked with needed someone to take their side, to explain the realities of their lives, and to push as hard for answers as a family member would.

Journalists were writing about life on the streets. One of the best was an article in current affairs magazine *Magill* in November 1983. Journalists Mark Brennock and John McHugh spent twelve nights sleeping on the streets, hostels, bus stations and shelters. They ate spam sandwiches at Brother Kevin's, washed down with tea poured from huge teapots with the milk and sugar already added. They described their own fears and sense of despair at times, along with the voices, jokes and outbursts of the men and women they met. The length of time they spent living on the streets and the space given to the article, which ran over thirteen pages, is unimaginable in today's media. Stories about homeless people tend to be short, sentimental or sensational. The cynic in me sees how they have become a seasonal staple. Christmas is when editors seem to care most about people sleeping in doorways, especially if they can be photographed with tinsel-draped Christmas decorations nearby, to contrast their misery.

Those Magill journalists who went undercover as homeless young men met a bureaucratic blank wall when they were told they couldn't sign on without an address. When they pointed out that they couldn't get an address without money, no one listened. Supplementary Welfare Allowances were available as immediate and flexible payments for people in that situation, but they weren't offered it in the course of their investigation. The difficulty of getting a welfare payment without an address is still an issue today. People have told us they are being told to go back to their home county to make a welfare claim.

In the eighties, health boards and local authorities were shunting the problem of homelessness between themselves. The health boards were insisting it was a housing problem. The local authorities were insisting that shelters were the responsibility of the Department of Health, but we still had officials who were human enough to see someone in crisis and fill the gap to help.

Dr Brendan O'Donnell was the city medical officer. It's a role that no longer exists. If he got a call to assess someone from a hostel, he would ring me to see if I knew them. Like Fred Donohoe, Dr O'Donnell could see when a flexible official attitude was needed to help someone.

Getting a letter to see Dr O'Donnell was like getting a winning lottery ticket. He could recommend people for housing based on their medical need, and he was a compassionate man who sat down with people face to face to assess them.

Colm was a man who came to us around that time. He lived with his brother in a flat and was very difficult. The flat in Dolphin's Barn had bare stone walls, with just a cooker, two beds, a table and chairs. They had no home comforts, no central heating. The wind whistled through the flat so viciously it was almost as bad as living out in the open. A lot of people living in that kind of poverty depended on the goodwill of neighbours to look out for them. Along with a lot of other problems, Colm was diagnosed with TB. The danger with TB was that he would infect other people, so it was vital that he take his medication, but Colm could not be guaranteed to take it without daily supervision.

Dr O'Donnell agreed that he could come into Trust to get his medication, and Paddy Gallagher would come in at the weekends to give it to him or visit him in his shell of a flat. The unorthodox arrangement meant Colm could be treated effectively and would not spread TB around. I can't imagine it being allowed to happen today. A carer would have to liaise with the public health nurse or a doctor to be allowed to administer medication.

Louisa was a woman who came in to us frequently. I took her to the Gaiety one night to see a play. I remember the people looking at her strangely. She reeked of her beloved cat, with whom she shared a small flat on Benburb Street. Her parents had been Seventh Day Adventists, and she had had a very strict upbringing from a fanatical religious alcoholic father and a dependent frail mother, who died of TB in a locked ward.

'I'll never forget seeing her there behind the glass, Alice,' Louisa told me as we walked down Grafton Street after the show. I had planned to get a taxi straight home, but I could tell Louisa wanted company.

We walked into the Coffee Inn in South Anne Street and got a table. Louisa stared into space as she started to talk, as if she wasn't with me at a table in Dublin any more. She was re-living a night a long time before when she ran along the platform of London's Euston Station, to jump onto a departing train and run down through the carriages to find the Irishman she was in love with. He was leaving London to return to Ireland, and he was the only man who had ever given her any love or attention. Louisa had decided to follow him to Ireland, where she hoped he would look after her.

I don't know how their relationship went, but Louisa never returned to London. She worked as a cleaner in St James's Hospital at one stage. I got to know her when she was living alone in a dark flat, curtains drawn, with just her cat pacing, like a caged animal, protecting his mistress. When I visited Louisa that first time, she had no food, apart from cat tins. Unopened letters lay on the table. She sat, birdlike, in a corner, shoulder bones protruding as she was hunched trying to keep warm. Her long fingers held mine, but there was no sense of warmth.

John Hayes, the supervisor in the nearby Model Lodging House and her local bank manager were very concerned about her. We all worked together to help her. She used to spend her nights walking around the streets feeding stray cats. She liked to come in to us in Trust, but she never saw herself as one of the people who needed help. She'd always bring something as a gift, a handkerchief or a bar of chocolate. Inadvertently, she had a tendency to insult some of the people, with a strange mix of snobbery and insecurity. We often had to smooth things over.

'Paddy, do you mind being called Paddy?' she'd say to Paddy Gallagher in her most imperious London accent. As far as she was concerned, Paddy was the generic term of abuse for an Irishman in London. Paddy Gallagher knew what she was like so he didn't bristle.

'I don't mind at all, Louisa. It's my name after all,' he'd say.

She told another man that only the bin men in London wore jeans. If people were sensitive or on edge, a wrong word from Louisa could unleash all hell in our waiting room.

Dr O'Donnell rang me about Louisa after complaints from neighbours about the smell of the cat who had grown old and incontinent.

'If you take the cat from her, she'll go before the cat,' I told him. John Hayes talked to neighbours to try to explain how much Louisa loved her cat, while understanding their concerns. We all turned a blind eye until the cat died naturally. After a fall, Louisa went to live in St Mary's Hospital in the Phoenix Park. Her home help, Liz, would call up to see her, take her a card and some chocolates on her birthday. Louisa loved *Hello* gossip magazine, especially spreads about Princess Diana. She kept small bits of china around her. She loved her nice things and she ended her days in happy comfort.

'I'm 81 years old now and still quite alert,' she wrote to me on cheerful yellow notepaper decorated with a butterfly and ladybird. 'I do crosswords and read a lot. I am reading Catherine Cookson's novels. I don't know how she thought it all up! I don't think I'll ever walk again, but I have a lovely comfortable arm chair. My electric mattress cost two

When paths cross great things happen. Paddy Gallagher and me.

Paddy busy in the store room at Trust.
A fresh set of clothes can mean a lot to those in need.

or three thousand, as you see how hospitals spend so much money.'

In a later card, she talked about the 'lovely pot of snowdrops brought in by a nurse. Then later on she will return them to her garden. It's lovely to see them going to sleep each evening and strange to say she [the nurse] didn't know that flowers do.'

Before she was hospitalized, and all the time I knew her, Louisa's flat reflected the state of her mind. When she was well and happy, there were flowers on the window, friends' photos on the walls, china cups gleaming on the dresser beside the willow pattern dishes, her contented cat purring on a sheepskin beside the fire. She used her free travel to go on day trips, snoozed her afternoons away over tea and cake in Bewleys or the Kilkenny Design Centre. After her cat died and she was in pain from a missed fracture, the clock turned back. The flowers were gone and she sat motionless, looking at, but not seeing, the television; the space around her withered back into the drabness I had first seen.

Benburb Street was still home to vulnerable people like Louisa and it was also the centre of the Health Board's Community Welfare Office, which had operated beside us in The Hut in the seventies, before it was moved to Benburb Street, where it became Homeless Persons' Unit. The Unit made emergency payments to the homeless people who didn't have the paper work or address to claim social welfare.

They administered the Supplementary Welfare Allowance, which was put in place in 1977 to replace the home assistance service, which dated back to the thirties. Supplementary welfare was designed to be a stopgap, an emergency payment for people in dire need because they could not access social welfare payments. It was a support for the most vulnerable people in the city.

As more psychiatric beds closed, more people were thrown into the system. Community welfare officers could requisition beds, bedding, clothing and shoes from welfare stores. They paid rent supplements and made exceptional needs payments for fuel or clothing. Three and a half thousand payments were made every week in 1977. By 1984 the Health Board was making nearly 9,000 payments a week under the scheme. The stopgap had become a staple and growing part of the welfare system.

Community welfare officers used to visit hostels and B&Bs and worked from health centres, alongside public health nurses. They were a visible part of the system. Since 2011 they have been subsumed into the Department of Employment Affairs and Social Protection, where they were reassigned as higher executive officers, administrators behind desks rather than outreach people meeting those whose cases they were dealing with. They knew people personally and had an important role in beds in hostels in the eighties and nineties, and they ran the freephone number homeless people used to find a bed. Now finding accommodation has become a local authority role. The freephone service is run by Dublin City Council, funded by the Dublin Region Homeless Executive.

In 1983 when Fred Donohoe had decided to move the Community Welfare Service from The Hut on Lord Edward Street to Benburb Street, it was the move that sparked my letter to politicians to try to lobby against the change and led to my falling out with Fred. Although the move across the river wasn't a great distance, it left a gap in our area, where so many of the hostels were clustered. For the 200 residents of the Iveagh, many of whom had lived in the hostel for the past twenty to forty years, and never moved out of its immediate environs, it meant unnecessary hardship. The move also saw more bureaucracy come into the system. They appointed different officers for the south and north sides of the city. If the officer for the southside wasn't available, someone based in a hostel on the southside could not receive a payment.

Just before Christmas 1987 the Homeless Persons' Unit moved from Benburb Street to Charles Street West. Community Welfare Officer Sheila Gibbs was the heart of the homeless unit, alongside Pat Doogue and Sally Shovelin. Sheila would always take a phone call, talk to anyone, and do a host of things to help the homeless people who came to her. She regularly worked late into the night and had an unshakeable belief in the humanity of everyone.

Charles Street was notorious among Health Board workers. The building was a mess, where Sheila and her colleagues soldiered in Dickensian working conditions. Sadly Sheila died too young, in 2002, and her colleague joked how one of her dreams had been to stand on the balcony of Dublin Corporation, having a wine and cheese party, watching Charles Street being demolished.

Life was changing in the city around us as the eighties shifted into the nineties. The days of factory workers coming to find employment in the heart of the city were ending. Industrial jobs were moving out to the suburbs. The docks became increasingly mechanized, with single forklifts and later cranes replacing the work of the many hands that used to load and unload ships' cargoes. The city centre became the domain of office and shop workers. Homeless people still drifted into the centre, to live in hostels or on the streets, but the casual work that they might get on the docks or in the markets disappeared. The downturn in eighties' Britain meant that many Irish emigrants returned home without work and without housing.

In one case, in 1983, a social worker from The London Hospital, where I had gone to research the intensive care system, contacted the Emigrant Welfare Bureau, which was based in Dublin's Harcourt Street. She was getting in contact about a man who had left Dublin in 1950, had only come back on three visits in the intervening thirty-three years and had decided now to return home. 'I feel he may be somewhat unrealistic about life in Dublin but feel he should have a try at going home,' the social worker wrote, 'especially since there is very little quality of life here for him in the East End.' They referred him to us and we were able to help him get a bed in the Iveagh Hostel.

I was still doing the daily tasks like washing peoples' feet, cleaning and dressing their wounds and helping them to get bathed and smartened up again. We were able to link them in with social welfare payments and other social and medical services. But someone also needed to speak out, to be their voice at the table. And those tables were getting increasingly large and polished and removed from the dirt, suffering and isolation that I still saw every day.

Fifteen years after the setting up of Trust, I saw how distant the people in charge were beginning to be from these realities. The days when senior Health Board officials worked in draughty ramshackle offices were coming to a close. Those officials were far less likely to be visiting hostels, much less volunteering in them and working shoulder to shoulder with people like me. Layers of bureaucracy and the jargon of management speak were growing around some senior officials like moss on stones. Empires were being built and large amounts of energy spent defending them.

The city was losing a web of connections that people on the margins could link into. Just as the voluntary hospitals in the city centre were going dark and being knocked or redeveloped, senior health and housing officials were retreating into suites of offices, surrounded by staff whose job it was to keep them even more removed from life at street level. The loss of the small voluntary hospitals in the city centre meant so much more than simply shifting a set of hospital beds from one part of the city to its hinterland.

As our doctor in Trust Laurence McGibben understood that casualty departments in these smaller hospitals were often places to spend the occasional night or a few hours where homeless people could have a cup of tea and a chat with a member of staff they had gotten to know. It was another resource, a pool of kindness that was drying up.

In a report to the Council for Social Welfare of the Catholic Bishops Conference Laurence talked about how important it was for the decision makers to build up a relationship with homeless people. Such a relationship would allow these decision makers to 'see and believe in the person behind the drunk, dirty, aggressive and self-destructive behaviour. If, as an authority figure, all one sees are the outward manifestations of the homeless person's behaviour, and acts on the basis of this, then one is merely reinforcing the hurt and distortion which gives rise to the behaviour in the first place.

'The job of people working with the deprived is to believe in the person, to link in with their long-forgotten sense of self-worth and encourage its emergence,' he said.

Bringing his psychiatric experience together with his experience of caring for the medical needs of homeless people, he was clear how those in authority could reach people thought to be unreachable. 'By giving of their interest, attention and expertise the health care professionals can re-awaken feelings of self-worth in the clients, and by showing that we think they are worth working with as people.' We had seen this happen. We had seen people like Louisa with her cat in Benburb Street who seemed so closed off from everyone around them blossom and open themselves up to human contact again. It took slow and painstaking amounts of work and care to achieve. And it could not be done from the bunker of a plush office.

Laurence McGibben described how the challenge of our day to day work had its own reward. 'Providing medical care to homeless people is like chipping at a coal face. Progress is slow, cramped and dirty but the results are real and produce a liberating heat and light which is a glowing alternative to some other types of social and professional interaction.'

'The work being done in Trust has neither pretence nor artificiality; no images are being maintained and no sensibilities protected,' Laurence said. 'Being brought in touch with the reality of being human is a privilege under whatever circumstances. I wish more people would allow themselves to become aware of this privilege and learn the qualities of transparency and vulnerability from homeless people.'

In the eighties that vulnerability became more acute. Drugs, and their awful effects, started coming through our door. Cannabis was always around, in small amounts. But, until then, the drug of choice was alcohol. Brasso, shoe polish and perfume were all substances I'd seen homeless people drinking. In recent years antiseptic handwash, now in pump dispensers throughout public buildings, is being stolen for the same reason.

We were used to dealing with people who took an awful lot of alcohol, but that was very obvious. People came in very drunk or very hungover. With drugs the behaviour changed.

People addicted to heroin visibly lost weight. At the beginning they'd be edgy, jumpy and angry. Then the anger went and they slumped into a passive state. It is a frightening plummet over the edge, a loss of control that is more overwhelming than alcohol. The quote that often comes to mind is by the late John O'Donohue. The drug becomes like a god 'a simplicity sinister in its singularity.' Nothing else matters. Everything else falls away.

We have a man coming into us, as I write this book, with infected needle marks. There is something about heroin that hollows the humanity out of a person. There's another man we've known for years. He's very bright. He has become a shadow and lost all dignity. Infected needle wounds are common. In May 2000 two homeless heroin addicts, both aged just forty, came to us for the first time with badly infected buttocks. One infection had spread to the man's genital area. We took them straight to hospital. One of them died thirty-six hours later.

People are so out of it that they don't think about using clean needles. There is something so pathetic about seeing people so abandoned to a drug. They lose all interest in themselves, their families and the world around them. Often truth becomes the first victim.

The political response has been patchy to none. Drugs go off the agenda until somebody is found dead. And if they die near the Dáil their death will be more relevant than somebody who dies in a room, cut off, struggling and isolated.

Intravenous drugs also brought awful health risks. In September 1985 David Magee and I wrote to the newspapers to warn about the high risk that AIDS posed to homeless people. 'We appeal to all relevant bodies and in particular the government through the Minister of Health, Barry Desmond, to be open to making the necessary resources available to deal with this growing tragedy.'

Powerful criminal empires began to be built around the Irish drug scene and the people at the top are not being caught. Educated, well-informed people with a lot of money see nothing wrong with using recreational drugs. They conveniently forget those drugs are supplied by people oblivious to the damage they're doing to entire communities and generations of drug users.

Methadone was introduced in Dublin in 1971 at the Drug Treatment and Advisory Service in Jervis Street Hospital, a centre that had been established two years earlier. A handful of opiate addicts, abusing prescription opiates, attended for treatment. Most of the people who attended were suffering alcohol addiction.

The opiate epidemic hit Dublin in the early eighties. Virtually overnight, hundreds of people arrived with heroin addiction problems to Jervis Street, the majority of them injecting the drug. Hospitals saw a huge increase in hepatitis B cases, including in one 1982 case, reported in the *Irish Medical Journal,* of a twelve-year-old boy who had started injecting heroin when he was just eleven years old.

The late Tony Gregory and other local activists started organising meetings in Dublin's north inner city highlighting the effect the drug trade was having on their communities. The Government responded with the methadone protocol in 1998. This was designed to stop the widescale leaking of methadone onto the black market and a situation where GPs known to dispense generously had addicted people travelling from all over the city to their clinics.

It was a typical single-solution response, and I don't think people realised the dangers of methadone, its addictiveness. We have a great tendency to look at one single solution and not to see what is required alongside that solution. Methadone was meant to be a stopgap to get people off heroin and then get on with their lives, but the support services needed to get people past that first step were never put in place with enough resources. We created a lost generation of people. Today around 10,000 addicts receive methadone, a third of them have been on the drug for over a decade.

Methadone clinics, like homeless hostels, were concentrated in poorer parts of the city and locals naturally reacted angrily to the idea of a methadone clinic in their area.

You could be overwhelmed by the problems of addiction and mental health. But if you're overwhelmed by it there's no space for creative ideas. Sister Consilio of Cuan Mhuire, an addiction treatment centre in Athy, County Kildare, is someone who has responded with creativity and compassion to addiction. She's someone with whom I feel a great sisterhood. Our hearts are close, as we used to say in Tipperary. She trained as a nurse and midwife before joining the Sisters of Mercy. In 1966 she set up Cuan Mhuire, (the Harbour of Mary) which has grown to five centres, including one in Northern Ireland and six transition houses.

They run a very structured programme and look at the deeper questions of what life is about and where addiction starts. She has saved the lives of countless people. The problem with all rehabilitation is that when people are back on the streets their only friends are people they were drinking or taking drugs with. It can be easy to fall back into addiction when your friends are still in its grip.

Dermot was a quiet, gentle man, who struggled with drink and drug addiction over many years. He was medium height and had beautiful blue eyes and clear skin. The last time I saw him he came in to Trust as we were about to leave for the day. There was an acrid smell of burning wood from his clothes. His skin was blackened from smoke. The last identifiable part of him those clear and piercing Paul Newman eyes, glittered out from his smudged face. He told us he had spent the previous nights and days sitting over a fire to stay warm.

Dermot died on the banks of the Dodder in 2011 after being released from prison. His brother Gerry spoke to *The Irish Times* about Dermot's case, and I wrote to the paper to point out how frequently people like Dermot found that 'a bed in prison is all too often the only one available to them.'

At his funeral another brother, Kieran, talked about Dermot's addiction problems, quoting Olivia, one of Dermot's close friends: 'Addiction is a terrible thing. Unfortunately it put its hands around Dermot and wouldn't let go of him.'

It is always sad when someone we work with dies. We are sometimes the closest people they have to family. Their families often turn to us to find out about their last days, how they were and what they did.

Sometimes the deaths of homeless people make a difference. Pauline Leonard and Danny Lyons's deaths resonated beyond our walls in the basement in Bride Road. They were a turning point, the moment when homelessness became a political football and was treated for a few weeks as a national crisis. The homelessness industry was born in the bitterly cold winter of 1992. Such was the sense of emergency around the death of Pauline, Danny and a third younger man, Pat Feery, in December 1992 that the army was called in.

I picked my way over a rubble of tiles, gravel, muck and broken bottles on a derelict site near Benburb Street with RTÉ reporter John Egan in early December 1992, nearly a quarter of a century ago. There was a yellow outline showing where Pauline's body was found. About four feet away another yellow outline showed where Danny Lyons had been lying when he died. 'There's nothing soft there,' I remarked as John recorded an interview for the Pat Kenny radio show.

I talked about how disturbing it was to see this place, written about in all the reports of Pauline and Danny's deaths and to imagine two people lying down on the rubble of sticks and slates. 'Our dog wouldn't find comfort here,' I said. 'It's dreadful. It's dreadful. Something good has to come out of this.'

Pauline was forty when she died. I had known her since she was a very young woman coming into the Simon Shelter. She was my height, with lovely dark brown hair. Sometimes she would come into us with her hair matted and filthy. She would wash it and brush it till it shone again. Pauline cared for people deeply. She had a strong motherly instinct but had not been able to care for her own children. They had all been taken into care and their loss was a deep source of pain to her.

Like Louisa, Pauline had grown up in London. 'I knew the Kray twins,' she used to say to me. I never knew whether to believe her or not.

Her letters to me from prison could have been written by a child.

'I have some coloured felt pens and paper which I can draw pictures with, it helps pass the time,' she wrote. 'I will be getting out on Tuesday. I have spoken to the Governor he said if I behave myself I will be out before then.'

Pauline's childlike nature reminded me of another woman, Gloria, who we worked with over the years. Gloria used to love the Christmas window in Clery's on O'Connell Street. One December, I came upon her dancing on the street, her face glowing with delight, moving in time to some mechanical dancing dogs in Clery's window.

Pauline loved to help us put up Christmas decorations. Her favourite thing to do was gluing cotton wool snowballs to the glass door. I have a collection of letters Pauline wrote to me from prison in the eighties. 'How are the two budgies?' she asked in one letter. 'I'll be glad when I get out so I'll be able to teach them to speak.' She would sign off Pauline Catherine Leonard with a line of kisses. Her relationship with Danny Lyons, who died beside her, went back to those prison stays. In one letter she complained that he hadn't been to visit her. 'That shows he can't think anything of me.' Danny was more than thirty years older than Pauline. In another letter she asked me not to tell Danny where she was.

'I miss the children very much and I am always thinking of them,' she wrote in another letter, 'but I do know they are in safe hands.' She compared the grief at losing her children to that of losing her parents, who had died within two weeks of each other years earlier.

Hours before she died, we saw her in Trust. She mentioned again that she wanted to put up the decorations for Christmas, maybe do the cotton-wool snowballs on the glass door again. We had a sheepskin coat in our clothing store and I offered it to her. She put it on shrugging her shoulders into it and buttoning it snugly across her front. It fitted her perfectly, but she said it was too heavy and she didn't want it. Clothes that are warm to someone with a home are not always suitable to someone homeless. If you're walking around all day in the rain and you've no place to leave a heavy wool or sheepskin coat to dry, it just gets wet and sodden, weighing you down with its heavy coldness. Still, I often wonder what might have happened if she had worn that sheepskin coat.

Danny Lyons was a tall man who wore a cap. We knew him as Danny Lyons but his real name was Michael O'Meara. He lived in the St Vincent de Paul hostel in Back Lane. He was a fiercely proud Kerry man and could talk about the pedigree of every footballer in Ireland. I realised that he wore the cap to cover a hole in his forehead. I tried to give him letters to refer him to hospital to have it looked at. Eventually I decided to confront him.

'Look, Danny, you have cancer,' I said as gently as I could. 'And it will get worse. Why don't you accept treatment?' The doctor I took him to see was a famous Meath Gaelic footballer. That connection clicked and Danny agreed to accept the treatment.

Pauline and Danny met up some time after she left the basement in Trust and they went to drink at the derelict site where they were later found, hidden from the street. Pauline had talked about how she had secret places around the city, where she could drink in peace, without being moved on by the guards. This may have been one of them.

It was a bitterly cold winter, with temperatures dropping to just above freezing. Some time that night Pauline and Danny fell asleep after drinking on the open ground behind Martin and Joyce's, the Benburb Street butchers where I used to call for bones for Simon soup. Neither of them woke up. Their bodies were seen by someone on the upper deck of a passing bus. They had died in a busy bustling part of the city hidden behind a hoarding on waste ground. A block of new apartments has been built there since.

A week later a twenty-five-year-old man, Patrick Feery, was found dead in a disused building in Grangegorman, the grounds of St Brendan's Hospital. Three people dying from cold in December hit a huge public nerve. Dublin Lord Mayor Gay Mitchell called an emergency meeting and asked a three-person group to propose a plan of action. The group, the city manager, the programme manager for community care and Bishop Des Williams were asked to report back in seven days. Taoiseach Albert Reynolds was reported to have ordered a search for empty buildings that could be used as temporary overnight accommodation.

In the end Albert Reynolds called in the troops. It was a sobering moment. Irish people were more used to seeing Irish soldiers sent on humanitarian missions to help stricken people in war zones or desperately poor countries far away. Here was a humanitarian mission right on our own doorstep.

A twenty-five-bed temporary shelter was opened by the army in the grounds of St Brendan's on 16 December, less than a fortnight after Pauline and Danny had died a short distance away. It was a big story. Ed O'Loughlin of *The Irish Times* described its first hours of business: 'The first customer was an ex-soldier who wandered in at 9pm. He was met

Photograph of a painting of Generous and jockey Alan Munro, winner of the Budweiser Irish Derby 1991 and English Derby 1991, by Paddy Gallagher, presented to me and Trust.

by three officers, seven other ranks, a dozen civil defence volunteers, a television crew, two reporters and a photographer. He ate some of the Civil Defence's food and went to bed. The man in charge was Captain Fergal Spain (32). He had turned up with his men, a mobile phone and 30 beds at 6pm and was ready two hours later. 'We're trained to deal with all sorts of situations,' he said. In this case the training consisted of a one-hour briefing from a Simon worker who "told us to treat people sensitively, to ensure that dignity was preserved."'

Calling in the troops might have looked like an impressive response, but the reality was that it did little to alleviate the problem. Lots of the homeless people who stayed in the hostel had beds in other hostels but moved to the army hostel because it was free and easier to access if drunk or barred from other hostels.

Towards the end of its days the hostel was used almost entirely by drug-addicted homeless people. In 1998 the Health Board said over a third of Dublin's homeless people were drug addicts. I saw the depressing effect drugs had on young men in their twenties. They would come in to us all enthusiastic about looking for a flat. Then six months later that would be forgotten.

I felt that medication was being used to control people. I saw young, angry men turning bloated and passive. They became like children, dependent on a system that made them spend all their energy on getting a bed each night rather than pulling themselves out of homelessness. Heroin addicts not on methadone spent every waking hour finding their next fix, constantly on the move, walking around the city until they were skin and bone, every bit of their energy used chasing a dealer or the cash to buy drugs.

Homelessness is not a just a housing problem but with the supply of housing contracting in the eighties, more and more people were pushed to the margins. Dublin Corporation began evicting those suspected of dealing drugs in response to community anger. It was rough justice. A whole family could be evicted, even if just one family member was dealing. New laws allowed the Corporation to evict people without court orders. The late nineties also saw the property boom begin to push people who were no longer able to buy houses into the rental market. That pushed others who might have been able to rent privately into local authority housing, and even though the country was beginning to boom we were building fewer local authority houses.

It's staggering to look at the figures and realise the extent of the catastrophic failure in public housing. Local authorities built nearly 9,000 homes in 1975 the year we established Trust. In 2015 they built a total of 64. That's 64 flats and houses across the entire country. A decade passed with little or no local authority housing built, every year the deficit growing larger. It is a truly deep hole that we have to get ourselves out of to solve a housing and homelessness crisis. The seeds were sown in the late eighties when local authorities went from building thousands of homes to hundreds. In 1989 local authorities built just 768 homes. That dramatic decline was starting to be reversed a decade ago, but then the crash came and the building of social housing fell off a second even steeper cliff.

By the end of the nineties the homelessness industry was in full swing. Voluntary and co-operative agencies were building houses, trying to plug the widening gap where the State was failing. Charities who had never intended to become housing agencies had done just that. Much of our work in Trust remained unchanged. People still got sick, injured themselves, became lice infested and needed a hot shower and a clean change of clothes. But up the steps out of our basement on Bride Road the city was transforming, faster than I could have imagined.

CHAPTER ELEVEN

The Homelessness Industry

'Where is the wisdom we have lost in knowledge?
Where is the knowledge we have lost in information?'
TS Elliot, 1934

I first met Peter in The Morning Star Hostel. He was from the west of Ireland. He shuffled along the corridor to meet us, avoiding our eyes, dressed in a long heavy coat, big boots and a hat that covered his dark hair. He kept himself well, but, at times, his thin frame seemed lost in his big coat, miserable and in pain.

Peter had a friend called Declan, who was more outgoing. One cold bright morning Declan ran into Trust and threw his arms around me. 'Come as fast as you can,' he said, panic in his voice. 'Peter is dying on the waste ground'.

I called a taxi and a young clerical student came with me, sitting quietly in the car as we drove the short distance to the Grand Canal. I got out and the taxi man asked me was I sure I should go in there?

Was it safe? I climbed over the wall and pushed through the briars and saw Peter. There was one lone tree growing in the wasteland and he was slumped against it. The ground was littered with broken glass, stones, tins, signs of lonely drinking. He seemed to be dying with his life lying around him in a detritus of bottles.

I held his hand and talked to him, told him I was there. The young cleric joined me and we said a prayer as Peter's breathing became more ragged. This was nothing like those deaths in Baggot Street Hospital, where curtains were drawn and calm privacy created. At one point I looked up and saw women in an office typing away, talking on the phone. There were flowers in the office window; everything looking bright and warm. They were busy and had no idea what was happening. Their world seemed so far removed from this place where Peter's life was ending in the cold brightness. The ambulance men came with a stretcher, lifted Peter onto it and took him to hospital, where he died a very short time later.

I have met people, mostly men, who have drifted so far away from everyone that it is only in their dying days or hours that they come back to the shoreline. John was one of those men. There was a shopkeeper in Fairview who contacted us about him. John was sleeping rough in an outhouse. He never claimed money. Local people gave him the food and shelter he needed. The shopkeeper was worried about John. He felt John had cancer and was dying.

After shutting up Trust for the day, Paddy Gallagher and I went to see him. He was huddled in an outhouse with a bottle of whiskey beside him and visibly in great pain. He told me to fuck off. He didn't seem to like women. He was probably from that generation of lost men who never knew their mothers. They had been reared in institutions. Women represented officialdom to this generation. Many social workers, nurses and doctors they dealt with were women. Attitudes to women are still challenging even among a younger generation. It makes for another bridge that we might have to cross to reach people.

That day I left a box of Complan for John with the shopkeeper and a bottle of Orovite for him to take and arranged to call again with a doctor.

The shopkeeper managed to talk him into going to hospital. There they gave him a chest x-ray and said he was fit for discharge. He had bad teeth, they said, but his chest x-ray was normal. Paddy and I picked him up from the hospital in a taxi and took him to Trust, where he had a bath and a change of clothes. We reassured him that he was safe and asked the Iveagh staff if he could go up to a bed and go on a liquid diet. We contacted the Corporation to see if they could get him a flat in Fairview. We felt doubtful he would ever need it.

John needed more than a warm clean bed. I talked to the local hospital staff and explained about his pain and his attitude to women. He was admitted and given pain relief. Local people from Fairview visited him. The hospital staff said that by dealing with John they got some sort of understanding of what could drive a person to leave behind the norms of polite interaction and become so abusive and difficult. For some nursing staff it was the first time they had met someone who had slept rough for years.

We got a call shortly afterwards to say John had died quite suddenly but in comfort. The funeral was arranged in Fairview Church. The undertaker John Kirwan agreed to take care of him. The church was packed. It was very moving to see a community of people coming to mourn the passing of an outsider, someone who lived off the grid, without much money, relying mainly on the kindness of other people. Today the message we get is that outsiders like John are a burden and

SYBIL CONNOLLY

71, MERRION SQUARE,
DUBLIN, 2.
TEL. 767281/2.

Sunday 24th Sept 89

Dear Nurse Healy,
I admire very much what you are doing. I am enclosing a small contribution to your work.
With kindest personal regards
Sybil Connolly

Note from the designer Sybil Connolly in 1989. Support for the work of Trust has always been given generously by people from all walks of life.

a bother at best, a danger and a menace at worst. We are told that they are people who need to be managed into a more compliant way of life. That's not how some of the people of Fairview felt about John.

Sister Lesaux Soizick was a nun from Brittany who taught craftwork in the inner city. She made a portrait in copper of John, which hangs today in our front room. It was in an exhibition opened by Minister Michael Woods and Bishop Des Williams. I told them that night that I wanted it for Trust and asked one or other of them to buy it at the exhibition and give it to us.

Lives lived on the margins and deaths that made us all think were so much more powerful than reports and statistics. A short time after

John died, another man came to us when he was dying, nameless and paperless. He was so far removed from mainstream life and yet a fellow citizen who needed our help.

The pressure was on to label people. In the mid-nineties the Health Board tried out the term 'eccentric adults', and sent around a research proposal asking if we would provide them with names of people using our services who would fit the category. 'While it is not intended to marginalise people further by labelling them, nevertheless it is necessary to find a working definition,' the covering letter said. Calling a 'label' a 'working definition' doesn't make it any less of a label. The culture of labelling was all about removing the need to talk to the people in person. Fitting complex and different humans into generic working definitions meant they could become part of the system to be shuttled around remotely by people who never felt the need to meet them face to face or ask them what they needed.

Artists are often better at getting to the truth of what it is to be a human. Singer songwriter Christy Moore has documented so much social history in song. I first met him years ago at a benefit gig for prisoners in the Belvedere Hotel. We are around the same age and we remind each other, whenever we meet, that happily we're still alive and still giving out.

His rendition of Floyd 'Red Crow' Westerman's 'Quiet Desperation' always chimes with me. It's not one of Christy's own songs, but he makes it his own. The lyrics 'my soul is in the mountain, my heart is in the land, I'm lost here in the city. There's so much I don't understand' capture the yearning of so many people I met over the decades who came from rural Ireland, and more recently countries further away. These are people cut off from the place where they feel they belong and drifting on lonely impersonal streets. Something about Christy's songs, and those of Bob Dylan and Leonard Cohen get the simplicity and complexity of those lonely lives of many of the people we have met.

Novelists allow us to walk in the shoes of outsiders. They can give us a chance to feel what it is to be at odds with the world, not to fit in. Maeve Binchy was a great friend of Trust. My husband Charlie knew her. He often drove her to events in his taxi and they were very fond of each other. My favourite book of hers was *The Glass Lake*. It's not one that gets talked about, but I think it's her best. It's the story of a woman who goes missing from a close-knit village in fifties' Ireland. Much of the book is about the effects that her disappearance has on her family. Writers like Maeve, Sheila O'Flanagan and Deirdre Purcell have a freedom to say more than those of us who are confined by structures and rules. They can reach people and pose questions in a non-threatening way.

Maeve understood our work so well; I asked her to write the introduction to *Not Just a Bed for the Night*, my first book written with journalist Anne Dempsey and published in 1995.

'There are dozens of Dublins,' Maeve wrote. 'And we all think we know our own. But sometimes we can be jolted in a realisation that we don't know our city at all. All around us there can move backwards and forwards people whose lives have a different heartbeat, whose hopes and dreams and expectations are wildly far from our own.'

Writers could convey truths across time and distance. Russian playwright Maxim Gorky's *Lower Depths* was a spine-tingling theatre experience in the Abbey in 1989. Dublin audiences hated the bleak play about characters living in a shelter. Theatre goers stayed away in their droves. I went to see it twice. Paddy Gallagher and I sat transfixed in the almost-empty theatre seeing such familiar personalities on the stage for the first time.

The City Morgue was in Store Street beside the garda station. Built in 1901, it was a replacement for an older morgue in Marlborough Street, which had been incorporated into the old Abbey Theatre. Death and theatre cheek by jowl brought a new meaning to jokes about dying on stage.

Humanity and personal contact is my touchstone when it comes to working with homeless people. On my rare visits to the City Morgue I would be struck by the kindness of the men who worked there and their respect for the bodies of people who had died, some in desperate circumstances. Derek Kirwan worked as the Coroner's Court Registrar in the Edwardian building where the City Morgue was based on Store Street back then. He had a wood-panelled office with a coal fire. The only other person who seemed to work there when I visited was a porter whose name was Frank. He washed and prepared the bodies. Frank brought the coal in for the fire that burned in Derek's office. They were two of the nicest public servants I ever met.

Despite their kindnesss, my visits to the morgue were always sad and disturbing. I would be called to identify a body when it was felt that it was someone we knew. The first body I identified was a young man from the west of Ireland who had drowned in the canal. It was a real glimpse of how terrible an experience it must be for a young guard or emergency worker to be called to a drowning or another awful scene. My experience as a nurse helped, but it was gruesome.

The morgue was a cold, forbidding place, lit with a stark light. You went down a bleak corridor to the room where the bodies were held in refrigerated drawers. It always amazed me that Frank and Derek could be so nice. There was a gentleness about them and they were professional. They spoke about the dead with great respect. I don't know where Frank is these days. He was the kind of worker that gets forgotten about when we talk about the public service. These people weren't the high fliers. Their voices were rarely heard. Being quoted on the media can make you feel very important but there are lots of hidden people in the city who do major work, and have terrible jobs. The toughest filthiest work is often the least well paid and comes with the fewest plaudits.

The morgue has since moved again from Store Street out to the Malahide Road. The Coroner's Court remains in Store Street. It is an unusual courtroom because it feels almost like visiting a sacred space. It's quiet, clean and sombre as if the sadness of the stories had seeped into its walls. It must be an awful experience for people to go in and hear the details of the death of a loved one. I visited the Coroner's Court to appear as a witness to confirm that I had identified someone. Having a professional job to do made it feel easier. But I felt for those stricken relatives.

One of the saddest cases where I had to identify a body and give evidence at an inquest was John. I was ironing one Saturday afternoon in late autumn 1993 when I heard the news bulletin. A man had been seen walking off the pier in Dún Laoghaire into the sea. Hours earlier, a woman taxi driver had been sitting in her car outside Clery's on O'Connell Street. She was grieving for her father who had just died. A man with long red hair and a beard opened the door and asked how much it would cost to go to Dún Laoghaire.

'Would it be £20?' he asked, clutching a plastic purse tied with a rubber band. At the inquest the taxi driver said her passenger looked just like Jesus. He sat motionless in the back of the car. Later that day, the taxi woman heard that same 4pm bulletin and contacted the gardaí. Something told her the man who had walked off the pier had been her Christ-like passenger.

We had known John for six years. He drifted in and out of flats over the years but always kept in touch with us. He had been reared by his mother, and had met his father only once. He worked as a cook in the army for a time and then, unable to find work, he had gone to London. He worked in the West End as a postman, enjoyed delivering nice post to nice people in nice houses. He read a lot, went to concerts, spent one Christmas in a hotel in Cornwall and had taken a bus holiday to Moscow.

His life started to unravel when he felt a change coming over him. He started smashing windows and couldn't explain the outbursts. He lost his job, his flat and slept rough for the first time. He ended up in court and eventually in prison until a judge referred him to a psychiatric hospital. 'This man is not a felon. He is a sick man,' the judge had said. John was transferred to Dublin and discharged, like so many others into rundown rooms in houses or a bed in the Iveagh Hostel. His only possessions were his radio, the clothes he wore, his watch and his Post Office book. 'I am not penniless,' he once told us. He was a proud man.

John had a clockwork routine. He woke at 5am and took his medication with a cup of tea. We discovered after his death that he had visited a cafe in Parnell Square for more than fifteen years, helping the owner open the grills and collecting things from the wholesalers, always returning the exact change. The cafe owner used to open on Christmas morning just to see if John was around and would insist that John take some money. John would return to his room after walking back through the city. He loved classical music and would listen to the radio for the rest of his day until the next morning at 5am when it began again.

In later years John's mother was in a geriatric hospital and our friend physiotherapist Catherine Pearson would take him to visit her. Just as Anne Rush had brought Kitty to the Phoenix Park to see the deer, Catherine regularly drove John in her car to visit his mother. John would arrive down to us and get shaved and spruced and dressed up with a clean white shirt, suit and tie. In the summer of 1992 his mother was transferred to a general hospital when her condition deteriorated. In the autumn of 1992 she died and was buried before John heard about her death, thanks to a lapse in the paperwork.

The nurses in the geriatric hospital knew about John, but when his mother's condition had deteriorated and she was transferred the information that John was her next of kin wasn't passed on. A ward sister in the geriatric hospital who knew John best had been off duty when his mother was transferred. She was deeply upset at this oversight. She visited John later to reassure him and talk about his mother's last days.

We held a prayer service in Trust with a priest we knew. Catherine and I sat there and two hostel dwellers who drifted in. Later, I went into the room and John was alone with tears streaming down his face. I tried to reassure him that it was good to cry, that it was a sign of strength rather than weakness. He sat alone smoking for a while, wiped away his tears, straightened his shoulders and walked out and back up to the hostel. He never mentioned his mother to us again.

Two years after he died the psychiatric nurse who arranged his funeral contacted us to say they had John's watch and they wondered did we know anyone who would wear it. The watch lay in a brown envelope in a drawer until another John I had come to know well, Paddy Gallagher's son John (Gino) asked me the time in Ballyfermot at his uncle's funeral. I offered him the watch, which was still in perfect order. It seemed fitting that a watch owned by one John should be given to another John. Gino Gallagher was shot dead in Belfast a few years later.

The last person I had to identify in the mortuary of The Mater Hospital was Kevin. Another proud army man, Kevin, wouldn't accept any help or rarely take anything we offered him. My brother had given me some money one Christmas and asked me to give it to someone who was sleeping out, a loner. I persuaded Kevin to take it. He was standing in the doorway of our office. We had been able to give him a good pair of boots for his walk. He was setting off to walk down to Glenstall. A rugby fan all his life, Kevin tried to explain the difference between the Heineken Cup and the Magner's League to me. 'Alice we'll go down to Thomond Park,' he said that day before he left.

Kevin was killed in an accident on the northside of the city. One of our volunteer nurses saw a notice in the paper looking for help to identify the victim of the car accident and called to tell me. We got on to the guards and discovered it was Kevin. I met his sister and I went to the inquest with her. A young man, who was on his way to the Italian embassy, had accidentally knocked Kevin down. No speed or drink was involved. Kevin's sister went over and put her arms around the driver. 'Look, it's not your fault,' she said.

Sport has always been a great way to connect with people. On a Monday morning it was the way to chat about something cheerful or exciting, the outcome of the weekend's hurling, football or rugby matches. Many of the men we saw had been talented sportsmen in their younger days. Jimmy grew up with his granny in Inchicore and had been a great soccer player. He was sleeping out in a makeshift skipper (temporary home) under the stands on the Shamrock Rovers soccer pitch in Milltown when we got to know him. Jimmy had great acting abilities. When he wanted attention, he could collapse very convincingly. One night he wanted to go and tell his story to Vincent Browne, but when it came to the time he got choked with emotion and couldn't go on.

Jimmy loved the Dublin football team and we used to keep a Dub jersey for him for the match days. He'd get drunk if they won and

Jimmy in a skipper, a makeshift shelter, under the stands at Shamrock Rovers in Milltown in the 1980s.

drunk if they didn't. A draw invariably ended in drink as well. I saw him one day sitting on the footpath outside a city pub watching a World Cup match through the window.

It was always a relief to us when we could get Jimmy off the streets. He spent one Christmas in comfort in the Meath Hospital after I promised him a new pair of glasses (his third pair) if he stayed in. He did and was later moved to a convalescence home but couldn't cope with the confinement. Some patients, he said, were allowed drink and he wasn't. He longed so much for some.

Jimmy started drinking after his granny died when he was thirteen and began sleeping out soon afterwards. Jimmy always talked about a guard who had rescued him out of a car in Smithfield when he was a teenager suffering from pneumonia. He never forgot the guard who saved his life.

Jimmy was in my mind when I talked to Joe Dowling, the senior garda who had managed to talk Robbie out of his hunger strike back in the eighties. He had moved down to the garda training college in Templemore, County Tipperary. Joe always felt the young trainee guards would benefit from a placement somewhere like Trust. It would really help, he felt, if they had a better understanding of the people they might be asked to arrest or move along in the street.

We arranged a two-week social placement training for student gardaí, and we began taking the young recruits on placement in 2000. We were very clear that people didn't come in on placement to sit and drink tea in a corner or lick envelopes. They were here to learn, not to pry into people's lives but to see a different side to people they might have written off as troublesome or violent criminals.

We took gardaí in for a decade on a very structured programme. They always came to us without uniforms. At the start, most of the students came from rural Ireland but more Dublin guards came as the course went on. We had some women. One in particular was very beautiful. Noel who lived in the Iveagh Hostel and works with us here still talks about her and she comes in to visit us. The young guards felt like part of the Trust family. If I hear of something awful happening to a guard, I think, 'Oh God, I hope that wasn't one of ours.'

We got great feedback. Asked if his perception had changed, one young guard said he recognised half the waiting room as people with whom he had had negative experiences. 'I've seen a different side to those I knew and those I might have been wrong to pre-judge if at all.'

Another trainee guard, a former nurse in a major hospital, talked about his nursing experience with homeless people, where he was 'unable to treat them as people, but only treat their condition which more often than not is as a result of their lifestyle. This is the uniqueness of Trust, in that it is not a treatment centre for a condition, but a people centre.'

Before we took the guards on placement, we took student nurses from the Adelaide. One nurse talked about her placement helping her to not be afraid to talk to a homeless person on the street. 'Now I know that they would be happy to have someone to talk to.'

Another gave a no-holds barred account of her morning with me visiting a women's hostel. 'We met Alice at 7.40am for a visit to the Regina. She had a few ladies she wished to try and help so we went early before they all left. Wow. Filthy. Stinking. Got told to f... off (by resident) and got told something similar (but much politer) by one staff member. I don't think they are at their best in the mornings. Alice told both ladies to PLEASE try and come to Trust as they wouldn't or couldn't be helped there. They both said, 'maybe'. Still Alice felt it wasn't a wasted visit.

'This week I've spent in Trust and out on the streets with Alice is one of the best things I've done since I started nursing. One of the most important things I discovered is the number of prejudices I had and, until confronted with them, was unaware of.'

Those nurse placements finished when the Adelaide closed. More recently I went up to St James's to give a talk to nurses. I arrived on time. They were late coming in and the room wasn't prepared for a speaker, so I said, 'Leave everything and come on with me down Thomas Street.' And they did. I brought them into Trust to see the reality of what I would be talking about to them.

We have had architectural students, one of whom drew up the plans for our public showers. It still only exists today on paper as a set of architect's plans.

We have been forced to stop Transition Year or lengthy placements in recent years because of fears about safety. My concern is that training is done away from people. And the further you are away from homelessness the bigger expert you may feel you are. Expertise can be easier at a distance from complicated human situations.

* * *

Uncomfortable truths began to be airbrushed out of the official response to homelessness in the nineties. A new Housing Act came into force on 1 January 1989. It defined a homeless person as someone living in a hospital, county home, night shelter or other such institution. The Act shifted the responsibility from health boards to local authorities.

By their nature local authorities tended to define homelessness in terms of housing. But the next decade saw a property boom that would push social housing off the agenda in favour of hotels, holiday homes and 'mixed use developments' of apartments, shops and offices. Property developers would be allowed to buy their way out of providing social housing in their developments. The country would become richer (briefly before a catastrophic property crash), but our housing stock would become drastically poorer.

As the decision makers in the homeless industry became more removed from the realities on the street, there was a corporate creep into the language around homelessness. People became 'service users' to be recorded and moved from one service to another and finally to the sunlit promised land of a 'positive outcome'. It might sound like a minor problem but language is important. I was working every day in a world where people said exactly what they thought, sometimes offensively. It wasn't always acceptable, but it was always real. I would go to meetings where the opposite was happening. People around the table seemed to be muting distinct voices and human responses under a suffocating layer of corporate speak.

At one meeting I suggested that homelessness was complicated and had a lot to do with addiction. A senior voluntary sector worker rounded on me and told me that addiction had nothing to do with homelessness. It was much easier to talk about building houses than to put the long-term supports there to keep people coping successfully in that accommodation. As the social housing provision dropped lower by the year, it was clear that it was much easier to talk about building homes than it was to actually build homes.

Corporate speak meant you did not exist if you did not fit the template. By the middle of the nineties Trust was under pressure to move out of our location in the Iveagh, to grow bigger and to start providing housing. We regularly sat down to try to figure out where Trust fitted into the growing homelessness industry, whether we were needed or whether we were taken for granted. If we grew into a housing agency, would we be forced to play the same games competing for funding, adopting the jargon, spending a fortune on advertising and producing the glossy reports? Who would continue our hands-on work with people who were living at the very bottom of the ladder? These were the people less likely to provide an agency with 'positive outcomes' to be reported on at the end of a financial year.

The work we do in Trust does not fit neatly into boxes that get ticked. As I write this book, a man is coming to us who is very troubled and won't fit neatly anywhere. He likes our service, and he came in with a wound from his groin to his knee which had been stitched with around sixteen stitches. It was infected and his leg was out like a balloon. We were afraid he would lose his leg and we sent him in a taxi up to St James's Hospital with a letter. He came back the next day with a prescription. We told him to come in every day to have his wound dressed. I dressed it one day myself when our nurse was busy. Matt Geoghegan who works with me said afterwards 'Alice, you enjoyed doing that dressing because you were back doing the hands-on nursing.'

We found the remains of six stitches in the wound. We've often come across cases where people have removed their own stitches rather than returning to hospital to have them taken out. I felt we should have contacted the hospital to discuss his case, but they would probably have told us they could only discuss it with the man himself or his GP. We're not his doctor, and if we sent the man to complain, he might get angry. So we dealt with it and the wound has healed. That's not the kind of thing you can put a price on or put in a glossy report. We saved his leg and saved the State an awful lot of money.

Charities were given a tough choice. Should they continue to lobby the State to provide the services people needed or knuckle down and do it themselves? In 1983 the Simon Community stated clearly the pressure it was under to shoulder responsibilities that should not be those of a charity. 'Simon Community is there to help the homeless, to befriend and provide basic needs by its shelters and soup runs,' they said in a report. 'But it is not a housing agency, nor should it or any other voluntary group be seen as such.'

Today Simon is a huge housing agency, along with dozens of other charities and voluntary groups, providing homes with a mix of State and charitable funding. Many of the best known national homeless charities established after Trust was set up, have gone down this road of becoming a housing agency. They build, manage, refurbish and run accommodation for people on the Housing List, with excellent intentions.

Charities have shouldered responsibilities with good motives. It is an understandable response to a growing crisis. We see the need every day and jump in to fill the gap. In Trust we drew the line at changing what we were and what we do to fill a gap that was becoming a chasm. But by filling that chasm the charity sector has unfortunately helped create an unwieldy and inefficient system. There are 8,000 registered charities in Ireland raising money for everything from hospital equipment to housing. The multi-million euro homelessness industry is letting the State off the hook, duplicating services and allowing our politicians to avoid having to commit proper long-term resources to our social infrastructure. It's a mess.

I met a former senior Health Board official recently who is now working in the charity sector. He pointed out how the State is getting services on the cheap from his organisation which provides basic healthcare. The employees and volunteers of charities are not pensionable State employees. Their labour is cheaper and more expendable. The charity sector has allowed the State to privatise the poverty industry and large tracts of public healthcare. The system creates waste with duplication and competition for resources among increasingly ambitious organisations who are more and more removed from the people they were set up to help.

I started saying this in the nineties, loudly and as often as I could. At one meeting around a polished table in Dr Steevens' Hospital, I talked about the dirt, violence, hope and pain I saw every day. The woman in charge of the meeting told me coldly that it wasn't appropriate to talk about those things. If the people who were supposed to be helping to solve the problems didn't want to hear these things, then who would?

Saying what I was saying didn't make me many friends. Today The Alice Leahy Trust receives no funding or other support from the State. We don't fundraise and we never ask for money. We are entirely funded by the generosity of donors. Our accounts have always been audited and we have never had a credit or debit card. Our cheques are signed by two trustees, never by me. Our only State support came from my salary, which was paid by the Health Board until the nineties, along with a very modest annual grant, medicines and cleaning supplies. It became clear that the Health Board official who attended our meetings only took an interest when we were criticising the Health Board. In the end, we decided we valued our independence more than the idea of being subsumed as some kind of partner NGO, so we cut that last tie.

It was a lonely place to go. From the mid-nineties we began to feel ourselves being sidelined. In 1996 the Government set up the Homeless Initiative to bring Dublin Corporation, the Eastern Health Board and the various voluntary bodies working with homeless people under one umbrella.

'The voluntary sector has long played a vital role in providing accommodation and services for homeless people,' Labour Minister Liz McManus said in a speech at the launch. 'I believe that the effort and commitment of voluntary bodies will be enhanced in this co-operative arrangement with the statutory bodies.'

Charities and voluntary bodies were being brought into the fold, given parcels of funding to do the job of the State. We resisted being sucked into the homelessness industry, not out of contrariness or stubbornness, but because we could see that a ball that did not belong in our court was being bounced our way. In answer to the Health Board's repeated questions about whether we were involved in resettlement I was adamant that this was not our responsibility. 'We do not have flats, but we do refer people to your service,' I wrote to one Health Board official, underlining the words 'your service'.

As the economy began to thrive politicians were keen to promise

Breakfast in the Mansion House for Mother Teresa in June 1993 with Iveagh Hostel residents (from left) Tim, me, Noel and Paddy D.

an end to homelessness. Homeless charities stood alongside them in a concerted effort. A voice like ours pointing out the hollowness of such a promise was not welcome at the table.

At a meeting of the Homeless Initiative in 1998, two years after it was set up, our work was said not to meet their definition of 'outreach' work, despite decades of visits to hostels and people sleeping rough when we were the only people doing it. By the end of the nineties we stepped down from the Homeless Initiative. 'Success defined in business terms is meaningless when dealing with human beings,' I wrote telling them that we did not have the time to attend meetings where the issues were being ignored.

We were beginning to be seen in the same light as the people we were working with, outsiders in the real sense. What was really happening on the ground wasn't reaching the people in power. It stopped at middle management, where exposing a real problem was seen as personal failure.

The more difficult people were falling out of the system, where the emphasis was on the dreaded performance indicators. We and the people we were working with were being swept under a carpet somewhere.

My views about homelessness weren't welcome at meetings that took place behind closed doors. But during the nineties I was asked to take part in more public conversations around the social exclusion that led to crime.

In 1994 I was part of the Lord Mayor's Commission on Crime. Chaired by High Court Judge Michael Moriarty, we held weekly meetings in the mansion house. We sat around the boardroom table in the same building where the first Dáil met, in 1919, and where the truce was signed after the War of Independence, in July 1921. Crime was an issue that was really beginning to exercise public opinion.

There was great energy in the group, which included barristers Paddy McEntee and George Birmingham. Our meetings were professional and focused. Gossip and small talk did not feature as we had much to get through and a tight deadline in which to do it. Senior officials from Dublin City Council were there. Paddy McEntee said at one of the first meetings that we should use our energy constructively, that there was no point in trying to reinvent the wheel. They were wise words from a wise man.

People were beginning to question the social issues that led to homelessness. We heard dramatic accounts of families in local authority housing being terrified and abused by violent neighbours. Dublin City Council was beginning to take a strong line on eviction of these problem tenants. We produced a report which, I'm sorry to say, went on a shelf to gather dust.

Four years later, public panic about crime reached a peak. In 1996 Garda Jerry McCabe was shot dead in an IRA robbery in Adare, Co Limerick. A short time later, journalist Veronica Guerin was murdered in her car as she sat at traffic lights on the Naas Road.

In February 1998 I was a member of The National Crime Forum, which sat for nine days of town hall meetings in Dún Laoghaire, and later went on to hold meetings around the country. Judge Bryan McMahon did a good job of managing the diverse group of people who were on the forum. In the opening session, we outnumbered the members of the public who actually attended. Lots of voices were listened to over the days of those public hearings.

Bryan McMahon commented in the final report at how reasonable the debate was. The strident tone of much of the media coverage wasn't a feature. There were much more balanced and nuanced views. We received 250 submissions from individuals, organisations and interest groups. The dominant idea that emerged was that any measures that would tackle crime successfully needed to be comprehensive, and that they should start in areas of life other than the criminal justice system, like schools, homes and hospitals. Crime prevention was related to social, health and education support for the communities who made up the bulk of our prison population.

There was space and time to get a truer picture of crime. In the report, we noted that those most at risk of attack are young men in urban areas, not elderly people in rural Ireland. Yet the fear that elderly isolated people had, and still have, was no less real or in need of attention. I was confident that what I had to say as part of the Crime Forum was every bit as relevant as anyone else. We produced a report and a Crime Council was established. It felt like a worthwhile exercise, the kind of public democracy that the country needed, but I wonder if it had any real legacy other than window dressing. The bulk of the resources continued to be pumped into prisons and security.

Another era came to an end in Annesgift when the house and estate was sold to Coolmore Stud in 1999. The 562-acre farm and house had been put on the market at £2.5 million. It sold for £7.1 million, almost three times the asking price. I still walk around the estate whenever I visit Tipperary. It still feels like home.

Back in the basement in Bride Road, we were encountering real brick walls with the health service. The Health Board we had first started working with was replaced in 1998 with the Eastern Regional Health Authority. This, in turn, morphed into the Health Service Executive and each new incarnation brought a new layer of high-octane bamboozlement and management speak.

We were losing touch with the individuals who ran things. We found ourselves not knowing the key personnel or being able to find out who they were. Bureaucracy and jargon were silencing debate, and hospitals became more difficult to deal with. I would write to consultants to talk about people we saw. Professor Patrick Plunkett who recently retired from St James's stood out as a wonderful empathetic consultant who was brilliant at dealing with people. However, other consultants and GPs seemed to disappear behind secretaries, who wielded enormous power in deciding whose calls to put through.

People like us who had hands on contact with other humans were being pushed aside in favour of management consultants whose value was gauged by the size of their fee. The bigger the fee the better they must be. 'The voice of the nurse working on the ground who can be a midwife welcoming a new life to the world or holding the hand of someone leaving it, is a voice we need to hear more of if we are to keep

Launch of With Trust in Place *in City Hall, 2003. From left: Charlie, me, Maeve Binchy (front), Pat Kenny and Hannie Leahy, my mother.*

in touch with humanity,' I wrote in a letter to Department of Health in April 2001.

A system was growing which alienated those, like Joe, that it was supposed to help. Joe was a man who came to us from rural Ireland. He was born in 1916, a few months after the Easter Rising, and worked all his life. He paid his way in the Iveagh Hostel after years in England. He liked to visit his local pub, have a chat, and watch the races. He dressed well and kept his only suit hanging in a wardrobe and his shoes polished. He wanted to live independently for as long as he could. But, when he was in his seventies, the twinkle in his eye dulled and pain altered his gait until he was almost completely bent over. Reluctantly he decided to move to a nursing home. We promised to help.

Simpson's Hospital in Dundrum was where some former residents of the Iveagh were living and a bed came up there. Joe visited and was accepted. All he needed now was the paperwork to allow for nursing home subvention. Trust nurse Geraldine McAuliffe worked for three weeks trying to secure the funding. It was an endless series of soul-destroying, unanswered phone calls, messages not passed on, hours on hold with nerve-jangling hold music. Eventually she secured the commitment to fund his nursing home, but only if Joe was examined by a geriatrician. The trouble was the waiting list for an appointment was lengthy. The HSE finally agreed Joe could be examined by a public health nurse but insisted it had to be a nurse attached to his GP practice. The nurse agreed to examine him the day before her holiday if the forms could be faxed to her by the HSE. Geraldine got a promise on the phone that they would be faxed urgently. They arrived four days later.

Joe eventually got his paperwork and his place in Simpsons but spent six weeks in an acute bed in hospital while the expensive, time wasting and spirit-sapping rigmarole was played out.

If we weren't sure the bureaucrats had taken over, then an advertisement in July 2006 for the newly-created position of Head of Process and Operations in the HSE crystalised the daftness. The job, the ad said, involved 'executive leadership of cross-pillar operational and process change, sponsorship of process developing projects and the cascading of process excellence throughout the HSE.'

George Orwell would turn in his grave. The English writer was the scourge of meaningless language. He pointed out in his 1946 essay 'Politics and the English Language' that obscure language is a tool to hide the truth. Euphemism, jargon and management drivel bring with them a danger of contagion, Orwell warned. People who use them start to hide their own thoughts from themselves. Woolly language leads to woolly thinking. And we needed all the clear thinking we could get.

If the HSE and the City Council weren't going to listen, I had other ways to have my voice heard. The media was a big help. John Quinn interviewed me on RTÉ radio as part of his 'My Education' series. It brought home to me the importance of communicating what we had learned about life from the people we helped and I felt sure others could too.

We commissioned Esperanza Productions to make *A Fragile City*, a powerful film about homelessness in Dublin. The title came from a book of poems published by poet Micheal O'Siadhail. I was excited about the potential for education that the film gave us. It was important, that people saw it. If they couldn't come into our basement, then they could hear the voices and stories we knew in this wonderful film.

I met Department of Education officials to ask about sending a DVD of the film to every school in the country. It was one of the most dispiriting meetings of my career. The officials showed no enthusiasm for the idea, and we went ahead without them.

Along with journalist Anne Dempsey and City Council community worker Miriam Flynn, we put together a training day on the homeless experience for health workers, guards and anyone else who was involved and interested. We held it in the City Council offices, charged nothing for the day and gave people lunch and free parking. We got great feedback, but again I wonder if the programme would have been more valued had we charged a large fee.

As the boom turned to bust, we saw many of the casualties of the building crash come down our steps. Like the Irish workers who went to London in the fifties to work on the buildings and fell into street life, we had a generation of eastern European workers who came with a dream of work that fell through. In some months we have people from twenty-six countries in our waiting room. Racism became a problem.

It was a challenge to go into our waiting room and have people speaking languages I didn't understand. It meant we had to reach further to make that connection. Feuds could flare that we couldn't understand or anticipate.

The difference between nationalities is usually outweighed by the similarities.

You look out in our waiting room and see people staring into space with a cup of coffee. It's a familiar terrible sadness in the lives of people who come from abroad. They're thinking of their families, what might have been. A lot of them would stick together and drink together. We know a lot of them who would have died on the street.

We had always dealt calmly and quietly with shouting or violence and I was never afraid, but one day it all came to a head. We found a large carving knife in the toilet. Another day there was a stash of drugs hidden there. Shortly afterwards a man who had been in touch with the psychiatric services walked in and upended the table scattering everything. A couple came in another day and he was having a shower. She was in the other bathroom and they were shouting and roaring at each other. I went out to ask them to cool it, and Alan Best, who works with us here, took me to one side and said, 'Just be careful, Alice. He's wearing a stab vest'.

The final straw was the day a man said to someone outside the door: 'I'll come in tomorrow with a gun,' after he left disgruntled because he didn't get what he wanted. I rang the superintendent in Kevin Street on his mobile and he sent his biggest guard around fast. The man denied it. 'What would I be doing with a gun?' he said.

In July 2010 we closed and locked the gate at the top of our steps. Callers rattle the gate and tap the lock to ask to come in. We can see them on CCTV before we let them inside.

Ending thirty-five years of an open door policy was sad but necessary. We were worried about our staff and so were our trustees. Their work is hard enough, emotionally draining and the kind of work that few other people would do.

We are in the heart of a concentration of drug services. People attending methadone clinics were dropping in to sit in our front room and fall asleep. We suspected some of them were dealing. One lunchtime, before we closed the gate, a man stole someone's bag outside on Bride Road and ran in the door. He was trying to get through the hostel and escape. Locking the gate hasn't ensured we are always safe. One man jumped the locked gate with a bike recently and tried to break down the door because he wanted a shower.

Our waiting room is a reflection of life on the streets, which feel more violent and drug-fuelled now than forty years ago. The majority of people who come to use our service are as frightened by it as we are. And it is for them that we continue boiling the water for tea, putting out the plates of scones and biscuits, sorting through the bags of clothes to replenish our stores, dressing wounds, handing out the disposable razors for men to wash and shave, taking people to hospital, making phone calls on their behalf, trying to link them in with services or work, listening to them and making them feel like they are known, at least by me and the wonderful people I work with in Trust, or The Alice Leahy Trust as we became known in 2016.

CHAPTER TWELVE

Walkabout

'Age is a number. It's something imposed on you. It drives me absolutely spare when people say, "Are you going to retire? Isn't it time you put your feet up?"'

Actress Judi Dench

There's a grey steel grill over the window that used to be Louisa's flat on Benburb Street today. You can't rap on the glass, like I used to when I called to see her. Louisa would raise up the sash window and come out to the main door to let me in. The photographs of 1916 volunteers are hung on a hoarding across from her old flat. Each volunteer is shown above a colour photograph of a living relative. Louisa would have loved looking across at them.

The volunteers all seem to have the same profound look in their eyes, a seriousness that comes probably from being photographed in black and white at a time when portraits were more formal. I wonder what they would think of the world now. The Luas glides past what's left of Benburb Street flats, past all the echoes of lives lived here and all the people I once knew.

Geraldine McAuliffe in Trust with Spike, given to her by Eddie to care for (a very lucky dog). The little things that matter.

All hands on deck encouraging new growth at Glencree. A group of us that all worked together in the early days of VSI, celebrating their 40th anniversary, May 2004.

This was where the work that led to Trust began. It was a place of hardship, some of the last of the city's slum blocks. But it had pockets of comfort. The four-storey redbrick block where Louisa used to live with her beloved cat and her careful collection of china is boarded up and derelict, one of the city's sadly neglected buildings. Sheets of steel are in the window frames to stop anyone breaking in. Buddleia is sprouting from the roof.

This was once a more bustling part of the city. The large Crean and Son soap company was nearby on North King Street and the Windsor Motor company, who gave us the room for our washing machine in a house across from the flats, had a large garage here.

Homeless men still live here in Oak House, or the Model Lodging House as I knew it. It's west of Louisa's derelict flat and faces Collins Barracks, now the National Museum. The army used to cook a great Christmas dinner for the residents in the old Model Lodging House.

Oak House is no longer run by the City Council. Simon is running it since the summer of 2015. A pigeon is flapping around the dining room because someone left the back door open when I pop in for a look. They have thirty-two long-term residents and two emergency beds or 'cold weather initiative' beds as they're called. Both emergency beds are normally used by the same two men every night. The building houses less than half the number of men it housed when I started visiting in the seventies. Then there were eighty-four residents living in basic cubicles with nowhere to keep their belongings other than under the beds or hanging on the paper-thin cubicle walls.

The other end of what's left of Benburb Street flats faces onto Queen Street and has been spruced up. You can still see the words 'A Block' carved into the facade. Martin and Joyce the corner butchers where I got bones for the Simon soup pot was the corner shop on the ground floor of the block. It's now called The Old Butcher Shop Studios. You can buy Irish linen cushions, napkins, table runners and scented candles there. Mr Sweeney's the chemist was down from there on the quays. He was always called Mr Sweeney, never addressed by his first name.

The only sign that Benburb Street used to be one long line of Victorian flats is the skirt of granite that runs the length of the street along the footpath. The remaining two blocks of the nineteenth-century flats stand like tall brick bookends at either side of nineties' private apartment blocks that were built after the publicly-owned flats in the middle were demolished.

Another apartment block has been built facing the river on the site where Pauline Leonard and Danny Lyons (Michael O'Meara) died behind Martin and Joyce butchers. The date on the front reads 1994. The bulldozers must have moved in not long after December 1992 to dig the foundations out of the rubble where they died.

Today you can cross the Liffey just opposite Benburb Street over the new James Joyce Bridge. It's a modern steel and glass white bridge, which opened on Bloomsday in 2003. Designed by Spanish architect Santiago Calatrava, it looks beautiful in blue-sky photographs, all elegant, white curves and a walkway of clean green glass.

But up close on a dank December morning, the curved steel is in need of a paint job. Leaves and dirt have darkened the glass walkway into a grimy murk. Some of the panes are shattered. Between dirt and damage it's impossible to see the river moving below your feet when you walk over it, as it quivers underfoot whenever a heavy truck goes by on one or other quay. What happens to us that we let our city grow dirty and shabby around us, even the shiny new bits that don't come with any historical baggage?

Back on Usher's Island in the south inner city I have crossed the

James Joyce Bridge, past the house, where Joyce set *The Dead* to call into the Usher's Island centre, the HSE Mental Health Day Centre for homeless people. It's set back from the quay. Nothing on the building tells you what it actually is. There appears to be a huge difference from when it was a workshop in the nineties. Back then, residents made chessboards and chessmen to be sold at craft fairs. In another workshop they chopped and packed kindling to be sold to local shops.

In spite of all the plans to bring psychiatric care into the mainstream, places like Usher's Island have the feeling of a Cinderella service starved of funding or leadership, or both. There can be an exhaustion of enthusiasm that grinds good people down. It's almost palpable as a weight on your shoulders when you step through the door of somewhere left struggling to cope with an overwhelming problem.

Further up the quays I meet a man who has been running a business in the area for many years who shows me shocking CCTV of people smoking and injecting heroin, violent attacks and drug paraphernalia and discarded needles in the area. 'This girl could have been saved,' he says as he plays a video of a young woman smoking heroin, explaining how he and his employees watched her go downhill rapidly as she huddled in a doorway but they felt powerless to help.

It's been a long time since I visited hostels in a professional capacity, walking or cycling over this river at the heart of Dublin's poverty district. I walk for pleasure now every day, for at least an hour. Recently I sat down for about ten minutes in Palmerstown Park. In the midwinter stillness I could hear the birds chatting with each other in the trees on either side of me. It's moments like that I would miss if I didn't walk.

I walk to work most mornings and sometimes I'll take the bus. A bus driver got out of his bus recently when he saw me at the door and waved up at me to see if I wanted the bus. A lifetime of not driving

Time to reflect and relax after a hard morning's work. From left: Karen, Matt, Noel, Alan, Jeanette, me and Mary.

The Alice Leahy Trust team, spring 2018, up the steps from the basement with St Patrick's Cathedral spire just visible in the background. From left: Alan, Mary, Noel, me, Karen, Jeanette and Matt.

doesn't feel like I've missed anything.

People on the streets have their own routes and patterns. My route from the top of Rathmines to Bride Road takes me past older men with rolled-up towels going into the Swan Leisure Centre for their morning swim. It's a wonderful building, almost squashed by the property crash, but the City Council pushed ahead and made a terrific community resource in the centre of the urban village that is Rathmines.

Down the straight long road to the Grand Canal I see prosperity coming back into view. The cranes are back on the skyline, the coffee shops are going a bomb. People juggle smartphones and takeout coffees. I had stopped seeing men sweeping the streets, but they've recently made a comeback after litter and dirt got out of control. Machines, it seems, are not the perfect replacement for people. I see the postman and the children going to school with their parents. Men are pushing buggies in a way I never saw decades ago.

When I throw bread to the swans who paddle around the lock at Portobello Bridge, flocks of gulls and pigeons swoop down, so I almost feel I'm going to be gobbled up in a clatter of feathers and outstretched talons.

Every now and again I see someone we know chatting with the passing people. Ann is one of our regulars. She sleeps out in a tent. She used to sit outside a supermarket with her dog, Jim, but Jim has disappeared recently. I regularly see people stopping to talk to her. She never asks for money, and I see people leaving with concerned looks, maybe wondering if anything is being done for her as they head to work. I always go into the shop and buy my paper and have a chat with her.

I sometimes stand and look at the solid bulk of St Patrick's Cathedral and the impeccably kept St Patrick's Park. Then on Bride Road I walk in through the basement corridor of the Iveagh Hostel, where breakfast smells and the steam from showers waft along. The postman is delivering letters to the hostel; the breadman comes with a wooden tray of freshly made sliced pan. The hostel feels like an unchanging world. The staff are always busy and the tiles on the floor are always sparkling.

We sit for our daily ten-minute discussion, hot mugs of Barry's tea in our hands, before we open the doors to whoever the world has given us today. We plan for the morning but we don't know what will happen and who will come to the door.

I have spent the largest part of my life in Dublin. Sometimes I feel very much part and yet not of the city. In Tipperary I have that same feeling of being part of it but slightly separate. I'm an oddbod, I suppose, a perpetual outsider, a happy misfit. I love the city. I love Grafton Street. The rest of the city centre I don't like as much. It's changed dramatically.

I love the freedom of being able to walk into a euro shop or stroll through Brown Thomas. I feel I could go into either of them. I buy my earrings for €15 from a lovely Polish woman in the George's Street Arcade and people stop me on the street to admire them. When I'm there, I'll usually drop into Vinny in Urban Picnic and have a bowl of his homemade soup. Walking through the city is part of my day; it's part of my life. Sometimes it's difficult if you have a very busy morning and you want to switch off and people come up to talk to you.

Recently a woman who writes a fashion blog approached me when I was wearing my tweed coat and a hat with a flower in it. I turned down her request for an interview and photograph. I probably should have done it, but I felt like I was in another world when she spoke to me, away with my thoughts as I tend to be when I walk.

I often stop on Grafton Street to chat to my friend Michael Kavanagh, who has been on the street selling newspapers for forty-eight years. He has seen Grafton Street transform around him, and the age profile of his newspaper buyers grow older and greyer.

U2 guitarist The Edge used to sit on Michael's wooden stool waiting for his girlfriend to finish work in the shop beside Michael's pitch. Former Taoiseach Charlie Haughey once sat on the same stool. British comedian Tommy Cooper was a daily customer for a week in 1972 when he did a run in the Gaiety Theatre. Before his show Cooper would buy a copy of the *Evening Press* and take it into Bewleys, to read over a milky coffee. On the last night Michael asked the comedian how the show had gone. Cooper was delighted and said he had sold out every night. 'Have a drink on me,' he said, slipping something into Michael's top pocket. After Cooper had ambled away, Michael pulled out what the comedian had given him, expecting to find a folded note. It was a teabag. The day Tommy Cooper gave him a teabag with a punchline is one of Michael's favourite anecdotes from a life on Grafton Street.

I ask him about the Berni Inn, the old steakhouse that used to be on Nassau Street and Switzer's, the department store that still has a wall sign on the side of its old building, where Brown Thomas is now. 'That was in the early days, Alice when you were rocking,' he says grinning.

'I'm still rocking, Michael,' I tell him.

At my age and with my white hair, I'm put in a box labelled 'harmless' when people first set eyes on me. Then I start talking to them and they come away with a dramatically different set of notions. I can be blunt when there's something on my mind and I tend to ask questions that people don't always want asked.

I get called a saint, but find that annoying. I don't believe in that idea of sainthood. And neither do I believe that you should be driven by a sense of martyrdom. People say I look well. Women are always judged by how they look. I think my face reflects how I've lived, telling people how I feel and what I think.

If you're not able to express how you feel about things, it eats into you. I think that's why there are an awful lot of people out there who are depressed or down or feel life is useless. They're not being heard in a family situation, in a community or work situation. That leads to ill health. I feel energised mentally every day because of how I work or how I say things.

It's fashionable today to trash every State enterprise and Government quango as useless and croney-ridden. But one of the best groups I worked with in over forty years of seeing the criminal justice system up close was a group that few people knew or heard about. Our work was done entirely in private, in meeting rooms in prisons all over the country, where I sat across the table from some of Ireland's most notorious criminals.

I was appointed to the Sentence Review Group by Justice Minister Nora Owen in 1996. The group was set up to advise the Minister for Justice on whether or not a long-term prisoner should be released after serving at least seven years. It was a huge responsibility. We could also make a range of recommendations around maintaining a person's family contacts, therapeutic services, education, work training, transfer to another prison or temporary release.

It was the first time that my experience of visiting prisons could be put to good use. I knew how prisons worked and they didn't frighten me. Many of the people, especially the women I knew, saw prison as something of a safe haven, where they would be warm and fed and have human contact that they might lack for days on the streets.

In earlier years in Trust we had worked with Frank Murtagh, one of the longest serving prisoners in the State. He was convicted for the

1964 Ballybough murder of shopkeeper Jenny Murphy. In the eighties the prison governor in Arbour Hill asked if we would allow him to come down to Trust once a week with a prison officer to try and get him used to being outside before he was finally released. Frank came down one morning a week. He told Paddy Gallagher one day 'the Branch (Garda Special Branch)' were out there following him around. Paddy was able to relate to his paranoid fragility.

'For God's sake, will you catch yourself on?' Paddy told Frank.

'The Branch have more things to do than following you around.'

I took Frank to see a play in the Gaiety, with the Minister for Justice's permission. It was Brendan Behan's *Borstal Boy*. At one point Frank went out to the toilet. He didn't come back. Then I heard a loud bang. I jumped in my seat and thought: 'Oh God, this is my whole reputation gone.' But the bang had been on stage and Frank did come back to his seat. He was released from prison in 1986.

The work of the Sentence Review Group brought me into all the prisons in the State over the years that I served on it with chairwoman Judge Mary Kotsonouris. Visiting prisons has taught me about the reality of society's problems more than any other aspect of my work. Prisoners live in a very isolated world. It's the one area of the criminal justice system that I still feel energised around. Prison has the potential to help people or to destroy them. Many prisoners have practical skills that don't fit into mainstream life. A spell in prison can be a mark of success in certain areas or the destruction of your reputation in others.

I feel education should be mandatory in prison. Very often the prisoners who avail of education are those who've already been educated outside. So the people who need it the most are the least likely to get involved. Community service is a much more positive option for minor crimes. Restorative justice, where offenders and victims meet, can provide huge healing. We agreed to take people on community service recently. They were working with the Iveagh Trust. They painted our centre. I went in to meet them one weekend morning, to sit down with them and talk to them. They did a very good job.

I was appointed chair of the Sentence Review group before my term came to an end. There was a very strict routine around prison visits. Before you travelled, you got a box of files on the prisoner. Mine were delivered to my house on a Friday. The files made for difficult reading. These were people convicted for some of the most disturbing crimes in Ireland. When you went to meet the prisoner, you had to allow them to tell you their story. I think my nursing experience helped me to look at people dispassionately. We returned the files to the Department official after the visit.

I was part of a panel of people. The Sentence Review Group was made up of people like me with experience of working with prisoners, and a representative of the medical or psychiatric profession, a senior officer with the Probation and Welfare Service and a representative from the Department of Justice and others with relevant experience.

I often thought it must be very difficult for the prisoner sitting there in front of a wall of listening strangers. I was very impressed with the humanity of the people sitting alongside me. We had to weigh up the safety of the community and how dangerous the person was going to be with the idea of this person being given a chance. There were very few opportunities for people released from long sentences and that hasn't changed.

It wasn't a surprise to go from reading a graphic set of files on a set of crimes to seeing the person who had committed them in the flesh. I was used to thinking that no matter what the crime was, there was a human being inside the criminal. You're always left with the question of what

My right-hand woman Jeanette multitasking in the engine room of the Alice Leahy Trust, as usual, where teamwork is key.

happens to people along the way. Is it the social circles they're in? Is it due to a mental health issue?

These are some of the people that are labelled evil. It's an idea I struggle to understand. No one is born evil. Something must happen. It's almost too easy to say it's evil, rather than face up to the idea that humans are capable of doing terrible things. The big question I was left with after serving on the Sentence Review Group was whether you can ever decide if someone is going to be a real risk. We had to make efforts to measure it, but you don't know what's going to happen to people along the way. The Sentence Review Group was replaced by the Parole Board in 2001, but the final decision on a prisoner's release still rests with the Minister for Justice.

As I write this book the world is facing the horror of terrorist attacks. We see cases of minor alienation where people are difficult, open to exploitation and neglectful of their mental health. Extreme alienation can drive someone to take a truck into a crowded French seafront or a German Christmas market. It has to be something that happens to them or their loved ones or community along the way, which is why we all need to support all families that are struggling or marginalised.

Other public bodies were less inspiring. In June 2006 I applied for a role as a Human Rights Commissioner and was appointed. I came away from the meetings of the Irish Human Rights Commission (IHRC) feeling that they were all very committed people with their own life experience, but the discussions were academic and technical. It was always hard to see how you could bridge the gap between academia and real contact with people who are suffering. Their pain, isolation and anger doesn't translate into legalese and has to be felt to be understood.

The IHRC concerns itself mainly with legislation surrounding rights and this is essential work. However, I felt, for me, that the gap between academia and the practical work was too wide. I represented the IHRC on the National Action Plan against Racism chaired by Lucy Gaffney. It did good work, but that monitoring group has since been dissolved. The IHRC was replaced by the Irish Human Rights and Equality Commission in 2014.

At one conference I was struck by a quote from the leading human rights expert Professor Conor Gearty. He described human rights as 'the phrase that comes to mind when we want to capture in words a particular view of the world that we share with others .... That view is one rooted in the simple insight that each one of us counts, that we are each equally worthy of esteem. Human rights is, in this sense, a visibility project, forcing us to see the people around us.' It summed up not only human rights but the decades of work we had been doing in Trust. We were a visibility project forcing ourselves and a wider world to see the people around us, and to see past their difficulties to the humans that they are, to know them as people rather than a set of problems and statistics.

I wrote to the IHRC president Maurice Manning in 2009, calling on the Commission to review the law around the protection of whistle-blowers. I wanted to see the protection in the Health Act of 2007 for 'protective disclosures' extended to workers in the homeless sector and in other areas of life, including private and voluntary sectors. Five years later, we got the Protective Disclosures Act, which widened protection for whistleblowers outside the health service.

When my five-year term as a Human Rights Commssioner ended, I stepped down wondering if my membership had been of any use. The IHRC seemed to operate in a parallel world where my experience of what I saw on a daily basis was not seen as relevant. 'A lot of time has been spent by the IHRC attending conferences abroad,' I wrote in my final letter to them. 'Yet, the absence of feedback from these events makes it impossible to assess its usefulness in relation to the domestic situation.'

In December 2008 I joined the board of management for the three child detention centres in the Oberstown campus in Lusk, in County Dublin: the Boys School, Girls School and Trinity House. Oberstown seemed so much more progressive than Loughan House in Cavan, which opened as a children's prison in 1977. We all protested about Loughan House. At the time, the criminal age of responsibility started aged seven. In the PRO we described Loughan House as a 'savage and reactionary response to the problem of child delinquency'.

Oberstown was set up to help rather than punish troubled children and get their lives on the track through stability and education. I am no longer on the board, but I'm saddened to see reports of violence against staff and widespread unhappiness among workers there.

Some roles in the homelessness industry became stepping stones for a lot of the people I've met along the way. Their enthusiasm shines out of them when they first step into the arena. They know the answers to homelessness; they have the solutions and are certain the problems will be solved. I understand their enthusiasm, and it can be a refreshing reminder of how I felt the same way myself when we first set up Trust in The Hut in Lord Edward Street.

But many of them don't last a wet week. They mean well, but how do you turn your energy and commitment into a lasting effort in the face of sometimes heartbreaking human sadness? Long-term work with homeless people can feel like a thankless nightmare once the news agenda has moved on and you're struggling to shore up people who are often being helped by multiple agencies already.

New arrivals into the homelessness industry can get burned out very quickly because results are hard won. If you're focusing on changing peoples' lives, failure becomes a reality. The tough truth is that you can't change people unless they want to change.

I believe in the power of people. There is a humanity that crosses religion, borders, languages and ethnicities. I once spoke to a Danish psychiatrist about Pauline Leonard, the woman who died behind Benburb Street in 1992. 'I know that woman,' the psychiatrist said. 'Oh have you been to Dublin?' I asked surprised. But, no, he meant he had met women like Pauline in Denmark. There are many Paulines in the world. I was struck reading *The New York Times* account of a homeless woman living and dying on the streets of Manhattan in 2018 how her story could be just as easily a story about a woman in Dublin. Another Pauline lost to the world.

At the risk of reducing Pauline and others like her to a type or a label, I understood what the psychiatrist was trying to say. I thought of Pauline recently when I read a report from the Children's Court from former journalist Dr Carol Coulter's Child Care Law Reporting

Project. It outlined the circumstances in which a teenage mother had her son taken into care in 2013 after she was seen, with her baby in a buggy nearby, smoking heroin down a lane by a garda. It was late evening after a very hot day, and the baby was grubby and distraught. The court heard the mother had a tough start in life. Her own mother, a long-term drug user, had died when she was a child. The young mother had her son taken into care under an emergency care order in 2013 and she was placed in a residential unit.

A clinical psychologist and a key worker in the mother's drug treatment programme both gave evidence that the young woman had a beautiful relationship with her son and innate parenting skills. 'If she could successfully attend residential treatment and supports were put in place for her, it was possible she could care for her son. However, it was up to the mother to make the decision to attend residential treatment and move away from her circle of friends who were using drugs.'

During the final hearing, the court heard that the woman had been 'immensely overwhelmed by her addiction', had been evicted from private rental accommodation and was living in a tent to avoid other drug users in hostels. 'She is emaciated and not wearing clean clothes. Part of the reason she is not presenting [at court] is that she would be embarrassed by being dishevelled. She is in full denial about the extent of her addiction,' the court heard.

The judge granted a full care order over her son until he turned eighteen. 'She is a very good person in a very bad place,' the judge said. 'She is a very good mother but she is not in a position to be a mother at this time. This could change, if she got a toehold she could approach the [Child and Family] Agency to bring an application to discharge the care order.'

I think of the two lives damaged by this. A woman, herself the daughter of a woman addicted to heroin. Maybe she's filling the hole that her mother's loss left in her with the drug that destroyed her mother. And now her son left with a mother-shaped hole in his life.

There are no easy answers to how you give people that 'toehold' where they can steady themselves and climb out of addiction. The only answer I have is not to give up on people, but to keep on trying.

Human hurt is at the heart of addiction. So many of the alcoholic men who have come to us over the years had to leave where they came from because they were gay, even up to recent years. They started drinking to blot out the pain. They were linked in with one counsellor after another but the root of the problem is the pain of rejection. Despite the passing of the Marriage Referendum, there are still pockets of misunderstanding about gay life in Ireland. The word remains a playground insult even today.

One autumn, in recent years, I met Joe, a man who had been known to us for years. He had moved in a familiar spiral from the streets to a hostel to transitional housing and finally to an apartment. He was getting some education and then everything crumbled. We don't know why. I think his drinking had something to do with it. There's often more than one reason. His friends were gone; most of them had died and he fell back into homelessness. He was deeply ashamed of the fall from a regular life back onto the streets.

'Put your pride in your pocket,' I told him. 'And start again. You did it before. You can do it again.' I hope that is true in Joe's case. The reality of our work is that we're not their family. We don't have any control over them or any right to know the direction their lives took after we saw them. It is frustrating to hear of a death of someone we worked with. All of us need to realise that patchwork nature of our work. You meet certain people at certain stages in their lives and then they move on. No one person or organisation should see themselves as the only one dealing with a person and their problems.

I still call on Professor James McCormick's wisdom when I come up against the sadder cases. 'Ill people are not just disordered machinery,' he said. 'If therapy always promised cure, if ageing and death were not a fact, if human beings were not dependent on others, a mechanistic approach would answer their needs. In reality, they need love as much as they need therapy, particularly as so much therapy is needless or ineffective.'

'Successful living depends upon the ability to adapt to change: for many it is necessary to adapt to different climates and different cultures. All of us have to cope with bereavement and ultimately with death. Health is the ability to live autonomously. Health is successful coping,' James wrote.

We all have to figure out ways of coping with loss and getting older. I no longer think of myself as a nurse. If I did, I would be just talking about antibiotics and illness. Nurses who are not afraid to look past the patients to the social determinants of health can have a much broader view and make a great difference. Nurses still have the privilege of working with fellow human beings at a time when their need as humans is at its greatest, whether it's a midwife attending a birth or a nurse holding the hand of someone who's dying.

I gave a talk this year to nursing undergraduates in Trinity College about the past, present and future of nursing. I really wanted it to spark debate and was looking forward to talking to my young counterparts who were studying nursing more than half a century after I first struggled into my uniform in Baggot Street. But the talks overran their allotted time and my lecture wound up without any time for discussion.

Sometimes we meet people who find those toeholds and step back from the edge. Our nurse Geraldine was in a supermarket some years ago and she went to the checkout to pay her bill. 'Nurse Gerri, do you not recognise me?' the woman on the till asked. Gerri didn't.

'Do you remember the day I was in with you?' she said. 'After that, I listened to what you said. I went back home. I've got my life together. I have a lovely partner now and I've a job.'

Good things do happen. If we don't see people again, it doesn't always mean that they're dead or in prison. It might mean that they're getting on very happily with their lives.

We have a panel of black and white portraits by the late *Irish Times* photographer David Sleator in our office. They are head and shoulders shots of some of the men we work with. David took them for an *Irish Times* millennium supplement and they are wonderful. They are very useful if you have visitors and you want to make them think about the people we meet. I always position visitors sitting directly opposite those photographs. One of them is a man we knew as the Flour Man.

The Flour Man was rumoured to have been a former New York policeman, and we discovered that he was going around the chemists in the city, buying DDT powder. It's banned now as it's carcinogenic but we used to shake it on beds in Simon to kill fleas and lice. The Flour Man caked himself and his clothes in a white layer of it so that he looked like he was covered in flour. I had to go around to the city centre chemists and ask them not to sell it to him. He is still alive, and living in supported housing, without having to powder himself in poison every day.

Who are the other people I will never forget? Paddy Gallagher is one of them. Another unforgettable character was Eddie and his three dogs: Tina Turner, Jezebel and Bruno. Eddie worked with the Corpo and would sit around braziers at night, doing security. He had a home, but he came to us for friendship and support. Those dogs were his life, and you had to watch and make sure none of them snapped at you when he brought them in, either Eddie or one of the dogs. Eddie had a huge cyst on his forehead. Children used to call him Mad Eddie and throw stones through his window.

Geraldine and Maurice Guéret, a GP and one of our then Trustees, took him up to St James's Hospital, to have the lump removed. It made a huge difference. Eddie shuttled between coping and not. The only person he would let into his flat was Geraldine Halpin, who worked for Dublin City Council. She was from Dublin and he could relate to her. Geraldine Halpin linked in with us and together we ensured he was comfortable as possible. He would come to us when his gas or electricity was cut off. Jeanette O'Brien would take him down to sort out the bills. Eventually he had to make more regular visits to James's as his health went downhill.

Geraldine Mitchell, who wrote an inspiring book on Olivia Hughes's wonderful friend Muriel Gahan the founder of The Country Shop, gave us two lovely leather chairs that had belonged to her late father, Professor Mitchell from the Adelaide Hospital. One of them was a reclining chair. We don't do much reclining in Trust so we gave the chair to Eddie, along with some blankets and pillows we'd been given by a church in Malahide. Eddie made a comfortable bed for Tina Turner, Jezebel and Bruno out of the chair. I don't think Professor Mitchell would have minded.

Eddie's consultant would ask us how it was that he always looked so well. We told her he'd always come to us before his hospital appointment for a wash and clean clothes. Towards the end, he got into the Hospice in Harold's Cross. I went up one day to visit him with a tape recorder. He had so much to say about what it was like to live in the city. He was very wise. He would regularly ask us, when he came in, 'What are you all running around for? Will you just sit down, take it easy.' But I couldn't bring myself to tape him. His spirit wasn't something that could be captured like that.

The morning Eddie was dying, the nurse rang and Geraldine went up and sat with him. He said to her before he died, simply, 'Thank you.'

Tony Gill, the street poet whose poem inspired the name of this book, visited regularly and challenged us every time. He'd come in at least twice a week, sometimes daily. He was often in a terrible state and it would be everyone's fault but his own. He was in very poor health. He was set alight where he slept in Westland Row in the autumn of 2004, whether it was a cigarette or a malicious attack nobody could be certain. He was taken to St James's Hospital and walked out. He arrived into us on the Monday morning. When he took off his shirt, we noticed the burns. We cleaned him up and escorted him back up to the hospital, to hand him over to the staff. We knew that he wouldn't wait to be seen unless one of us went with him. He was admitted and he went downhill very quickly. He requested that we would be his next of kin. When he died, efforts were made to trace his family, but the guards couldn't find anyone. So he was buried in our plot in Glasnevin. A few years ago, we got an email from a brother of Tony's in Australia, who had googled his name.

In 2006 Tom Crilly, a man who knew Tony and a lot of his friends, put together Tony's poems into a book. It was great to get the voice of a real outsider into the pages of a book. Tony often brought poems into us, and I'm sure a lot of his writing was lost along the way. When he died, we realised so many people knew him and really loved him.

Louisa from London impressed me with her independence and her stubbornness. I would see a touch of that in myself. The list of unforgettable people is a long one, including those nurses and consultants who were compassionate professionals. My friend and former colleague David Magee, now a practising psychotherapist, is a huge part of the story of Trust. The late Professor James McCormick, a GP and first head of the Department of Community Health in Trinity College Dublin, and our long-time chairman and mentor was a powerful hero of mine. We wouldn't be here today only for him.

Having someone like James in my corner was a huge source of strength and resilience. He validated what we do here with a brilliant independent mind and rounded vision of what healthcare should be. I would love to know his thoughts on injecting rooms for drug users. The legislation has been passed and they are going to be introduced. The debate around them felt starkly black and white. Anything that helps to address the drug problem is important, but there needs to be more lively and engaged discussion about these ideas. Somehow we don't get to this stage until after these things are set up.

It has been a strange time to be writing this book. Kindness and integrity seem on the wane in the face of darker human instincts. I appeared on *The Late Late Show*, still a central programme in Irish life, to talk about my work at the end of an extraordinary year of looking back. The following morning, a visitor could come into Trust and might find me at the door with a mop, or on the phone to a Minister. I feel secure in myself, a strong sense of purpose that has come in a direct line from my childhood in Annesgift.

I love that Jenny Joseph poem 'When I am an old woman I shall wear purple, With a red hat that doesn't go and doesn't suit me.' I don't pick flowers out of other people's gardens and I haven't learned to spit, as the poem says, but I have reached a feeling of freedom about who I am. It comes from the enormous number of people I've met and people who supported and impressed me in a way maybe they don't even realise.

Perhaps that sense of freedom hasn't come with age; it was there all along, partly inspired by those strong independently-minded women of my childhood: my mother, grandmother, aunts, great aunts, Olivia Hughes and Muriel Gahan, who saw things that needed doing and did them.

I believe in what I'm doing in this basement in Bride Road. I don't see our work as a waste of time. I still wish we didn't have to be here. And I wish there were more people like us. I have Jeanette O'Brien, my right-hand woman, who comes from the heart of the city and runs The Alice Leahy Trust with a care and commitment I can't imagine finding in anyone else. Our colleagues Mary Kelly, Matt Geoghegan, Alan Best and Karen Ryan and our volunteer nurses: Mairead Hever, Angela O'Rourke, Mary Merriman, and Eilish Keegan, have a kind of patience and compassion that is uniquely special. As I write, Noel Byrne, who we first met when he lived in the Iveagh Hostel and who now lives upstairs in the apartments overhead, has inspired and challenged us from our early days and has just turned eighty.

The Alice Leahy Trust is as much them as it is me. Everyday people visit us with donations, some of it weird, most of it wonderful. It's a lovely part of the day, and I often wish I had more time to give people but often we're busy with the work at hand. People like calling in and seeing how clean, bright and pleasant The Alice Leahy Trust is, with the soft music from Lyric and the candle in the fireplace. It feels like a refuge. Sometimes people think places like ours are chaotic and noisy. But we're different. That difference in tone was the spirit of the place from the first day we opened our doors and we all work hard to keep it like that.

The South Africans have a philosophy of Ubuntu, or the inter connectedness of humans. The idea that 'I am because you are' sums up my decades of work. I've learned to ask for help all along the way and to look for support by looking past the labels, whether someone came from a big house, a doorway, the senior public service or a religious background. The older we get the more we are seen by our labels. I would be seen in many quarters now as an even madder nurse than I was when I first handed in my notice and went to live in a homeless shelter. It's easy for people to dismiss you as mad when you're doing things differently and when you believe anything is possible. But that doesn't bother me. My work has been supported by a wonderful patchwork of people, many of us misfits in our own way, not all of whom agreed with each other or came from the same background or identity.

Community is a word we use very glibly. People talk about 'the homeless community' all the time. Homeless people are not a community.

I see community at work all over the country and I see it being taken over by people who want to protest. I'm in favour of protest. I have been on many protests, but I'm not in favour of exploiting frustration and anger for political aims. That's what has happened with Brexit and with US President Donald Trump, and I can see little shoots of it starting here. We have serial protesters who do little else but protest. They need to be asked why they're protesting, what they really believe in and whether it's right to hijack human misery for their own empowerment.

The media has a huge responsibility to keep asking those questions and education is key to keeping people from knee-jerk reactions that do more harm than good.

Politics is the only system we have, but I struggle to find thoughtful conversations happening in Leinster House. The Senate should be the place for thinkers, but it has become a place for people who are going to run for election, have failed in election or are aiming for a post in

Europe. They're given a seat in the Senate so they have a platform.

We live in a democracy and a wonderful country. I can still feel a rush of joy and enthusiasm for our sports people, our countryside, our writers and artists, our animals and our food culture. We have to be optimistic, cherish our democracy and the basic decency of most people. If I felt bleak about everything, I would have been dead long ago.

It's helpful to just stop for a few minutes to look at nature, how the leaves die, they rot, the worms love them and then in the spring it blooms again. You have a whole cycle. We've grown away from that connection with nature. We've lost the capacity to lift our heads up and see things at all levels.

I would hope that this book is a way of encouraging people to say life is great. We've only one life. We've all kinds of opportunities to live it and not to be confined by labels and bureaucracy.

Ireland is a wonderful country, and we have a strong and wide streak of decency and compassion that I see in Bride Road almost every day. We need to be a lot more positive, have a can-do approach, be aware of how society works and aware of our limitations. If I met my younger self today, I would tell her to stay outside the system. I've been an outsider probably all my life and I feel blessed to have had such a broad view of things, to know how the world is and not feel down about it. Life is a jigsaw and in our rush to put all the bits together we miss out on the positive bits of the pieces that don't always fit in.

I was listening to one of the players in the Icelandic football team who went so far in the European Championships in 2016 being interviewed by John Murray on RTÉ. John asked, 'How did you win?' And the footballer said, 'it was the power of us working as a team.'

I think a team is made up of different parts but everyone has a point of view. We're lucky to have a great board of directors. We're not getting any younger, but destiny has led me and The Alice Leahy Trust to where we are. I have to let the gods look after everything after that.

More than twenty years ago, at the conclusion of my 1995 book, I wondered if 'perhaps in twenty years' time someone somewhere will pose the same questions.' That someone somewhere is me and many of the questions are still as relevant and even more urgent today.

I think there is a force out there. I don't know what it is. I can't describe it. But there is something. Even in writing this book, I was talking about the City Medical Officer Dr Brendan O'Donnell, and his former colleague Carmel Hickey walked in to give us a donation shortly after I had remembered him. There's something very connected, a shared spiritual resonance to life that I feel sustains my own spirit.

Singer and songwriter Bob Dylan says, 'We're all prisoners living in a world of mystery.' We need to have time to see the mystery. I don't think you get it in the institutional church, but you can get it in other ways. I enjoy life. I need space to lock myself away to listen to music or read a good novel where everyone lives happily ever after. I believe the newspapers are not as challenging as they should be. I meditate and I've been doing that for years. I find it keeps me focused.

I'm much better at saying no these days. Charlie helps me with that. My life isn't all about The Alice Leahy Trust. It happens to be a bit about this.

Every morning I say the same simple prayer of gratitude. It sums up how I feel about my life: 'Dear God. Today is the day you have made and I am grateful to be part of it.'

Leabharlanna Fhine Gall

Photograph Credits

The authors and publisher thank the following for permission to use photographs and illustrative material: pp 5, 93, 115, 132, 138, 166, 170, 177, 202, 211, 213, 228 (photo of painting by Paddy Gallagher), 233, 237, 248 (photo of painting by Paddy Gallagher), 256 (both), 258, 262, 279 (top), 293 (both), 307 (photo of painting by Paddy Gallagher), 321, 343 (both), 350 Derek Spiers; pp 1, 142, 183 (bottom) Peter Orford; p183 (top) Pat Cashman, *Evening Press*; p195 Alan Betson; pp16, 22, 25, 35, 38, 45, 51, 59, 73, 77, 80, 97, 102, 121, 122, 156, 192, 244, 253, 255, 279 (bottom), 313, 329, 333, 339 (both) The Alice Leahy Trust and author's private collections; p8 *RTÉ Guide*.

Text Credits

The authors and publisher thank the following for their kind permission to quote from their published material: Dr Damien Brennan and Routledge for permission to quote from *Irish Insanity 1800–2000*. First edition (2014); Robert Frost Estate; Hanna Greally and Cork University Press, for material taken from *Bird's Nest Soup*; Graham Greene Estate; Jenny Joseph Estate and Johnson & Alcock Ltd; Eugene McEldowney and *The Irish Times*; Ed O'Loughlin and *The Irish Times*; Seamus Purseil, *The Irish Times*; Michael Viney; Floyd Red Crow Westerman.

If any involuntary infringement of copyright has occurred, sincere apologies are offered, and the owners of such copyright are requested to contact the publisher.

The Alice Leahy Trust

Trust was founded in 1975, growing out of work carried out by Alice Leahy and a group of volunteer doctors. In November 2015, after forty years in existence, the then trustees decided to rename Trust as The Alice Leahy Trust.

We operate from the basement of the Men's Iveagh Hostel on Bride Road, Dublin 8 (between St. Patrick's Cathedral and Christ Church) with our own entrance to the basement. We open each weekday morning from 9.00am to 1.00pm, closing at 12 noon on Fridays.

We have both paid staff and volunteers. Teamwork is crucial to the day-to-day running of the agency.

Some mornings we meet between twenty and thirty people who come from doorways, squats, skippers (temporary shelters), emergency one-night only hostels, parks, tents, garda stations and casualty departments.

On a given month we could meet people from up to twenty-six different countries who are homeless in our capital city. Many of these people would have come here, like our own Irish of a generation ago who left our country with a dream of a better future.

Some people we meet cope with very serious addiction problems, including drugs, alcohol and gambling. Many people call on an ongoing basis and then disappear; many call just once and others reappear after many years. Time with people is spent on providing a wide range of care, from applying dressings, advising on medication, housing and entitlements, referral to specialist services, assisting with washing/showering, foot-care (extremely time-consuming yet hugely beneficial to those sleeping out), contacting families, healthcare professionals working in hospitals and the community, gardaí and welfare officers and workers in the voluntary sector. Human contact is a vital component of the work of The Alice Leahy Trust and this entails an enormous amount of time, which is difficult to quantify and increasingly not easy to provide.

The provision of showers is the first step to linking in to other services, statutory and voluntary, keeping an appointment in a hospital, in the Courts, even to access accommodation or reconnecting with family or friends. Our submission for public showers in our capital city can be viewed on our website www.aliceleahytrust.ie.

The Alice Leahy Trust is governed by a Board of Directors who meet every four to six weeks. We meet the requirements of the Charities Regulatory Authority, the Companies Registration Office, Revenue and the Data Protection legislation.

The Alice Leahy Trust is not grant aided and not actively involved in fundraising. The running costs of the agency are met in full by unsolicited voluntary donations which are receipted and gratefully acknowledged. Accounts are audited annually by Chartered Accountants Deloitte.

Our website www.aliceleahytrust.ie is updated regularly and only used for educational purposes.

The philosophy of The Alice Leahy Trust is based on the recognition of every individual's right to be treated as an autonomous and unique human being. The Alice Leahy Trust accepts people as they are, in the spirit of Article 1 of the Universal Declaration of Human Rights, and recognises that everyone is entitled to be treated with dignity and respect. No information on people using our service is kept on computer or shared.

Thank you for buying this book. You join the many people from all walks of life who continue to make our work possible while recognising that in an ideal world there should be no need for our service.

Contact details
Postal address: Alice Leahy Trust,
Bride Road, Dublin 8.
Tel: 01 454 3799
Email: info@aliceleahytrust.ie
Website: www.aliceleahytrust.ie
Charity No: CHY7014